THE NEW INVESTMENT FRONTIER III

THE NEW INVESTMENT FRONTIER III

A Guide to Exchange Traded Funds for Canadians

Howard J. Atkinson
with Donna Green

INSOMNIAC PRESS

Library and Archives Canada Cataloguing in Publication

Atkinson, Howard J., 1958-
    The new investment frontier III : a guide to exchange traded funds
for Canadians / Howard J. Atkinson and Donna Green. -- 3rd ed.

Includes bibliographical references and index.
ISBN 1-894663-88-8
Exchange traded funds. 2. Stock index futures. I. Green,
Donna H. II. Title.

HG6043.A85 2005   332.63'228   C2005-904341-5

The publisher and the author gratefully acknowledge the support of the Canada Council, the Ontario Arts Council and the Department of Canadian Heritage through the Book Publishing Industry Development Program.

Printed and bound in Canada.

Insomniac Press, 192 Spadina Avenue, Suite 403,
Toronto, Ontario, Canada, M5T 2C2
www.insomniacpress.com

For my parents, who continue to make the investment of a lifetime;
to my children, who make a lifetime worthwhile;
and to Deb, who helps me keep it all in perspective.

Acknowledgements for the Third Edition

The success of this book owes a lot to the enthusiasm of my colleagues at Barclays Canada who, though in no way responsible for the content of the book, gave me the benefit of their collegial encouragement and some very useful fact checking. In alphabetical order I'm indebted to Marie Amilcar, Ravi Chelliah, Warren Collier, Adam Deif, Bobby Eng, Geri James, Meahgan Li, Gerry Rocchi, Rajiv Silgardo, and Ruby Velji.

This edition was once again helped by the invaluable research and number crunching of Norman Rothery, Ph.D. of *www.stingyinvestor.com*. I'd also like to thank Matthew Elder and his team at Morningstar Canada who always had time for Donna's inquiries and gave us the generous use of some valuable proprietary information. I've drawn quite heavily from Paul Mazzilli and Deborah Fuhr's research work at Morgan Stanley and want to thank them and Morgan Stanley for their generous permission to use their research here.

Lea Hill at CIBC World Markets and Dan Hallett of Dan Hallett & Associates Inc. were free with their time and are models of passionate commitment to their areas of study. I'm happy to be able to acknowledge Don Vialoux's substantive contribution to the market timing section. (He knows what I mean.) Peter Haynes and Marty Gillespie at TD Securities were a pleasure to confer with. Earl Bederman and his excellent team at Investor Economics were helpful with numbers not easily found elsewhere.

Thanks also to Chris Adair of Fundata Canada Inc. and Gary Hannusch of TD Waterhouse.

The people who find themselves the subject of end-of-chapter interviews were very good sports about it all—John Bogle, Bill Fouse, Jamie Golombek from AIM Trimark, AMEX's Kevin Ireland, Paul Mazzilli, Steve Rive of Standard & Poor's, and Cliff Weber from AMEX.

Erica O'Keeffe is responsible for the detailed ETF information in the appendices, all of which she did in her spare time, along with much help in formatting charts and text. As my long time associate at Barclays, I'm grateful every day for her contribution.

A big thanks to Donna Green for working with me again and to Mike O'Connor and his many arms at Insomniac Press.

And finally, to my family, the biggest thank you of all.

Howard J. Atkinson
Toronto, Ontario
June 2005

Table of Contents

Introduction

Exchange traded funds are a fundamentally better way of delivering a diversified portfolio than conventional mutual funds. Since the first edition of this book came out in 2001, exchange traded funds (ETFs) everywhere have grown explosively in number and size. They've gone from a cool, sophisticated investment vehicle to the standard family coupe. The reason is simple: like a dependable car, ETFs are both practical and liberating. They're also completely cheat-proof. ETFs have the prudent diversification of mutual funds but with razor-thin management fees, completely disclosed holdings and perfect price transparency. No "market timing" worries here. Because they trade on a stock exchange, ETFs are bought and sold with the speed, ease and public price disclosure of an ordinary stock.

At an almost breathless pace, ETFs are evolving into ever more useful, versatile tools: ETFs that specialize in dividend paying shares, ETFs that verge on active management, and ETFs that hold commodities, like gold, instead of a basket of stocks or bonds. More and more brokerage firms and investment advisory services of all descriptions are re-engineering their client portfolios with ETFs. It's not only investors and advisors who have been liberated; fund manufacturers have too, and the plethora of new products based on the ETF structure will continue to expand and develop.

Competition around these innovative products reflects the revolution they have spurred. U.S. exchanges are competing fiercely for ETF listings and giant U.S. mutual fund companies are responding defensively. Fidelity Investments has lowered the management expenses on its index funds to an unheard of 0.1%. And in a let's join 'em, not fight 'em move, Fidelity has launched its very own ETF, taking a page from Vanguard, the world's leading index fund company, which offers 23 ETFs of its own—now with even lower management expenses.

I'm passionate about bringing knowledge of these productive tools to Canadian investors. It makes no sense for investors to put up 100% of the capital and over a long holding period get less than 50% of the return because of the corrosive effects of sales charges and management fees. The next generation of mutual funds has arrived. With our retirement savings soon to be fully open to the nearly 200 ETFs on North American exchanges, I hope this book helps you make the most of your money so you can drive off safely into your dreams.

Howard J. Atkinson
Toronto, Ontario
June 2005

How to Use This Book

The New Investment Frontier III is divided into four sections. Part One explains what ETFs are and how they work, explores the concept of indexing and the alternatives to ETFs for implementing an indexing approach. Part Two explores investment strategies using ETFs, their tax implications and tax-saving strategies. Part Three looks to the past and future of ETFs. Where did they come from and what will they evolve into? Mutual funds are going to rise to the competitive threat and you'll be best equipped to understand the new products that will inevitably spring forth by knowing a little bit of history and stealing a peek at the future. Part Four is an aggregation of vital statistics on ETFs, their universe, and related information sources. Part Four on its own is an invaluable ETF Resources Centre.

Feel free to skip around to the chapters that most interest you. This material, and ETFs themselves, should be used to complement existing investment strategies or help to develop new ones, whether you invest on your own or with the aid of an advisor.

It's easy to forget that financial products are invented and run by people; people who often face obstacles in making their product come alive. To capture this human dimension, there's an interview at the end of each chapter with product pioneers or industry experts intimately in touch with the birth pangs—like Bill Fouse who invented the first index fund and whose patriotism was questioned for doing so, or John Bogle, the founder of the world's largest index fund company who has made it his mission to challenge the fund industry to justify their management costs. This is an unusual element in a personal finance book but one I'm particularly proud of.

A Note about Foreign Property Restrictions

At the time this book went to press, the Government of Canada had not officially declared an end to the foreign property (commonly referred to as "foreign content") restrictions on Registered Retirement Savings Accounts. Given the general consensus that these restrictions would be lifted and not wanting the book to be instantly dated the minute the ink dried, we designed our portfolios with full freedom. If the 30% foreign content restriction is still in place as you read this, stay mindful of that limitation.

Disclaimer

The author is Head of Public Funds and a principal with Barclays Global Investors Canada Limited.

The opinions expressed in this book are exclusively his and do not necessarily reflect those of Barclays Global Investors.

While every effort was made to ensure the accuracy of the information herein, the authors and the publisher assume no responsibility for errors, omissions, or inconsistencies, and they disclaim any liability arising from the use of information in this book. Information, regulations, and methodologies change. Every investor's situation is different and it is always prudent to consult qualified financial professionals.

Part One

The Powerful Case for ETFs

Chapter One

What Are ETFs?

Exchange traded funds (ETFs) are the investment world's equivalent of a nectarine—part mutual fund, part stock, but a marvellous improvement over both. Simply, an ETF is a portfolio of securities that trades on a stock exchange. As a basket of investments, ETFs offer the broad diversification of mutual funds, but at a fraction of their cost. And, because they are traded like a stock rather than being redeemed like a mutual fund, ETFs are generally more tax efficient than mutual funds.

The differences between ETFs and mutual funds are significant because they can have a big effect on the overall cost of your investments and, as a result, your returns. Probably the best way to understand ETFs and their advantages is to contrast them with conventional mutual funds, the kind sponsored by big-name companies like AIM Trimark, Fidelity, and Mackenzie. So here's a rundown of the similarities and differences between mutual funds and their more delectable hybrid, ETFs.

How Are Conventional Mutual Funds Different from ETFs?

A mutual fund is a basket of securities owned by a number of investors but managed by a professional money manager. Because the fund holds a basket of different investments, you spread your risk among a plentiful number of bets. Both mutual funds and ETFs enjoy the single biggest advantage of funds—their broad diversification, but the two diverge in a number of ways.

Buying, Selling, and Pricing

Once a day, after the close of trading, a mutual fund's assets are priced and the mutual fund is given its daily value. When the fund has been priced, all fund unit buy and sell orders that have been queuing up through-out the day are transacted by the mutual fund company. (The mutual fund company does the redeeming and selling of its fund units.) Whether you are buying or redeeming, the price you get is strictly related to the value of the underlying assets of the fund without variance; however, because the fund's value is calculated only at the end of each trading day, this pricing arrangement doesn't allow you to know beforehand just what price you are going to get when you place an order to buy or sell a mutual fund.[1]

ETFs, on the other hand, trade on an exchange exactly like a stock and can be bought and sold any time the market is open. That means you can know exactly what is going to end up going into or coming out of your pocket when you execute a trade. It also means that all the devices used for stock trading can be applied to trading ETFs: price limit orders, stop loss orders, short selling, margining, and in some cases even option strategies.

In addition to the real time bid and offer quotes provided by the stock exchange, the value of an ETFs underlying portfolio is priced and broadcast every 15 seconds. This permits you to check if the price you are paying for an ETF is close to the value of its underlying securities. Unlike mutual funds, an ETF can trade with some small discrepancy from its underlying assets.

Since ETFs trade on an exchange, a brokerage commission applies on their sale or purchase. That's different from most mutual funds, which usually impose no transaction fees to do a sale or purchase, though such transactions can trigger "loads." A load is a sales commission payable to an advisor and his company. Front-end load funds pay the sales commission on purchase of the fund directly from your investment money. Back-end load funds ding you for a sales commission on the sale of the fund if you redeem before some specified holding period—usually six or seven years.

If you buy or sell a mutual fund through a discount broker, you may have to pay a flat transaction fee. Don't confuse this transaction fee with loads or charges from the mutual fund company. A transaction fee in this case is imposed by the brokerage and has nothing to do with the mutual fund company itself.

Conventional Mutual Funds Are Actively Managed— ETFs are Not (Yet).

A conventional mutual fund uses a manager to select the fund's investments. The manager actively buys and sells securities in hopes that he or she can outperform the market. The sad truth is that the cost of active management is frequently greater than the value that management adds to a fund's return. As a result, most fund managers don't often surpass their benchmark indices—especially over the long haul. That sticky little fact has prompted many investors to turn to a passive style of management in which a fund manager simply replicates the market he's in—with the more modest ambition of merely keeping pace with the market as represented by an index. This is called "passive management," and so far, most ETFs are passively managed. But then, index mutual funds are passive vehicles, too. So what's the difference?

ETFs Most Resemble Index Mutual Funds

ETFs don't have all that much in common with actively managed funds but they are very similar to index mutual funds. An index mutual fund is one whose portfolio is intended to track a target index. An index is a collection of stocks or bonds that reflects the movement of a broader market. The S&P/TSX 60 Index, for instance, is a collection of 60 of Canada's largest and most widely traded stocks. The movement of those 60 stocks is indicative of the broader Canadian market as a whole—or at least the larger companies that make it up.

Index fund managers generally buy the same stocks in the same proportion as the index they are tracking, put their head in their hands and watch it work. Good index funds will mimic the performance of their index, minus the management expenses. That's pretty well how ETFs work. The difference is that ETFs do it better. ETFs can track an index with bloodhound precision because they are burdened with very small management fees compared to index mutual funds, and they positively scoff at the bloated management fees of actively managed funds.

ETFs Are More Cost Efficient Than Mutual Funds

ETFs are renowned for their low management fees. This is a critical advantage in an industry that pays itself out of the investor's returns whether those returns are positive or negative. Obviously, the lower the MER, the more closely any index product will track its target.

The management expense ratio (MER) is a standard measure of fund costs. It is an annualized figure that captures a fund's operating expenses and management fees, stated as a percentage of the fund's assets. The bigger this number, the less of the fund's return you see. The median Canadian diversified equity fund carries an MER of 2.62% (or 262 basis points).

Although it varies, as much as 40 to 50 of those basis points go to paying the manager for investment research and decisions. A much larger portion typically finances sales and distribution.

Index funds, free of the expense of active management though not always entirely free of paying sales commission, typically shoulder a much lighter MER. Canadian equity index funds have a median MER of 0.78% because all they've got to do is hold on to an index.[2] That may seem like a bargain until you see the parsimonious MER of their rival ETFs.

Each ETF tracks a specific index, domestic or foreign, and they do it even more cheaply than index funds. Canadian-based ETF MERs range from 0.17% to 0.55%, a fairly ascetic lot. Canada's most popular ETF, the iUnits S&P/TSX 60 Index Fund, otherwise known as the i60, has a sporty MER of 0.17%.

Why Costs Are So Important

If you don't think saving 1% or 2% in MERs over the lifetime of your investments is anything to worry about, consider the chart below. It shows the difference of a few percentage points on what you get to keep of your own returns. It's chilling.

What Funds Keep (fig. 1)

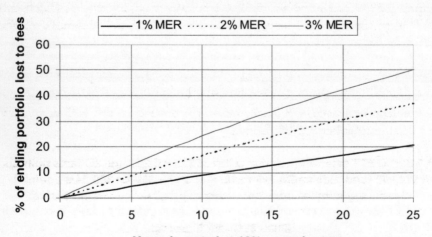

Source: www.stingyinvestor.com

After 20 years, a 2% MER consumes 30% of what your portfolio value would have been without the MER.

In an interview for this book, John Bogle, the famous U.S. pioneer of low-cost index investing, didn't mince words: "Take a look at the difference between 10% and 9% over an investment lifetime of 50 years. Just that little 1%. The difference is staggering. A dollar at 10% is going to be worth $117 and a dollar at 9% is going to be worth $74. If you want to put $10,000 around that, it's $1,170,000 vs. $740,000 to the investor at a 1% difference. That's $430,000 to the croupier. At a 1% difference. Think of that. A third of the return is taken by the croupiers. The investor puts up 100% of the capital and takes 100% of the risk, but gets two-thirds of the returns."

Fat MERs and back-end load commissions are the Black Jack dealers here. Your financial advisor's commission on a standard back-end load fund (otherwise known as a deferred sales charge fund or DSC) is around 5% of the value of your investment, and typically another 0.5% annually (on equity funds) for providing on-going service. That commission, though not paid directly by you, is financed through your fund's MER. The economics work because the MERs are high enough to make it work, and if you should have to redeem your fund before your declining sales charge schedule has run its course, you'll think ETFs, even with their trading commission costs, a real bargain.

As long as you hold a back-end load fund for the full course of its declining sales charge schedule, usually about seven years, you don't pay any sales charge on redemption. Most fund companies do allow 10% free annual redemptions and free switches among funds in the same fund company, but should you want to move your money out of the fund company altogether before the DSC schedule has run its inexorable course, you pay a "back-end load" that starts as high as 7% of your investment and declines over the schedule.

Back-End Load Charges vs. Trading Commissions. Which Do You Prefer?

Compare having a percentage of your assets clawed back on the redemption of a back-end load fund to the flat fee cost of selling an ETF at a discount broker for $25 a trade.

A $10,000 ETF sale with a commission of $25 = 0.25% (or 25 basis points).
A $10,000 fund redemption with a load of 3%* = 3% (or 300 basis points).
*insert any number from 7 to 0 here depending on holding period

$300 - $25 = $275 savings

You can avoid a back-end charge by purchasing front-end load funds. These are the second most popular commission option through full service and discount brokers. Under the front-load arrangement, your advisor's sales commission comes immediately and directly out of your invested dollars. You can often negotiate this charge to zero especially for large accounts, but the MER doesn't budge, and front-end MERs are little different from their back-end twins.

Why are front-end MERs so high when front-end funds don't have to finance the advisor's commission? Well, front-end load funds are paying out a sweet 1% annual trailer to your advisor (on equity funds). So with either front-end or back-end option, one whole percentage point of your MER is going to pay advisor compensation in one form or another. Trailer fees are reduced on the increasingly popular "low-load" funds, which have a far less punitive DSC schedule lasting just two or three years.

No-load funds, those that have neither front- nor back-end charges, will spare you hurtful sales charges, but they will not let you escape high MERs. With a few exceptions, no-load fund companies charge MERs comparable to their load counterparts.

Index mutual funds, sold almost exclusively as no-load funds, have MERs that are also hard to justify, at least compared to ETFs. Bank index funds easily range from 0.25% to 2.84% with the median being 1%. Some insurance company index fund MERs are right off the chart with MERs well over 2%.[3]

Once you understand the destructive impact these charges have on your returns over time, it's hard to feel indifferent to them. You must decide if you are receiving value commensurate with the cost.

Canadian Equity Fund vs. Index Fund vs. Index (fig. 2)

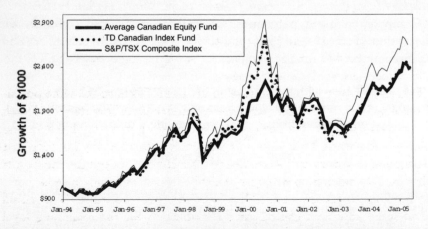

Note: MER on Cdn large cap fund, 2.3%, MER on TD Canadian Index Fund, 0.88%.
The longer management costs compound, the harder it is to beat the index

Source: www.stingyinvestor.com

ETFs Can Be More Tax Efficient Than Mutual Funds

Active managers sell securities at a profit, which is their job after all, but that has the unfortunate consequence of generating capital gains. The more active a fund manager is, the more likely she is to be racking up a tax bill for you at the end of the year (unless your holdings are in a tax-sheltered account like an RRSP). Mutual funds are now required to disclose their historical portfolio turnover rate in their prospectuses, and the numbers might surprise you.

Let's compare the 5-year average turnover rate for the ten largest Canadian equity mutual funds to the turnover rate for their benchmark index. As a proxy for the index, we can use the 5-year average portfolio turnover rate of TD's Canadian Index Fund, which gives us a baseline of 11.4%. The ten largest conventional equity funds had an average turnover rate three times as high, at 36.7%.[4] That's a significant difference, but one I believe understates the turnover rate of the majority of equity funds. Big funds move slowly so as not to move the market with them. Smaller funds react more spryly, jumping in and out of positions like a mouse running between the legs of an elephant.

In any event, capital gains from portfolio changes must be passed on, at least annually, to the fund investor. Not only is this likely to result in a tax bill, but sometimes you can find yourself paying tax on gains the fund made before you even owned it.

The less a portfolio trades, the fewer capital gains are realized and ultimately distributed. Since an index manager is most often sitting passively on her portfolio doing little more than trying to keep her portfolio as similar to the target index as possible, passively managed funds generally are more tax efficient than actively managed funds. Sure, a change to the underlying index will trigger a buy or sell within an index fund or ETF, but these changes are seldom momentous.

This isn't to say that index mutual funds and ETFs have the same potential tax liabilities. They don't, and the difference is in how they deal with redemptions. Imagine a popular index, like Nasdaq, suffering a severe and prolonged downturn. Push your imagination even further, and imagine that Nasdaq fund investors decided to flee to safer ground, redeeming their units in droves. The index fund manager would be forced to liquidate some portfolio holdings to get the cash to buy back the redeemed units. This could lead to some unwanted capital gains distributions for the remaining loyal unit holders who went on to see the value of their holdings diminish as the bear market continued to maul their index and their fund manager. Nobody wants a tax bill on top of a disastrous year.

ETF investors don't have to stay up late worrying about redemption runs because retail investors can't redeem their shares; they can only buy and sell them to other parties. These transactions on the secondary market don't directly affect the underlying portfolio and so have no tax consequences to other fund investors. This is the main reason ETFs should be more tax-efficient than index mutual funds. U.S.-based ETFs are decidedly more tax-efficient than U.S.-based index funds. In Canada, the tax-efficiency difference between index funds and ETFs is not as clear as it is for U.S. products. As we'll discuss later, institutional clients can cash in large ETF positions for their underlying securities. In the U.S. this redemption does not trigger tax calculations. In Canada it can. Three Canadian ETFs have periodically disgorged hefty capital gains to unitholders due to institutional activity. Most other Canadian ETFs, however, have not.

With the exception of these three Canadian ETFs, and I hope it is a temporary exception, ETF index investors have greater control over their own tax liabilities than their counterparts with mutual funds—conventional or index. Actively managed fund unit holders are at the mercy of the manager's selling activity. Index mutual fund owners are at the mercy of the redeeming millions.

What Mutual Funds Have That ETFs Don't

Mutual funds do have some attractive features that ETFs don't share.

Small Minimum Investment

Mutual funds can be bought with small minimum investments—often as little as $500, and it is easy to arrange very small regular monthly purchases (commonly known as a pre-authorized chequing plan, or PAC). ETFs, in contrast, are generally bought and sold in lots of 100 shares. Say the i60s were trading around $54 a share. Based on 100 shares, (a "board lot"), that's a $5,400 minimum investment plus brokerage commission. Of course it is possible to buy less than 100 shares, what's known as an odd lot, but the minimum brokerage commission still applies to these smaller orders which makes them less cost effective than a board lot purchase.

No Trading Commission

While ETFs have a trading commission associated with them, there is usually no transaction cost to buy or sell a mutual fund. The mutual fund company typically executes these transactions for free. Remember, of course, that mutual funds often have front or back-end loads, and even no-load funds and discount brokers can charge small transaction fees.

Dividend Reinvestment

Another nice feature of mutual funds is the ease with which dividends can be reinvested. Mutual fund owners can elect to have their dividends and other distributions sent to them in cash or reinvested into units of the fund automatically. ETF investors have to take the cash—unless their brokerage house has a private dividend reinvestment plan in place. To date, TD Waterhouse and the full-service and discount arms of RBC and CIBC offer dividend reinvestment programs for some of Barclays Global Investors Canada ETFs and the more popular U.S. ETFs. Canadian ShareOwner Investments Inc. does the same.

Certificate Form

For those interested in taking out an investment loan or using your investments for collateral, keep in mind that ETF distributors do not issue certificates. Your ETF holding is noted electronically and no physical certificate is required or produced. Most mutual fund companies, on the other hand, will provide share certificates upon request for a small fee. This permits you to hold the investments in a safety deposit box or to pledge them at a bank for a loan.

Closed-End Mutual Funds vs. ETFs

A basket of securities trading on a stock exchange is not a radically new idea. A certain kind of mutual fund has long traded on a stock exchange; known as "closed-end" funds, these are not to be confused with ETFs.

A Fixed Number of Units

Closed-end funds issue a fixed number of units that trade on a stock exchange or over-the-counter. Unlike conventional mutual funds, which continually issue and redeem shares (hence "open-end"), closed-end funds do not issue new or additional shares after the initial offering. That means investors wanting a closed-end fund must find someone else from whom to purchase their shares, just as they would for a stock—or an ETF. ETFs, though, do issue and redeem units with large institutional activity. No amount of institutional activity will make a closed-end fund sprout new units. They just can't do it.

Actively Managed

Closed-end funds are actively managed just like conventional open-end funds. ETF fans have long waited for an actively managed product, and the prospect still seems more than a year away at least. The fact that closed-end funds have the added advantage of trading on an exchange makes them sound like the Platonic ideal of a diversified investment product. Unfortunately they have had one stiff disadvantage in reality.

Trading at a Discount

Closed-end funds frequently trade at less than the value of their underlying assets. This is called "trading at a discount." (If they were to trade at more than their net asset value, they would be trading at a premium.) The average discount for closed-end funds in Canada was running at 2.9% at the end of March 2005.[5] It's not entirely clear why there is a discount and why it is occasionally of considerable magnitude. Some have suggested that discounts arise because of concerns about liquidity—the ease with which the investment can be sold.

In any event, to ameliorate this perennial problem, closed-end funds issued in Canada since the late 1990s have incorporated an annual retraction privilege which allows investors to sell back shares to the fund at their net asset value. This is an enormous structural advantage which should help to keep the newer closed-end funds far closer to their net asset value (NAV) than the sometimes 20-40% discount swings of the older funds.

Even with this modification though, closed-end funds can't match the slender discounts and premiums of ETFs. ETFs usually trade within a very narrow range of their NAV and rarely at a significant discount. There's a good reason for this.

ETFs Can Be Converted to Their Underlying Securities; Closed-End Funds Can't Be

With a sufficiently large number of units, ETFs can be converted at any time during market hours to their underlying securities. This requisite chunk is called a "creation/redemption unit" and generally consists of 50,000 shares. (The exact number depends on the specific ETF.) The ability to quickly distil an ETF into its constituent securities keeps ETFs trading very close to their net asset value. You can see for yourself how close to home ETFs trade by looking up the charts illustrating the historical discount/premiums of iUnit ETFs at *www.iunits.com*, under "Individual Investor," then "Tools and Data."

You'll often see closed-end funds grouped with ETFs and referred to as exchange traded funds. The contemporary crop of ETFs is then distinguished by the fetching phrase, "index-linked" exchange traded funds.

This is unfortunate and inaccurate because closed-end funds are not ETFs and ETFs are not all index-linked.

Some ETFs hold gold or bonds rather than index components, and all

Fund Structure Comparison (fig. 3)

Features	Index-Linked ETFs	Closed-End Funds	Open-End Funds
Management Style	Passive	Active Managed	Passive/Active
Management Fees	Very Low	Low	Moderate to High
Pricing	Intraday	Intraday	End of Day
Investment Restrictions on Illiquid Securities	No	No	Yes
Ability to Leverage	No	Yes	No
Premium/Discount Risk	Low	Moderate/High	None
Tax Efficiency	High	Moderate	Moderate
Redemption Feature	Yes	No or Annual	Yes
Investor Ability to Short	Yes	Yes	No
Transparency of Portfolio	Yes	Sometimes	No
Marginable	Yes	Yes	No
Limit Orders	Yes	Yes	No

ETFs are distinguished from closed-end funds by their ability to convert to their underlying basket of securities at any time during market hours. Take a look at Figure 3 to see the differences between ETFs, closed-end funds, and open-end mutual funds.

Closed-end funds have been around for a long time, and their new structure is giving them a second wind. The first closed-end fund in Canada was the Economic Investment Trust, launched way back in 1928. It took closed-end funds until 2001 to get to $6.7 billion in assets, but since then they've shot up to $22 billion in 2005.[6] This growth is in large part due to the bundling of income trusts into close-end funds to make an income trust fund of funds. ETFs, by comparison, have been around for only 15 years, and already have $10 billion in assets.

How ETFs Stay Close to the Value of Their Underlying Securities

Simply having some way to convert ETF shares to their underlying investments, and vice versa, means that ETFs almost always trade very close to the full value of their assets. It's the beauty of arbitrage at work and here's how it's done.

If the market price for an ETF share is cheaper than the proportional portfolio value, an investor with enough shares to form a creation unit, usually an institutional investor, can redeem the shares for the underlying securities. Since the securities are worth more than the ETF share, the investor then sells the individual securities and pockets the profit. That's basic arbitrage and it works in reverse just as well. Should the ETF shares be selling for more than the value of the underlying portfolio, an investor can independently buy up the individual securities and hand them over to the ETF administrator who will issue shares in the ETF. The investor can turn a profit by immediately selling those ETF units.

So arbitrage, in simple terms, is buying cheap and simultaneously selling what's dear and pocketing the difference after your costs. If you are arbitraging identical or nearly identical investments, there is little risk to this strategy provided you can execute your orders instantaneously.

Arbitrage Mechanism Results in Low Premium/Discount (fig. 4)

Premium
Market price > Indicative portfolio value

Sell ETF, buy portfolio basket

Authorized Participant

Discount
Market price < Indicative portfolio price

Buy ETF, sell portfolio basket

As a retail investor you'll never have to do this arbitrage, but the fact that somebody else can, and is willing to, keeps the price of the ETF shares cozily close to the value of the underlying investments. That's what really matters.[7]

"I've never seen a product as good at tracking its bogey as this one," says Steve Elgee, Managing Director, Equity Derivative Products, with BMO Nesbitt Burns Inc., referring to the i6o. Nesbitt Burns is one of the designated brokers for the i6o, and as such, is responsible for ensuring an efficient, liquid, and orderly market for Barclays Global Investors Canada's ETFs, known collectively as iUnits. "There are a lot of eyes on this. We are always watching for price discrepancies greater than a nickel because that presents arbitrage opportunities."

Arbitrage is made possible by two important features of ETFs—transparency and interchangeability. ETFs are transparent because their portfolio holdings are known at all times. Contrast that with the portfolio disclosure of mutual funds. Conscientious mutual fund investors know how hard it is to get current positions in a conventional mutual fund portfolio. The information is at best a month old by the time it is public. Quarterly portfolio reporting is in the offing, but so far regulations still permit disclosure that can be as old as six months. With average actively managed portfolio turnover of 40%-80% a year, that means that almost half of a mutual fund's portfolio could be different from the six-month-old snapshot—hardly a satisfactory state of affairs for those who would prefer to know exactly what they're buying.

ETFs are also interchangeable with their underlying securities and vice versa. You will sometimes see ETFs referred to as "fungible." This is another way of saying they are interchangeable, and it's the creation/redemption mechanism that makes this possible.

Even with this creation/redemption mechanism, however, ETFs do sometimes experience a premium or discount—most often towards the very end of the trading day. The price discrepancies are most often minor; nevertheless, it's best to trade ETFs while the market for their underlying securities is open. In the U.S., that means avoiding that tempting period from 4 p.m. to 4:15 p.m. when many ETFs still trade. For ETFs pegged to foreign markets, that means coordinating your trades with time zone considerations.

How can you be sure you are getting a fair price? With U.S. ETFs it's easy since the American Stock Exchange, where 85% of all U.S. ETFs trade, calculates the value of the underlying portfolio of securities every 15 seconds—as well as supplying real time quotes for ETFs themselves. The Toronto Stock Exchange doesn't have a similar NAV calculator so, if you're inclined, get your calculator ready for Chapter Seven where we'll lift the hood and take a good look at how ETFs run and how they're priced.

But before that fun, let me introduce you to the foot soldiers of the new investment frontier.

Getting to Know ETFs

With the exception of one Canadian bond ETF, and a U.S. gold ETF, all current ETFs are related to an index. Name an index and it's likely there is an ETF corresponding to it. ETFs are easy to use and make it simple to gain exposure to just about any geographical area, economic sector, or market segment. The sheer number of ETFs testifies to this. As of April, 2005, there were 197 ETFs trading in North America—181 in the U.S. and 16 in Canada. The global ETF population is booming at over 370 and counting.

The Varieties of ETFs

There's an ETF for all major indices: S&P 500, the Dow Jones Industrial Average, the Fortune 500, Nasdaq 100, S&P/TSX 60, and MSCI EAFE (Europe, Australasia, and the Far East.) Then there are ETFs for just about every industry sector known to analysts: financials, industrials, technology, utilities, internet, business to business internet, biotechnology, pharmaceuticals, regional banks, you name it. Global sector ETFs are also proliferating. (For a complete list of ETFs and their indices see the appendices.)

And if sectors aren't enough, there are ETFs to suit your taste in market capitalization and/or investment style. There's a U.S. ETF series based on the Dow Jones Index broken down according to a combination of capitalization and investment style. You can invest in a large cap value ETF, a small cap growth ETF, and many variations in between. Closer to home, Canadians can now select a growth or value ETF tied to a Canadian equity index.

In the U.S., you'll also find ETFs for a broad range of developed and developing countries, too, from humble Malaysia to languorous Brazil—24 country ETFs in all—each one trying to track their respective country's broad market. There are even ETFs that track the movement of real estate investment trusts (REITs), and ETFs that track U.S. bond indices. Most recently, ETFs have been introduced that track American Depositary Receipts (ADRs) Indices. ADRs are certificates that trade on American markets, but which represent shares of companies that trade on foreign markets. ADRs allow North American investors to have a direct interest in foreign corporations while still having the protection and convenience of dealing with a U.S. exchange. These products are well-established and are now being bundled into the ever versatile ETFs.

Although ETFs have found a comfortable niche in indexing, the ETF structure and concept lend themselves easily to other investments. One Canadian ETF, for instance, holds bonds. Well, one bond to be exact. Barclays Canada's iG5 Fund holds one Government of Canada 5-year bond which changes periodically to maintain a 5-year maturity. Actual gold bars can be found in two gold ETFs in the U.S., and more commodity-based ETFs are expected.

Beyond standard indices, bonds and commodities, you'll find ETFs pushing into unusual indices whose rules come close to mimicking active management. ETFs based on quantitative, rules-based indices have exploded on the U.S. scene as enhanced indexing products. Conceptually it seems a short skip to genuinely actively managed ETFs.

An actively managed ETF would have a basket of investments, which are actively bought and sold by a fund manager—exactly like a conventional actively managed mutual fund—just one that trades like a stock on an exchange. There aren't any of these in North America yet, but it's likely that actively managed ETFs will make their appearance here in the next few years. When that happens, the whole mutual fund industry will be looking over its shoulder, or getting itself ready to convert its own funds into more tantalizing ETFs.

What's in a Name?

For all their conceptual elegance, exchange traded funds have a nomenclature easy to confuse with a spoonful of vegetable soup. Take, for example, streetTRACKS DJ U.S. Smallcap Value, or even the simpler i60C Fund. Generally some letter or word in the name indicates the company that constructs and administers the fund. That company is known as the fund sponsor. "streetTRACKS" is the general product name for a number of ETFs offered by State Street Global Advisors, a U.S. investment firm. The rest of the name identifies the particular index the ETF is associated with, in this case the Dow Jones U.S. Small Cap Value Index, an index that consists of stocks in companies with small market capitalization and which are considered undervalued and longer-term holds—value plays in other words.

The i60C Fund has a similar name structure. The "i" stands for "index" and is the distinctive indicator of "iUnits," the brand name for all of Barclays Global Investors Canada Limited's ETFs. (iShares are Barclays' U.S. and global product.) The "60" refers to the S&P/TSX 60 Index consisting of Canada's biggest and most frequently traded companies. The "C" stands for "capped." A capped index sets limits on how large a percentage any one stock in an index can obtain—typically no more than 10%, which is the case with the i60C Fund. Capped indices became respectable when Nortel Networks Corp. made up a third of the TSE 100 in early 2000. So great was its concentration on the index that it was said when Nortel sneezed, the whole index shivered. Nortel ultimately caught pneumonia and investors and investment managers then realized the appeal of limiting index concentrations.

Canadian Exchange Traded Funds (fig.5)

Fund	Description	Symbol	Sponsor
i60	Oldest and biggest ETF in Canada. TIPS35 and TIPS 100 merged with i60s in 03/2000. Based on S&P/TSX 60 Index	XIU	Barclays Canada
iG5	5-year Government of Canada Bond	XGV	Barclays Canada
iBond	Tracks Scotia Universe Bond Index	XBB	Barclays Canada
i60C	Based on S&P/TSX 60 Capped Index (weights capped at 10%)	XIC	Barclays Canada
iMidCap	Based on S&P/TSX MidCap Index (The next 60 companies by market cap after the i60 companies)	XMD	Barclays Canada
iEnergy, iIT, iGold iFinancial iREIT	Five funds: Energy, Information Technology, Gold, Financials, REITs based on respective S&P/TSX sector indices All funds' constituents capped at a max. weight of 25%	XEG XIT, XGD XFN XRE	Barclays Canada
i500R	Based on S&P 500 Index	XSP	Barclays Canada
iIntR	Based on MSCI EAFE Index	XIN	Barclays Canada
TD S&P/TSX Composite	Based on the S&P/TSX Composite Index	TTF	TDAM
TD S&P/TSX Composite Capped	Based on the S&P/TSX Capped Composite Index (weightings limited to 10%)	TCF	TDAM
TD Select Canadian Growth	Based on the Dow Jones Canada TopCap Growth Index	TAG	TDAM
TD Select Canadian Value	Based on the Dow Jones Canada TopCap Value Index	TAV	TDAM

Barclays Canada: Barclays Global Investors Canada Ltd.; TDAM: TD Asset Management Inc.,owned by TD Bank Financial Group.

As of May 1, 2005.

TD Asset Management has an ETF based on a capped index also, the "TD S&P/TSX Composite Index Capped Fund." It's important not to confuse "capped" with "cap," a short form of "market capitalization." There are small, mid and large cap ETFs, all of which have "cap" in their name but are not necessarily "capped" in terms of their investment weightings. "Cap" refers to the size of companies that make up the fund's core holdings or emphasis. "Capped" means the fund has a limit on the percentage that any one company can represent in the fund.

Canadians can also buy any of the 180+ U.S.-listed ETFs. For a complete list of U.S. ETFs, please refer to the Appendix. The ten largest U.S.-based ETFs are listed below.

Popular U.S. Exchange Traded Funds (fig. 6)
See Appendix for complete list of all ETFs

Fund	Description	Ticker	Sponsor
S & P Depositary Receipt	Abbreviated as SPDR Based on the S&P 500 Index Oldest and biggest U.S. ETF	SPY	SSgA**
NASDAQ 100	Often called Qubes. NASDAQ 100 Index. Most heavily traded U.S. ETF	QQQQ	BoNY
iShares MSCI EAFE	Based on MSCI Europe, Australasia, Far East Index	EFA	Barclays US
iShares S&P 500	Based on S&P 500 Index	IVV	Barclays US
DIAMONDS	Based on the Dow Jones Industrial Average	DIA	SSgA
MidCap SPDR	S&P MidCap 400 Index	MDY	BoNY
iShares Russell 2000	U.S. Small Cap Index	IWM	Barclays US
iShares MSCI Japan	MSCI Japan Index	EWJ	Barclays US
iShares DJ Sel Divdend	Follows Dow Jones Selected Divdend Index	DVY	Barclays US
iShares Russell 1000 Value	Tracks Russell 1000 Value Index	IWD	Barclays US

**SSgA: State Street Global Advisors; Barclays US: Barclays Global Investors Ltd.; BoNY: Bank of New York

Just to avoid confusion, note that in Canada mutual funds and ETFs are sold in "units." In the U.S., they are sold in "shares." We'll be using the terms similarly in this book.

Sponsors, Index Providers, and Distributors

The company that constructs and administers an ETF is known as the ETF sponsor. Sponsors must pay a licensing fee to an index provider for the rights to use an index. In return, the index provider frequently grants temporary exclusives on licenses to give the sponsor an incentive to spend money marketing the fund. The i60 Fund, for instance, uses the S&P/TSX 60 Index which is administered by Standard & Poor's, the index provider. Continuing our example, Barclays Global Investors Canada, the originator and sponsor of the i60 Fund, must pay Standard & Poor's for the use of its index. As you might expect, fights over both exclusives and licensing fees have kept a number of ETFs from market—especially an S&P 500 VIPER from U.S. index fund giant, Vanguard Group.

And just to make things complicated, in the U.S., the company that sponsors an ETF is not the same company that distributes it. Barclays Global Investors manufactures the iShares series but they are distributed by a separate company, SEI Investment Distribution Co. Ltd. This isn't terribly relevant for ETFs in Canada, but knowing this can avoid some confusion when you're looking at U.S. ETFs.

Are ETFs the Death of Mutual Funds?

A major U.S. mutual fund industry intelligence company, Financial Research Corporation, did a study on the effect ETFs would have on mutual funds.

Gavin Quill, who co-authored the study, said in an interview for this book: "There is a compelling superiority to ETFs versus index mutual funds in most cases; nevertheless, you're not going to see the elimination of index mutual funds. In the real world, there is substantial inertia to investor behaviour. They stick with what's working well enough."

Quill believes the competitive threat will heat up substantially when actively managed ETFs become available. "People like actively managed funds—rationally or irrationally. Once you move to an actively managed option, now you've got a viable competitor to the mutual fund industry," he says. "We have been forecasting that in the first five years from the first actively managed ETF, we would get to about $200 billion in the U.S. Even under the very best case, that's only a small fraction of equity mutual funds and it would clearly still not annihilate the mutual fund industry. It would just be a respectable complement to the mutual fund giant."

"I expect over the next decade we will see ETFs and mutual funds all thrive together in the U.S., Canada, and around the globe," continues Quill.

"Growing wealth, increasing pools of financial assets, retirement privatization, and low interest rates will create a prosperous environment with plenty of opportunity for each of these vehicles to grow at a healthy pace without having to kill off one of the others to succeed."[8]

Just as television did not obliterate the radio, so ETFs will not completely displace mutual funds, but the world has changed forever and for the better.

Meet the First Spider Man

Now that you have a good understanding of ETFs and their prospects, let me introduce you to the man most responsible for bringing the first and biggest ETF to American investors.

An Interview with Nathan Most—Father of "Spiders"

A man who earned a living trading coconut oil in the 60s was the driving force behind the first successful ETF in the U.S., the now famous Spiders (SPDRs). Nathan Most had been responsible for the international trading of coconut and palm oil for a San Francisco company, Pacific Vegetable Oil.

When the company closed because of a falling-out between the owners, Most was approached by the Bank of America to start up a futures exchange in San Francisco to trade western commodities. It opened in 1970 and, as Most says with disarming casualness, he "finally ended up running it."

Then, says Most, there was a worldwide drought in 1974 that sent the price of coconut oil soaring. "Our principal contract was trading coconut oil from the Philippines. The price went from 13¢ a pound to 56¢ a pound in six months, and I had a lot of millionaires on my trading floor who thought they knew something about coconut oil."

"When the crop began to come back in," he recalls, "we got a market reversal that wiped out half my trading floor. Then the brokerage houses that were clearing for my floor traders said they weren't going to clear it anymore, so I had to shut it down."

That was in early 1976. Before he could dust off a pair of bell-bottomed jeans he was invited to Washington as technical assistant to the first chairman of the Commodities Futures Trading Commission.

Very soon thereafter, the American Stock Exchange (AMEX) asked him to help them put together a futures exchange, the AMEX Commodities Exchange. This was subsequently sold to the New York Stock Exchange and now runs as the New York Futures Exchange.

Most stayed on with AMEX, however, as head of new products. It was a splashy title, but Most admits he "pretty much made it up as I went." His job was to build AMEX's then languishing trading volume, and his first thought was to get mutual funds to trade on the exchange.

He approached Jack Bogle, founder of Vanguard Group and famed advocate for low-cost index funds. Bogle didn't have any interest in putting his funds on an exchange. The trading in and out of the fund that would result, he believed, would drive up fund costs. Most was aware of other attempts to trade baskets of securities, but he liked best an idea hearkening back to his commodities days, a warehouse receipt. With such a receipt commodities are bought and sold innumerable times without ever leaving the warehouse and with no additional expenses. Most applied that principle to a basket of securities, namely those in the S&P 500 Index— hence **S**tandard & **P**oor's **D**epositary **R**eceipts, SPDRs. To actually implement them, Most created an investment company as a modified Unit Investment Trust, and then spent three years and a million dollars of AMEX's money in legal expenses to break down the regulatory barriers.

Standard & Poor's Depositary Receipts, more affectionately known as "spiders," was launched in January 1993, and what was originally just a way to build trading volume has become an internationally popular investment vehicle.

Asked if the launch of SPDRs was a particularly gratifying personal moment, Most says, "When you work on something that long, it is sort of an anticlimax." But Most, still in the game as a board member for iShares Trust for BGI and Chairman Emeritus, says the gratification is coming now. "Looking where it's gone, it is almost unbelievable. They are spreading around the world very rapidly. It is just incredible."

This interview was conducted in 2001. Mr. Most passed away in December 2004, at the age of 90. When he died, there were about 175 ETFs in the U.S., with AMEX home to 85% of them. Like many pioneers, Mr. Most never received any monetary benefit from his role in the development of Spiders, but he left behind a great legacy indeed, one for which investors around the world are thankful.

Notes

1) With mutual funds, the price you buy or sell at is determined only at the end of the trading day and after you've placed your buy or sell order. The only exception is with some money market funds: their value stays constant at $1 or $10 a unit.

2) MERs in the U.S. are considerably lower than in Canada. According to *www.Morningstar.com*, the median actively managed U.S. large cap equity fund had an MER of 1.3% as of April 30, 2005. The most popular ETFs in the U.S., Spiders and Qubes, have a positively ascetic MER of 0.1% and 0.2% respectively. The median MER for Canadian equity index funds was provided by Morningstar Canada as of April 30, 2002. Insurance company index funds were excluded because their extremely high MERs have made the median MER too high to be representational of the overall retail market. The median diversified Canadian equity fund MER number came from Morningstar Canada's PALTrak as of April 30, 2005.

3) PALTrak data, courtesy of Morningstar Canada, as of April 30, 2005.

4) This finding based on work commissioned for this book and done by Norman Rothery, Ph.D. of *www.stingyinvestor.com* by reviewing fund prospectuses.

5) As per Lea Hill, closed-end fund specialist and Executive Director, CIBC World Markets Inc. in Toronto.

6) As per Lea Hill, closed-end fund specialist and Executive Director, CIBC World Markets Inc. in Toronto, as of May 2, 2005. The $22 billion figure for the closed-end universe excludes split share corporations.

7) This is how arbitraging works in principle. In actual practice, however, ETF arbitraging in Canada benefits from additional tools without redeeming fund units. What regularly happens with sophisticated players is arbitraging between the i60 and an index future on the S&P/TSX 60 index. When the future is cheaper, arbitrageurs will buy the future and sell the corresponding ETF, and vice versa. Since both investments have claim to the identical assets, the S&P/TSX 60 index, it is an easy and fairly risk free way to make money and help the market keep the price of the i60 in line with its underlying asset value.

8) Gavin Quill's report came out in 2000. He made these comments as Senior Vice President and Director of Research Studies with FRC.

Chapter Two

Why Index?

Exchange traded funds are almost all related to an index. You've got to be convinced that tracking the market is a good and noble pursuit, or ETFs, at least in their current incarnation, will have little appeal. Fortunately, the argument for indexing is very easy to make. The simple truth is that for most asset classes, indexing gives better investment returns over the long haul than active management, but somehow the perverse gambler in us all urges us to forsake the certain for the extraordinary. Here's why you shouldn't.

It's Too Hard to Pick This Year's Top Funds

Ask yourself just how many times you've had one of the top 25 performing mutual funds of the year—the year they were in the top. If you're like most, chasing yesterday's star means making a bed for today's tired dog.

A study done by Boston-based Financial Research Corporation (FRC) found that, on average, funds do about 20% better than most fund investors in those very same funds. How is that possible? It's the phenomenon of chasing returns. Most investors jump into a fund after it has made most of its gains, so a fund can have, say, a 15% return yet most of its investors will see only a 12% gain—or less. It's long been known that investors don't hold their funds long enough and have a nasty habit of investing just after a fund's top performing quarter when most of the gains have been made.

The FRC study found, on a 3-year rolling return basis from January 1990 to March 2000, the average U.S. mutual fund's mean 3-year return was 10.9%, while the average invested dollar gained only 8.7%. FRC also reports that American fund investors hold their funds for about 2.9 years. In the mid-90s, investors' patience lasted 5.5 years.[1] There's no reason to think the Canadian experience is much different.

"Investors (in aggregate) have poor timing and tend to *underperform* the very funds in which they are invested," says Dan Hallett in a report he wrote for FundMonitor.com Corp.[2] Hallett's study looked at two popular specialty funds with big sales and redemptions, AIC Advantage I and AIC Advantage II. He tracked the money going in and out of them and timed these cash flows to the fund's actual performance. Combining the figures for these two funds together, nearly 70% of the money in these funds to the end of September 1999 was invested in just the 36 months before. During those 36 months, Hallett says, "investors earned an aggregate annualized return less than one-seventh of the funds's own published performance numbers." This means that most of the money came into the funds after the funds had already made their gains and left before the funds got back on track.

Jumping around among funds is a form of market timing. It's ironic that mutual funds should have this problem since one reason investors have flocked to them is in acknowledgement that they can't time the market— yet investors continually try to time their mutual fund purchases. Clearly, market timing is just as difficult to do with mutual funds as it is with stocks. (If you're going to try to time the market, the best way is to invest in the market itself, and ETFs are absolutely the best way to do that. But more on that later.)

Winners Don't Stay Winners

Even if you are lucky enough to have picked a winner just before its glory, only a small fraction of today's stars stay in the top quartile of funds the next year. After two years, your chances of still having a fund in the top quartile are wispy. In 1999, there were 116 Canadian equity funds in the top performance quartile. Of those winners, six were left in the top quartile in 2001. These six turned out to be remarkably strong performers, making it to the end of 2004, the end of our study period. You may think the others just slipped quietly down into the second quartile, making respectable progress just beneath the radar. Hardly. By 2001, 65 of the first quartile funds in 1999 were fourth quartile losers. A mere two years later and 56% of the first quartile funds were an embarrassment.[3]

Durability of Performance (fig. 7)

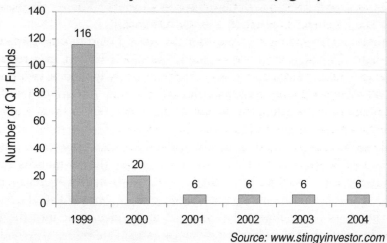

Source: www.stingyinvestor.com

First Quartile Funds in 1999 that Remained First Quartile in All Subsequent Years.

Where the First Quartile 1999 Funds Landed in 2001 (fig. 8)

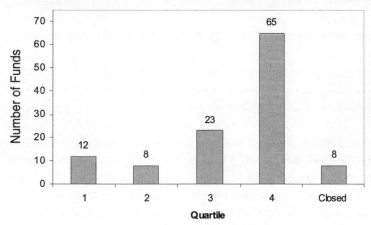

Source: www.stingyinvestor.com

Top performing funds don't stay that way for long. Of 116 first quartile funds in 1999, only twelve were first quartile performers after two years.

The more outstanding the fund, the worse its chances of remaining outstanding, too. FundMonitor.com Corp., a financial advisory support company based in Toronto, has discovered something they playfully call the "newspaper effect." They tracked the performance of funds from the first time they were advertised in one newspaper's mutual funds supplement. A staggering 92% of these funds did not subsequently match their advertised 3-year record, and 45% of these funds went on to do at least 10 percentage points less the year following the ad.[4]

This is called "reversion to the mean," and it is as unattractive a reality as it is an English phrase. Sooner or later, returns gravitate to the historical levels of their asset class. Of course, a few exceptionally brilliant managers have index-breaking 10-year records, but as their funds grow ever larger, their chances of continued success seem to diminish all the faster.

Although it's possible to beat the index—and to do so over a substantial period—it is unlikely, and it is even more unlikely that you are going to be fortunate enough to own the fund that does it. You need to ask yourself, to use Dirty Harry's famous words, "Do you feel lucky?" Do you think your luck will steer you to the winning active manager this year, and the one after, and the one after until retirement? Chances are your funds will have more mediocre years than exceptional ones, and a mediocre year with an actively managed mutual fund usually means getting returns below the benchmark index.

After Tax, Where's the Advantage?

Having an excelling fund does not necessarily mean it beat the index, especially after taxes. Fund returns are always quoted after management expenses are deducted, but take no consideration of the after-tax return. Because the average Canadian equity fund sells a large percentage of its holdings in any given year, a normal portfolio turnover rate for actively managed funds, there are usually taxes to pay. Too few investors scrutinize their after-tax returns. If they did, they'd realize holding a hot fund outside a registered account can be, if not a pyrrhic victory, sometimes an uncomfortable one. Of course everyone would prefer to pay tax if that means they're making money. The trouble comes when the outperforming fund becomes just a mediocre fund while its old, formerly winning, trading habits continue kicking out tax liabilities.

Using their proprietary software, PALTrak, Morningstar Canada surveyed a broad range of mutual fund categories to show the impact of taxation on average fund returns for a buy and hold investor. Their chart is an eye-opener. An abbreviated version is reproduced here.

Impact of Taxation on Fund Returns (fig. 9)

1 YEAR

IFSC Category	# Funds	Avg Return	Avg After-Tax Return	Percentage Lost to Tax*	% of Returns Lost to Tax (as a ratio)
CdnBal	271	6.99	6.14	0.85	12.19
Cdn Bond	141	6.44	4.58	1.86	28.90
Cdn Dividend	60	14.96	13.82	1.15	7.65
Cdn Equity	327	10.87	10.49	0.38	3.51
Cdn Small Cap	58	11.06	10.20	0.86	7.79
Cdn TAA	34	7.50	6.89	0.61	8.08
Global Equity	350	-0.26	-0.51	0.24	NA
Sci. & Tech.	84	-9.50	-9.52	0.02	NA
US Equity	281	-4.17	-4.43	0.26	NA

3 YEAR

IFSC Category	# Funds	Avg Return	Avg After-Tax Return	Percentage Lost to Tax *	% of Returns Lost to Tax (as a ratio)
Cdn Balanced	168	5.44	4.42	1.01	18.63
Cdn Bond	105	6.70	4.71	2.00	29.76
Cdn Dividend	37	8.86	7.78	1.08	12.23
Cdn Equity	236	6.49	6.24	0.25	3.81
Cdn Small Cap	45	10.44	9.70	0.74	7.09
Cdn TAA	27	5.31	4.80	0.51	9.62
Global Equity	239	-1.42	-1.60	0.18	NA
Sci. & Tech.	77	-5.63	-5.75	0.12	NA
US Equity	195	-4.41	-4.59	0.18	NA

5 YEAR

IFSC Category	# Funds	Avg Return	Avg After-Tax Return	Percentage Lost to Tax*	% of Returns Lost to Tax (as a ratio)
Cdn Balanced	130	4.48	3.19	1.28	28.68
Cdn Bond	83	6.49	4.30	2.19	33.75
Cdn Dividend	33	10.48	9.15	1.34	12.77
Cdn Equity	166	4.33	3.74	0.58	13.45
Cdn Small Cap	38	8.79	7.96	0.83	9.43
Cdn TAA	24	3.42	2.62	0.80	23.39
Global Equity	156	-4.69	-5.03	0.35	NA
Sci. & Tech.	39	-23.15	-23.38	0.22	NA
US Equity	125	-6.74	-7.08	0.35	NA

Source: Morningstar Canada

*Assumed tax rates: interest 48.6%, capital gains 24.3%, Canadian dividends 37.3%

All returns calculated on a before-disposition basis with the worst-case actual tax rates.

Taxes can take a big bite out of the returns you're paying a manager to get for you. A seminal paper in *Canadian Investment Review* calculated the performance penalty due to taxes on a Canadian equity portfolio with 80% turnover at a painful 4 percentage points.[5] Since that study, tax rates have gone down, and although the calculations haven't been redone, it's reasonable to estimate the tax bite is now closer to 2 percentage points of return. To overcome the taxes you have to pay on an actively managed fund with average portfolio turnover, your mutual fund will have to outperform an index by 2 percentage points, after management fees, every single year you own the fund. Just how likely do you think that is? That's why high turnover mutual funds, the ones that inevitably generate capital gains, should, at the very least, be held in a tax sheltered account like an RRSP.

After-Tax Returns (fig. 10)

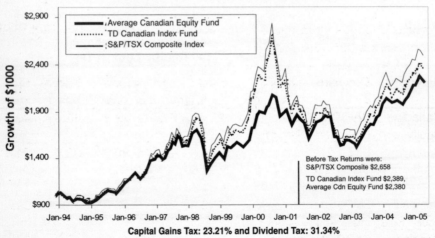

Source: www.stingyinvestor.com

An index and index products will usually have better after-tax returns than actively managed mutual funds.

U.S.-based ETFs are extremely tax efficient and generate few distributions. Canadian ETFs, on the other hand, can sometimes produce capital gains distributions that outstrip even actively managed funds. This is because Canadian tax laws have not quite caught up with the product. (More on that in Chapter Six.) Four Canadian ETFs, out of a total of 16, have a history of significant capital gains distributions, the i60 being the most prolific. Look at an ETF's distribution history before investing. Buy and hold investors might be better off holding the TD Composite ETF for a long-term position while using the i60 as a trading vehicle for short-term holds.

Management Fees Are Corrosive

If all your money is safely tucked away from the worrying touch of Canada Revenue, and you're reasonably content with consistent but not stellar funds, why should you consider indexing? For one thing, you'll still make more money in the long run with an indexing strategy because the large fees required to keep an actively managed fund going are corrosive. Over time, these fees will eat into your returns as surely as battery acid on aluminum.

No doubt fees play a big part in keeping equity managers from surpassing their benchmarks.

Active Managers vs. Their Index Benchmarks (fig. 11)

Percent of actively managed funds in Canada that outperformed their benchmark index 1999-2004

Category	Comparison Index	Last Quarter	Year To Date	One Year	Three Years	Five Years
Canadian Equity	S&P/TSX Composite Index Total Return	22.7	22.7	22.3	13.6	43.5
Canadian Equity	S&P/TSX Capped Composite Index Total Return	22.7	22.7	22.3	13.6	24.5
Canadian Equity (Pure)	S&P/TSX Composite Index Total Return	28.6	28.6	45.0	10.0	39.1
Canadian Equity (Pure)	S&P/TSX Capped Composite Index Total Return	28.6	28.6	45.0	10.0	8.7
Canadian Small Cap Equity	S&P/TSX Canadian Small Cap Total Return	63.4	63.4	69.8	41.3	28.8
U.S. Equity	S&P 500 Total Return Index C$	37.9	37.9	17.7	24.0	23.4

Data as of March 31, 2005
Source: Standard & Poor's, Fundata, www.spiva.standardandpoors.com

Most Managers Cannot Do Better Than Their Benchmark Index.

Except for the small cap growth sector, active equity managers struggled, and mostly failed, to outwit their relevant index in the most recent 1, 3-, and 5-year period.[6] That's the battery acid at work, not stupidity.

In the race for returns, the index wins the marathon mostly because fund management fees are a big obstacle even for talented fund managers to consistently overcome. Where a median MER for an actively managed Canadian large cap equity fund is 2.6%, the median MER for a Canadian equity index mutual fund is 0.78%.[7] The MER on a Canadian equity index-based ETF is 0.25% or less. Those little numbers make a big difference.

The miracle of compounding makes sure the longer these fees eat away at your returns, the greater the damage they do. You can find an MER impact calculator devised by the Ontario Securities Commission at their investor education site, *www.investored.ca*. The calculator shows the damaging effect of MERs on returns. Let's look at just one example.

An MER of 2.34% in a no-load mutual fund held for 20 years and earning an annual return of 10% will eat up 15% of your total returns. The absence of that money over the years ends up costing 25% in foregone earnings so that your final return is only 60% of what it would have been without any MER at all. At a 7% annual return you end up with only 56% of what should have been the total return. The smaller the returns, the more proportional damage the fees do, so every bit of return counts as does every bit of MER.

Are Actively Managed Funds Better in a Down Market?

The long-term superiority of indexing doesn't mean there aren't bursts when active managers come into the fore. In 2001, for instance, the median Canadian equity fund manager beat the TSE 300 Index by 2.2%. Her counterpart in U.S. equities underperformed the S&P 500 by 3.5%. A similar pattern held in 2000. By historical standards, 2000 and 2001 were exceptional years for professional Canadian equity money managers. The market was also busy tanking and continued doing so right through 2002. That year the median Canadian equity manager squeezed out a 0.1 percentage point lead over the benchmark while the median U.S. equity manager underperformed by 1.4 percentage points.[8]

If you ignore the performance of Canadian managers working with U.S. equities, you might be tempted to say that the good performance of

Distribution of Returns and Cost, 7% annual return (fig. 12) *

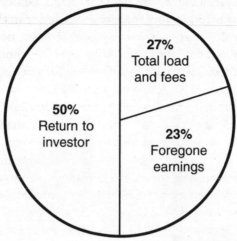

27%
Total load
and fees

50%
Return to
investor

23%
Foregone
earnings

Source: www.investored.ca

Distribution of Returns and Cost, 10% annual return (fig. 13) *

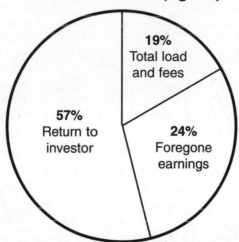

19%
Total load
and fees

57%
Return to
investor

24%
Foregone
earnings

Source: www.investored.ca

* Assumes holding a no-load mutual fund with a MER of 2.34% for 20 years.

Canadian equity managers is no accident: active funds protect against a falling market. That, at least, is the popular belief, but one that isn't supported by history. Yes, active funds did protect investors from the precipitous fall of the major markets that began in 2000, but they haven't always, and there's not much reason to think they will do so with any more consistency in the future.

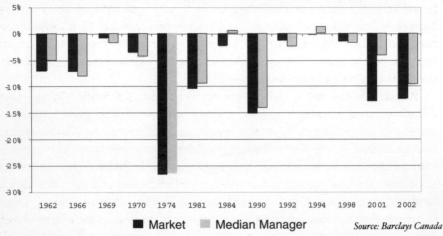

What Protection in a Down Market? (fig. 14)

■ Market   ▧ Median Manager   *Source: Barclays Canada*

This chart shows the performance of institutional money managers in 13 down markets from 1962.

Even institutional managers, as shown in the chart, don't consistently beat their benchmark indices in bad times. If anything, the collective performance of pension fund managers will be better than the collective performance of mutual fund managers because their management fees are much lower. As you can see, these active managers did better than the market in eight of those periods but in most cases they eked out only a minor differential. In four periods they did marginally worse.

It's often said that the cash component of an actively managed fund will pad the fall of a bad market. In fact, active managers are seldom prescient enough to throw a sizable chunk of money into cash at the right times.

Ted Cadsby, one of Canada's foremost indexing advocates, took a look at cash levels in actively managed mutual funds during the 1998 bear market in his book, *The Power of Index Funds* (revised edition). He found barely a difference in cash holdings throughout that dreadful year when the TSE dropped a painful 25%. In fact, the average Canadian equity fund went into the 1998 bear market with less cash than it started out with, though not by much (9.5% vs. 10.2%), which shows the managers didn't see what was coming. Overall, the percentage of Canadian equity funds with 15% or more in cash *decreased* immediately before the downturn (from 19.4% to 18.2%). Clearly, fund managers can't see into the future any better than anyone else.

In 2000, it wasn't cash that saved fund managers' bacon. It was regulatory fund restrictions that saved them from themselves. At the beginning of 2000, Nortel Networks Corp.'s huge price run-up had rocketed it to 36% of the TSE 300. But because Canadian equity fund managers are not permitted to buy a position that costs more than 10% of their assets, Nortel and its stunning growth was under-represented in Canadian equity fund portfolios. Managers were banging on security regulator doors to increase or eliminate the threshold because they were getting creamed by the TSE 300 index heavy with Nortel.

Regulators did not acquiesce for actively managed funds, though they did allow funds to exceed 10% in cases of spinoffs, and they did loosen the threshold for index funds. As you might expect, when Nortel plummeted later in 2000, the actively managed funds suddenly looked pretty smart in spite of themselves (though it didn't salvage their 10-year records).

It wasn't active management that served investors well in 2000, it was securities regulation. But one good benefit of the Nortel experience was the general acceptance of capped indices—as benchmarks for mutual funds and as indices for investment products like index funds and ETFs. Investors who want to index, but still see the prudence of moderation, can now buy a capped index product in which no single component of the index exceeds 10%.

You might think the amount of cash managers have in their portfolios would say something about their market outlook—a bearish outlook leading to more cash and a bullish outlook resulting in less cash, but it seems cash levels are mostly just a reflection of money coming into or out of a fund. In actual practice, a mutual fund's cash levels are more a function of investor behaviour than manager savvy. Cash often results from an influx of new money into a fund that can't be invested fast enough, or it can indicate that the manager is expecting a rush of redemptions.

You've also got to wonder why you want to pay a manager a high MER to manage your portfolio's cash position. Frequently, money managers plow excess cash into an ETF so as not to be handicapped by low interest rates. That means cash may not even stay cash for long. Determining your cash allocation is a basic and critical asset allocation decision you should be making and not deferring to a portfolio manager who knows nothing of your overall portfolio, investment objectives, or risk tolerance. Cash, too, is notoriously easy to manage at little or no cost; so why is a pricey equities portfolio manager taking charge of it?

Indexing Provides Better Portfolio Diversification

One of the biggest advantages of mutual funds is their diversification. Owning a great number of stocks diminishes the investment risk of a few stocks getting into trouble. In actively managed funds, the fund manager selects those stocks she likes and just a limited number of those. It's a fairly select universe, and investors have to hope her wisdom isn't flawed. In general, index funds and ETFs are more diversified than actively managed funds because they hold more stocks and in proportion to an index—not in proportion to the manager's favourites. The result is more portfolio diversification and less active manager risk.

Asset Allocation

The equity component of a well-constructed mutual fund portfolio will be diversified according to investment styles, capitalization, industry sectors, geographical regions, countries and so on. Trouble is, mutual funds don't always stay true to their original colours and this throws off those prudently assembled portfolios.

Active managers come and go but funds stay long beyond them. With each change of fund manager the fund can undergo an investment-style change. It doesn't happen all the time, but it is common. A large cap fund can start taking on more small cap, for instance, or a fund with a predominantly value orientation can start getting more aggressively growth-oriented. Even a continuing manager can feel pressure to adjust her style to prevailing market conditions to enhance performance. That's something called "style drift" and it was common during the tech run-up when value got left in the dirt and Warren Buffett was being called yesterday's man. Plenty of value-style funds bought Nortel Networks, the prototypical growth play in 2000, just so not to be left out of the party.

The issue of style purity is particularly complicated by the fact that mutual fund investors rarely know current portfolio holdings. Fund managers will soon be required to disclose their entire portfolio quarterly, but that disclosure can be dated before it is made public. Looking for style drift or manager signature in an actively managed mutual fund portfolio is a little like hoping to find your glasses in a quickly flowing stream.

Style purity and manager drift are never an issue with an index product. With a portfolio of index investments your asset allocation will be affected by only one thing—the changing proportional values of the indices themselves. The S&P/TSX 60 may go up relative to the S&P 500 and require you to rebalance your portfolio, but you'll never have to worry that your large cap index is slipping into small cap territory, or that your value index is slowly letting in more growth plays.

Index products also allow you to design exact asset allocations in your portfolio. Mutual funds are a mix of cash, and quite often, foreign stocks.[9] These are not pure asset pools. Furthermore, the percentage of cash and foreign equities can vary considerably without timely disclosure. Using mutual funds for asset allocation allows you only an approximation, but with an index product your allocation will be surgically precise.

A Zero-Sum Game

Perhaps the simplest argument for indexing is William F. Sharpe's famous one from logical first principles. Sharpe is a Professor of Finance Emeritus at the Stanford University Graduate School of Business and a Nobel Laureate. He argues that the average actively managed dollar will equal the return on the average passively managed dollar, but, after costs, the return on the average actively managed dollar will be less than that of the average passively managed dollar.

He begins with the self-evident observation that the market return will be a weighted average of the returns on all the securities within the market. Since each passive manager will obtain the market return (before costs), then it follows that the return on the average actively managed dollar must equal the market return. The market is a closed system, thus:

Before Costs
Average passive return = market return
Average active return = market return

Therefore: the average passive return must equal the average active return (before costs).

If the average active dollar outstripped the passive dollar, then the total market return would be increased—which isn't the case because it is a closed system. The market return is unchanged whether active or passive managers are plying their trade. Therefore, collectively, active managers cannot beat out passive managers.

However, our returns in the real world are after costs. Since active management costs are higher than passive management costs, then:

After Costs
Average passive return > Average active return

Sharpe naturally acknowledges that some active managers do beat the market, sometimes even after costs, but the trick is to find them just before they do it. Despite the great difficulty identifying these stars, and their greater difficulty staying stars, most people still place the majority of their money on active managers. No small reason for that is the shamelessly self-serving practice mutual funds have of comparing themselves to each other rather than to an index benchmark. Standard Canadian fund comparisons rank funds by their peer group performance—all large cap Canadian equities, for instance, or mid-cap U.S. equities, or balanced funds. If none of the funds managed to trounce their relevant index, being first among a group of underperformers is like graduating top of the class of a remedial program. It is better than nothing, but do you want your money there?

Canadian securities regulators require mutual funds to identify every fund's benchmark index so investors can compare the fund's returns with that of an appropriate index. This is a good first step, but appropriate benchmarking still has a way to go. Nevertheless, once it is understood that the real race is not for the best fund out of all funds, but rather for the best return relative to the proper index, indexing will seem less a counsel of despair and more a strategy of choice.

Ultimately, there are only two ways for a fund manager to beat their benchmark index: buy investments that aren't in the benchmark index; or over or underweight benchmark positions. If you find a manager who has successfully outperformed and you believe it will continue, you should own that manager—and not tell anyone else about it lest money rush into the fund and handicap your manager's performance. In mutual funds, success really can lead to an embarrassment of riches—for the manager.

As CIBC's Cadsby says, the decision to index is a trade-off. You trade off "the *low possibility* of doing better than the index, for the *high probability* of doing better than most other funds."[10] If the evidence has any sway, the probability of the index outperforming your active manager is a lot greater than your possibility of picking a winning fund. Add to that the tax burden of so many actively managed funds, and it seems anything but an index play is a gambler's folly.

Overall, indexing is cheaper, more tax efficient, less risky, better suited for fine tuning asset allocation, generally more tax efficient and gives more consistent returns than actively managed mutual funds. It's hard to do much better than that.

The Origin of Indexing and the Efficient Markets Hypothesis

You might think indexing as an investment strategy would be as old as the invention of a stock index, but indexing is actually a latecomer. The first stock index was invented by Charles Henry Dow in 1884. It was originally computed by adding up the price of 11 big U.S. stocks (most of them railroads) and dividing them by the number of stocks. The index was revised to 12 stocks on May 26, 1896 for an average of 40.94. Today, the Dow, which includes 30 blue chip companies like Wal-Mart and General Electric (the only remaining original Dow component), now stands at about 10,000. Of course, many more indices have followed, almost all of them weighted by market capitalization rather than the straight price average of Mr. Dow.[11]

For a long time, indices were used simply as a shorthand for broader market movement, rather like how a windsock indicates the direction and strength of the prevailing wind. But in the 1940s, an academic, Harry Markowitz, began to scrutinize index returns for what they could reveal about the risk/return trade-off among asset classes. His 1952 paper led to what is called "Modern Portfolio Theory," and the now widely accepted practice of asset allocation.

It's Modern Portfolio Theory (MPT) that says investors should pay more attention to getting their asset allocation right for their desired level of risk and leave market timing and individual security selection as very secondary considerations. An ideal asset allocation gives an investor the optimal mix of investments with the potential to get the return they need with the least fluctuation in their portfolio's total value. This is achieved by mixing together asset classes that react to market conditions in different ways.

Asset classes whose performances diverge under similar market conditions have what's known as a low correlation with each other. Real estate, for instance, goes up during periods of high inflation. Bonds, on the other hand, tend to wither away under those conditions. This counterbalancing of risk and return through asset class diversification (especially with low correlations) is the hallmark of asset allocation. According to MPT, diversification has a far greater impact on portfolio returns than smart investment selection or psychic market timing, and this wisdom is the foundation of all portfolio management today. Dr. Markowitz subsequently took home a Nobel Prize for those insights.

Around the time Modern Portfolio Theory was being propounded in the early 1960s, another market theory was taking hold—the Efficient

Markets Hypothesis (EMH). EMH says that stock prices reflect all past and present public information about a stock. In other words, the market is perfectly efficient and immediately factors all relevant information into a stock price. As a result, you cannot expect extraordinary returns from a stock. You may get extraordinary returns, but if you do, it is purely a fluke. Don't bother doing detailed fundamental analysis—it won't pay off. There are three versions of this theory—weak, semi-strong, and strong.

The weak version says you can't predict future stock price moves by studying past movements—so technical analysis is pointless. The semi-strong version puts the kibosh on fundamental analysis, too. It says that the current market price of a stock reflects all publicly available information about a stock and that scrutinizing annual reports, financial statements, and economic forecasts will not lead to consistent superior returns. The strong form of EMH holds that the market price of a stock reflects absolutely all information—including insider information. This means that even those trading on insider information will not be able to make superior returns.

Trading on insider information happens to remain illegal. A number of its practitioners have failed to make a profit from it, not so much because the market's utter efficiency defeated them but because they ended up in jail. Despite market regulators' skepticism about EMH, the weaker form of EMH had some popularity for a number of years and was one of the philosophical foundations of indexing. If the market is indeed as perfectly efficient as the theory purports, there's not much point in trying to beat it. You might just as well join it by indexing.

There have been, however, a number of demonstrated and perfectly legal contradictions to the weaker forms of EMH, such as the Value Line stock selection system, the January Effect, and the tendency of low price to earnings (P/E) multiple stocks to do better than expected. Interestingly, several current and some pending ETFs are structured to hold a basket of securities designed to exploit these well known anomalies. It seems then that no market is perfectly efficient. They all range between efficient and inefficient with some being efficient most of the time while others are efficient only some of the time.

Relative Market Efficiency of Various Asset Classes (fig. 15)

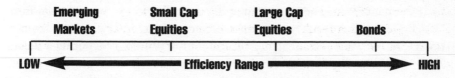

Asset classes vary by the efficiency of their markets.

Indexing: Is It Just for Efficient Markets?

It's often said that indexing works best in efficient markets and active management works best in inefficient markets. That may be true. At least it makes sense from first principles. Those poor, beleaguered active managers do have a better track record outpacing certain international and Canadian and U.S. small cap indices. Small caps and emerging market stocks trade within a wider band of fair market value than more actively followed stocks like large cap blue chips. This wider margin gives active managers an opportunity to add value.

Even still, it is devilishly hard for the majority of managers in these less dense waters to overleap their respective indices. A quick look at the chart below reveals the embarrassing truth.

The Number of Canadian Fund Managers Who Beat Their Benchmarks in "Inefficient" Markets Over One Year (fig. 16)

Global Equity	Int'l Equity	U.S. Mid & Small Cap
196 out of 603 (32.5%)	37 out of 252 (14.7%)	48 out of 80 (60%)
MSCI World C$	MSCI EAFE C$	Russell 2000 C$

Source: www.globefund.com for one year ending April 30, 2005. Universe excludes index funds.

Here's how they do over the somewhat longer term.

The Number of Canadian Fund Managers Who Beat Their "Inefficient" Benchmarks Over Ten Years (fig. 17)

Global Equity	Int'l Equity	U.S. mid & sm. cap
143 out of 271 (52.8%)	34 out of 106 (32%)	13 out of 41 (31.7%)
MSCI World C$	MSCI EAFE C$	Russell 2000 C$

Source: www.globefund.com as of April 30, 2005. Universe excludes index funds

Part of the reason these ratios are as good as they are is because of something called "survivorship bias." The bad funds are closed or merged with other funds, so the class of long-lived mutual funds decreases in a way that flatters the survivors. Limited data indicates a Canadian fund failure rate of about 9% a year. Recent U.S. numbers point to a similar story with about 8% of funds failing since the bear market began.[12]

Markets are not inherently efficient, and what efficiency they get is owed to an army of bright analysts identifying and acting on any mispricings. As markets continue to develop through regulation, increased competition among investment managers and robust security analysis, the opportunity to extract value diminishes. It gets to the point where the research costs start plundering the value added. The market may still be inefficient, but the inefficiency can't be exploited without self-defeating costs.

It isn't easy to know when this is going to happen in any given market though the proliferation of large actively managed funds in any one market might be a harbinger. The EAFE Index (Europe, Australasia, and the Far East) was long considered easy to beat, but the proliferation of funds, increased competition among fund managers and better index methodologies by MSCI, the index designers, has made EAFE less of a pushover now.

A skilled manager stays skilled just so long as she can capture the inefficiencies. As long as that happens, active funds should have a place in even a predominantly indexed portfolio. Actively managed funds aren't all bad, they're just a lot less useful than you've been led to think. In the next chapter we'll look at the various ways to do indexing—with ETFs, index mutual funds, index-linked GICs, equity-linked notes and futures.

Although indexing seems as though it should have sprung up immediately with the introduction of an index, it took almost 90 years and some determined personal conviction to bring the first index fund into existence. Bill Fouse is the one who did it.

The Inventor of Passive Investing: An Interview with Bill Fouse

Back in the early days of indexing, William Fouse's advocacy put even his patriotism into question. An investment research company, the Leuthold Group, adapted the famous "Uncle Sam Wants You" poster to read "Indexing is un-American."

"They sent these posters everywhere. Most trading rooms in money management organizations had one of those posters over the Marilyn Monroe poster," recalls Fouse.

He's laughing now, but in the early 1970s, the feelings were much closer to the nerve.

"It was just like an atheist trying to set up an operation in Baptist country," says Fouse of his attempts to introduce the notion of passive investing. "It was an emotionally charged thing."

His boss at Mellon Bank in Pittsburgh where Fouse had worked for 18 years was positively hostile to Fouse's suggestion that they start an index fund. The boss' reaction was just the first of many similar responses.

"It's an anti-establishment product," says Fouse, "because it doesn't square with the beliefs and intuitions and emotions of either the majority of plan sponsors or the investment bankers, brokers, traditional analysts, and portfolio managers. It attacks their fantasy system."

In 1970, Fouse found a more receptive employer and moved camp to Wells Fargo Bank in San Francisco. There he started a quantitative group, and in July 1971, he gained the pension account for Samsonite Corporation. (Yes, the luggage company.) That was, by all accounts, the first passive portfolio to be implemented. Fouse characterized it as an above average risk index account replicating an equal-weighted New York Stock Exchange Index. He says it had about a 10% higher risk than the NYSE capitalization-weighted index, and in 1972 and 1973, it did just what it was supposed to do: it lost money like the rest of the market.

In 1972, Wells Fargo started an S&P 500 index fund, originally funded by the bank's own pension fund. The next year they got their second client, Illinois Bell Telephone Company, an account they still retain. Together, the two accounts totalled US$10 million.

Eventually, Samsonite switched to the less volatile S&P product, too.

Fouse's study of market pricing and the efficacy of analysts' recommendations firmed his conviction that returns were random and that indexing was the surest way to consistently good performance. Thirty years later a lot of people agree with him although he complains that the pension management consulting community still gives little more than lip service to indexing. "It is certainly inimical to their interests. Through luck or through skill they've been able to classify indexing as a style, so logically you wouldn't put all your money in one style, would you?" In his mind, indexing rises above and encompasses all styles. They can't very well say, he remarks, "Put all your money in an index fund and go fishing, and then you don't have to pay us any more."

Asked why investors should put money into index products in a bear market, Fouse replies, "Historically, active managers have usually done worse in falling markets than the index funds and where they have done better by raising cash, let's say, they typically miss the market when it recovers. So there is no hard evidence that you're protected in a market decline by being with an active manager. I would say the only protection you can conjure up is a valid tactical asset allocation approach where you take a look at the alternative values in the marketplace between stocks, bonds, and cash."

The company Fouse co-founded, San Francisco-based Mellon Capital Management, does just that for over US$130 billion, more than $100 billion of which is indexed. At 77, the man who graduated in 1952 from the University of Kentucky with an MBA in industrial administration says he wouldn't hire himself today. It's a good thing Wells Fargo did because Fouse and other indexing pioneers revolutionized modern investing. Far from being un-American, Fouse says "It's Yankee ingenuity to take advantage of all the hard work and effort expended by others to make the market efficient and get a free ride." Mellon Capital still has the Samsonite account. Barclays Global Investors bought Wells Fargo Investment Advisers in 1995.

Notes

1) FRC's 107-page research paper, "Investors Behaving Badly: An Analysis of Investor Trading Patterns in Mutual Funds," by Gavin Quill, April 2001.

2) Dan Hallett, CFA, CFP is now president of Dan Hallett & Associates Inc., an independent investment research firm and licensed investment counsel in Windsor, Ontario. His paper was entitled "Distributions and the CGRM," published on *FundMonitor.com* on November 17, 1999. Also see Stephen L. Nesbitt, "Buy High, Sell Low: Timing Errors in Mutual Fund Allocations," *Journal of Portfolio Management*, Fall, 1995, pp. 57-60.

3) This finding based on work commissioned for this book and done by Norman Rothery, Ph.D. of *www.stingyinvestor.com* using data provided by FundMonitor and Fundata.

4) Duff Young, CEO of FundMonitor.com Corp., reported this finding in the *Globe & Mail*, May 9, 1998.

5) The 80% turnover figure comes from Michael Thorfinnson and Jason Kiss, "The Overlooked Piranha," *Canadian Investment Review*, Fall, 1996, pp. 17-21.

6) SPIVA Canada's 2004 fourth quarter report shows that a significant number of actively managed Canadian equity funds outperformed a blended index consisting of 70% S&P/TSX Composite (Total Return) and 30% S&P 500 (Total Return) calculated in Canadian dollars. Over three years, 47.6% of funds outperformed, and over one year ending Dec. 31, 2004, 52.2% outperformed the blended index. Clearly, the U.S. market's performance and the Canadian dollar's strength dragged down the group's performance, so by adjusting for these factors in the benchmark they did better as a group.

7) PALTrak data as of April 30, 2005 as per Morningstar Canada.

8) As per Norman Rothery, Ph.D. of *www.stingyinvestor.com* based on Fundata information.

9) Federal government regulations allowed foreign content limitations in RRSP accounts to increase by 2% every year from 10% in 1989 to 18% of book value in 1993. In 1999, the foreign content limit was increased to 20%; in 2000 to 25%; and in 2001, to 30%. Mutual funds, to be fully RRSP eligible, must not exceed the foreign content limit threshold and almost all take advantage of it to boost their returns. (The Canadian government has proposed eliminating the foreign content restriction, but the proposal was not passed into law when this book went to print. Should that restriction become history, it will be interesting to see how Canadian equity mutual

funds react to this new freedom and how their benchmarking changes.)

10) Ted Cadsby, *The Power of Index Funds*, Revised Edition, (Toronto: Stoddart Publishing Co., Limited), 2001, p.113. Emphasis is Mr. Cadsby's.

11) A capitalization-weighted index is one whose constituents are weighted according to the total market value of their outstanding shares. These indices will move in keeping with the price changes of the underlying stocks. The Dow Jones Industrial Average is a price weighted index. Higher priced stocks have a greater percentage impact on the index than lower priced stocks. Dow historical information from Dow Jones web site, *www.dowjones.com*.

12) The 8% fund failure rate is from John Bogle, the founder of Vanguard Funds, in a TV interview, August 2002. The 9% historical Canadian failure rate is from proprietary work done by Norman Rothery and Henry Lee using the *Globe and Mail* archives from 1978 to 1992. Also see John Waggoner, "Mutual Funds Vanishing at Record Rate: Failed Concepts, Bad Sellers Lead to Liquidations," *www.usatoday.com*, viewed September 9, 2002.

Chapter Three
Index Products: Which One Is Best for You?

If you're now convinced that indexing is the most sensible approach to prudent investing, what, then, is the best way to index?

Hulking institutional accounts can simply replicate the index by buying everything in the index and in the right proportions. Done. The rest of us have to rely on index products, of which there are many, though it's easy to narrow down the field pretty quickly. A number of index-linked products require a degree of sophistication few of us desire to cultivate—like index futures and index-linked equity notes. On the opposite end of the spectrum, index-linked GICs are just barely an index product at all. For most investors, index mutual funds and ETFs are the most accessible and practical way to index. I'd like to say unequivocally that ETFs are always the best choice, but, in fact, like most things, it depends on your circumstances. It depends most critically on how much money you want to give over to passive investments, but also on the product features that are most important to you.

If you've already made up your mind that indexing is the way to go, this chapter will help you decide what index products are best for you. We'll compare index mutual funds to ETFs and touch on index-linked GICs, notes and index futures.

Any index product should trigger the following questions:

• Does it track the index you need?
• How closely does it track that index?
• How much are the management fees and other costs?
• Are there tax implications?
• Is it easy to sell?
• What is the minimum investment?

- How are dividends handled?
- How do redemptions/sales affect the product?
- Is it efficient to invest and withdraw small dollar amounts?
- Is it best for short-term or long-term positions?

The answers to these questions should save you buying an inappropriate product that could cost you in returns, taxes, and aggravation. By the end of this chapter you should have the answers easily in hand for most of the index products available today.

Index Mutual Funds vs. ETFs

In Chapter One we discussed the differences between actively managed mutual funds and ETFs. Much of that discussion doesn't apply to a comparison of ETFs and index mutual funds because index mutual funds are passively managed. Where an active manager is buying and selling positions in the fund regularly in order to boost returns, a passive manager simply positions a portfolio to replicate the movement of a target index. Passive funds experience a lot less buying and selling, and when trades do occur, they are not for the purpose of making gains or preventing losses; they are made to better track the index. This difference in management approach makes index funds considerably different from their actively managed confréres, and more comparable to ETFs, but with some notable differences.

Index Tracking

An index mutual fund, like an ETF, is designed to track a target index. The best performing index product is one that most closely tracks its index. Any deviation either above or below the index return is a tracking error. Of course, nothing will perfectly track a target index because indices are abstract constructs. They don't live and breathe in the real world where trading costs add up. An index is calculated, but not actually implemented, by the index sponsor. That means an index and its returns are blissfully unaffected by trading costs or price run-ups when its securities are changed. Index mutual funds and ETFs are, however, real things with real costs. Take, as just one example, the addition of Fluor Corp. to the S&P 500 Index. The stock went up $4 on the day from indexers scrambling to buy the stock in order to match the completely theoretical S&P 500.[1] That's some real-world pressure at work. Index managers aren't exactly as idle as the Maytag repairman.

Tracking Methods

There are three different ways to track an index and both index funds and ETFs take advantage of all of them.

Replication

The most straightforward tracking method is to completely copy the index by buying all the securities in proportion to their weighting in the index. This is called, obviously enough, "replication."

Optimization

Instead of replicating an index, a fund could buy a representative sampling of the index's securities. This is known as "sampling" or "optimizing." Managers resort to this because of restrictions on portfolio concentrations and foreign ownership, or as a way of coping with thinly traded stocks on some indices. Markets in which many listed securities lack liquidity create a problem for those trying to manage a replicated index in real time. Managers try to avoid this problem by carefully selecting liquid securities representative of the market they are trying to track without actually owning everything in the index. It's never perfect, which is one reason why developing country index products have greater tracking errors than similar products in more efficient markets. Optimizing can also result from an attempt to save fund costs. The fund manager is betting that leaving out minor securities won't much affect tracking but will definitely reduce transaction costs.

Derivatives

Finally, a fund itself can buy other index products like derivatives or ETFs. Fully RRSP eligible foreign index funds, for instance, typically buy forward contracts or futures on their target indices and put the lion's share of the portfolio into staid Canadian T-bills (which is how they get to be fully RRSP eligible despite giving full foreign exposure). This is known as a "derivatives indexing strategy."

Not all tracking strategies work equally well. Portfolios that do not perfectly reproduce their index have a bigger chance of running afoul of the index returns than replicated funds. Indexing strategy, then, plays a part in tracking error.

Concentration Limits

Securities regulation also impacts tracking. Mutual fund regulators stay up at night worrying about excessive concentration in mutual fund portfolios since diversification is one of the biggest benefits of mutual fund investing. Conventional mutual funds (that is, non-index mutual funds) may not purchase a security if, after the purchase, the fund would have more than 10% of its net assets (at current market value) invested in the securities of any one issuer. Regulators relaxed this restriction for index funds first by capping them at 25%, then eliminating the concentration restriction altogether. This serves index funds well because any portfolio restriction always has the risk of throwing off tracking, though it can permit undesirable concentration.

ETFs in Canada have no regulatory restrictions on concentration, but that doesn't mean that all Canadian ETFs have no concentration caps. In fact, Barclays Canada's sector funds have a 25% cap on the weight of any single security. This restriction reflects the cap set by the rules of the underlying indices themselves.

U.S.-based ETFs are not so lucky. They're restricted by law from holding a position in any single issuer worth more than 25% of the ETF's assets. Other restrictions apply as well. Securities that have a weighting of 5% or more within the fund cannot collectively add up to more than 50% of the fund's assets. Sector ETFs can run up against this restriction easily. Take, for example, iShares Dow Jones U.S. Energy Sector Index Fund whose index once had a 38% weighting in ExxonMobil. The fund had to optimize its positions by buying other oil and gas producers with a high market correlation to Exxon's stock.[2] This is a common tactic for getting around concentration restrictions. It's not perfect, but it's the best that can be done.

Cash Flow

Cash flow is another reason index tracking can derail. The more cash in an index portfolio, the less well that fund will track its index. That's called "cash drag" and in a down market it can buffer the fund from a precipitous market crash. In a rising market cash holds the fund back from the market highs. Index mutual funds can be particularly hobbled by cash flow effects. Mutual funds take in and give out cash on a daily basis. A large rush of money into or out of a fund can create a pile of cash not tied to the index—always a risky situation.

ETFs don't have a similar cash flow problem. The reason is quite simple. ETFs don't have many sources of cash apart from dividends. ETFs neither redeem their units for cash, nor do they take in cash from new unit sales the way mutual funds do. Instead, what's called an "authorized participant" or in Canada, an "underwriter," uses their own capital to put together the stocks needed to constitute a creation unit. This basket of stocks is turned into an ETF unit in advance of market demand, so there are always new ETF units available, and no cash standing idly by.

Dividends

Stocks within an ETF portfolio do sometimes spit out dividends so ETFs can find cash a drag, too. Certain ETFs are able to reinvest the dividends into the portfolio immediately upon receiving a dividend, while others must segregate the cash for quarterly distribution. Which method is used depends on the structure of the ETF, and yes, unfortunately, there are different structures. We'll talk more about those differences in Chapter Seven when we look at Canadian and U.S. ETF structures. For now it's enough to know that ETFs which can reinvest dividend cash have better tracking than those that have to coddle the cash separately. Even with today's low dividend rates, how dividends are reinvested can make a difference. In 2005, i60s, for instance, had $6.3 billion in assets and received $15.5 million in dividends. That's almost 2.5% of the fund's assets—hardly insignificant.

Index mutual funds get dividends, too, but index funds can immediately reinvest the dividends in the fund when the dividends are received. Dividends are less of a tracking problem for index mutual funds than they are for ETFs.

Index Adjustments

The difference between index funds and ETFs is highlighted when there is a large addition to the index. Both index funds and ETFs must sell the stock leaving the index (triggering gains, if any), and both must buy the stock entering the index. But if the purchase amount is more than the sale amount, the index fund sells more of the other stocks in its portfolio and thereby triggers more gains. The ETF, in contrast, simply issues more units to the underwriters to finance the additional purchases. The ETF does not need to sell as much stock and so, theoretically, ends up triggering fewer gains. This isn't significant all the time, but big index changes will make the difference show.

Management Expense Ratio

With all the noted impediments to tracking, you may wonder how any product manages to keep hold of an index. It's not as easy as it may look, and we've not even come to the most major and inescapable tracking impediment of all—the management expense ratio. The MER pulls on an index strategy like an undertow. Even if a manager could perfectly manage cash flow, avoid concentration restrictions and fully replicate the target index, the fund will still fall short of the index's return by exactly the amount of the fund's MER. There are some mitigating circumstances, though, that may find an index fund occasionally squeaking out a better performance than its index. Sometimes fund managers can make (or lose) a little money relative to the index when trading the index changes. And sometimes cash flow comes to their rescue, too.

To see how well an index fund has tracked its index, go to *www.globefund.com*, select a specific index fund or all index funds generally and in "charts" you can compare their performance one by one to their respective index. Keep in mind that you will want the total return version of any benchmark index when comparing it to an index fund or ETF. (A number of total return indices are not available on the Globefund site.) You can check Barclays Canada's ETF tracking though Globefund, also, or on their Canadian site, *www.iunits.com*. For some reason, TD Asset Management's ETFs are not listed on Globefund.com., nor is their tracking graphically illustrated on TD's own web site. For U.S.-based ETFs, The American Stock Exchange has an on-line tracking comparison as does Barclays U.S.' site, *www.ishares.com*. ETF tracking should use the ETF's net asset value (NAV) and not the ETF's market value, which can fluctuate somewhat from the NAV, though arbitrage seldom allows this to happen to a great extent.

Obviously, the closer a fund's returns are to its target index return (after costs), the better the indexing strategy is working (unless it is an "enhanced" fund, which we'll discuss below).

In general, ETFs have better tracking records than index mutual funds, mainly because the new kid on the block has moved in with a lot less baggage; namely, much smaller MERs. MERs on U.S.-based ETFs range from 0.07% to 0.75% with most under 0.60%. Canadian MERs run from 0.17% to 0.55%. Contrast that with 0.78% for the median Canadian equity index fund and you can see why less onerous MERs mean ETFs can more closely track their indices. This is not just an academic observation either.

Look at how a good Canadian equity index fund with a long track record has tracked its target index.

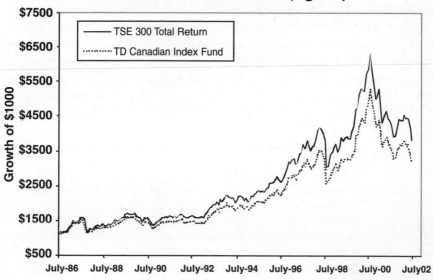

TSE 300 vs. Index Fund (fig. 18)

Growth of $1000

— TSE 300 Total Return
······ TD Canadian Index Fund

$7500
$6500
$5500
$4500
$3500
$2500
$1500
$500

July-86 July-88 July-90 July-92 July-94 July-96 July-98 July-00 July02

Source: www.stingyinvestor.com

The longer an index mutual fund tracks an index, the more its performance will diverge from that index because of the cumulative effects of a relatively large MER. *Note: The TD Canadian Index Fund currently has an MER of 0.88%.*

Compare the tracking of a good index mutual fund as we've just seen, to a good ETF. TIPs 35, the predecessor to the i60, tracked the Toronto 35 Index. There are four lines in the graph below, but if you see only three, that's because TIPs and the Toronto 35 Index are so close they are indistinguishable. That's why just beneath those two indistinguishable lines we've manipulated the tracking a little to show the marvelous symmetry of TIPs tracking. Not coincidentally, TIPs had an expense ratio of 0.04%. To see how iUnits ETFs have tracked their indices, refer to the Barclays Global Investors Canada web site, *www.iunits.com*. For U.S. ETFs, tracking comparisons are available through AMEX's web site, *www.amex.com*.

TIPs vs. Toronto 35 Index (fig. 19)

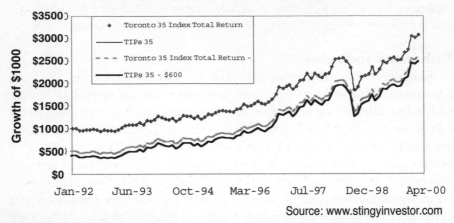

Source: www.stingyinvestor.com

TIPs 35 tracked the Toronto 35 Total Return Index so well, its line and the index line are indistinguishable.

ETFs Have Small Tracking Errors

Take a look at Canada's largest ETF, the iUnits S&P/TSX 60 Index Fund, compared to the S&P/TSX 60 Index itself. The tracking error is miniscule. (If you notice an overlap in the time periods from Figures 11 and 12, that's because the i60's started trading October 4, 1999 and TIPs and HIPs were merged with the i60 on March 9, 2000.)

XIU vs. S&P/TSX 60 Index (fig. 20)

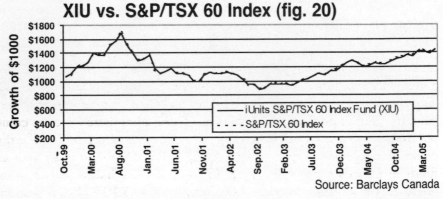

Source: Barclays Canada

According to a Morgan Stanley research report (January, 2005) the NAV of most ETFs tracked their respective indices very well, in many cases, not much beyond their MERs. "Tracking error in 2004 averaged 23 basis points (bps) for U.S. major market ETFs, 28 bps for U.S.-style ETFs, 57 bps for U.S.-sector ETFs, 75 bps for international ETFs, and 17 bps for fixed income ETFs." Canadian ETFs show similar tracking excellence. Over shorter time periods, the tracking will fluctuate more than the MER, but over five years or more, the tracking error comes pretty close to the MER, especially on replicated ETFs. Tracking error is slightly greater with optimized ETFs. Let's just say you're unlikely to lose any sleep over those tracking errors.

Enhanced Indexing

Enhanced indexing strategies try to second-guess the market. Sometimes this can be as simple as just overweighting certain securities within the index in the hope of enhancing returns. Other methods can be a little more complicated. The first crop of enhanced ETFs uses rules-based selection methods to chose and exclude securities in the hope of beating a conventional index. If it works, the fund will beat the market. If it doesn't, it will underperform the market by more than other index funds. It's almost a contradiction of the idea of indexing, but hope springs eternal in the hearts of some fund managers. National Bank's American Index Plus Fund is a good example of an enhanced index mutual fund. In April 2005, it had about 70% in Spiders, the remainder in individual stocks. In three years to the end of April, it did -8.58% compared to the S&P 500 composite index return of -6.08%. At an MER of 1.9%, this fund is no bargain.

Perhaps the quantitative, rules-based strategy worked out by PowerShares and other ETF sponsors waiting in the wings like Profund Advisors, will succeed in enhancing returns when more subjective methods have not been all that fabulous. Quantitative rules indexing is an exciting development in the world of ETFs, and is being seen as the first step toward actively managed ETFs.

Management Expense Ratios

Because of their enormous impact on tracking, MERs deserve a little bit more examination. From an investor's standpoint, management fees are a necessary evil: funds cost money to run and the manager has to get paid. The companies that record the securities and their transactions must get paid, too, and so on down the costly line. These administrative costs come out of the fund and are calculated as a ratio of expenses to assets, hence the name, "management expense ratio" (MER). The MERs on index mutual funds in Canada range from 0.31% for one of TD's index e-funds to an obese 4.03% for Transamerican Life Canada's fully RRSP eligible guaranteed (segregated) Asian equity index fund. Most non-segregated retail index mutual funds have MERs around 0.9% and under 1%.[3]

These MERs may sound like a bargain when you contrast them to actively managed funds, but they're still bloated compared to the MERs on ETFs. This is one important aspect in which ETFs shine. MERs on ETFs in Canada range from a slender 0.17% to 0.55%.

Management fees represent money slipping from your account into the pockets of fund managers. There's nothing wrong with that if you have a relative in the fund business, but most of us would prefer to keep our gains to ourselves. The longer management fees and ancillary fund expenses erode your investment, the more damage they do. On the face of it, 1% either way doesn't seem too much to be paying for management, but you'd hardly be blamed for being resentful once you see how harmful it is to your long-term returns. Saving even 1% in management fees increases your returns by an astounding amount over the long haul. Saving 1% over 15 years will mean a 16% improvement in total returns. Thanks to the miracle of compounding, that shoots to 22% after 20 years, 25% in 30 years and an astounding 49% in 40 years.[4]

Obviously, the bigger the MER, the less well the fund will track its market. In the indexing world, you get what you *don't* pay for. The more you pay in management fees and expenses, the less you get in returns. Period. Always scrutinize MERs. The lower the MER, the more money you make. All other things being equal, select an index product with the lowest MER.

Expenses

You might think the MER gives the full cost of running the fund; it doesn't, and to my mind, regulators have abetted the mutual fund industry in this misleading practice. In fact, the MER doesn't tell the whole story. Trading costs, the commissions the fund must pay to brokerage houses for transacting trades, aren't included in any MER calculation. This means your actual costs of holding a fund are always going to be higher than the posted MER, and adversely affect the fund's net return. The more active the manager, the more the costs pile up. Trading costs have been known in extreme cases to be double the fund's MER.[5] Gratefully, an index product normally has so little buying and selling that the trading costs are usually miniscule in comparison to the size of the portfolio. In Canada, Barclays and TD pay few if any stock trading commissions for their ETFs because of favourable brokerage arrangements, but it wouldn't be unreasonable to expect somewhat higher trading commission costs with ETFs if the current favourable arrangements changed.

Taxes, Redemptions, and the Index Funds vs. ETFs Challenge

Any security that holds a good number of different stocks is going to have dividends, and these dividends are going to have to be passed on to the investor. That can't be avoided. Capital gains, on the other hand, can be avoided. Index mutual funds and ETFs are generally tax efficient because they don't do much to generate capital gains. They are passive investments. Little selling is going on inside a passive portfolio, few realized capital gains are generated. That's good because index funds and ETFs, all mutual funds in fact, distribute their capital gains at least annually to unitholders who then must pay tax on those gains. Bottom line—the longer you put off paying tax on capital gains, the better.

When you do get a distribution from a Canadian ETF and mutual fund, the distributions retain their tax character. This means dividends from Canadian corporations are eligible for the dividend tax credit, and capital gains retain their tax-advantaged status. Canada Revenue Agency is not so favourably disposed, however, to dividends or capital gains from U.S.-based ETFs. All their distributions are dinged as income—more on this and other tax-related matters in a later chapter.

But even in a tax-lean passive environment, ETFs might be seen to have an advantage over index mutual funds. ETFs have something of a buffer from the onslaught of redemptions from retail investors. A redemption run on an index fund could force the manager to sell profitable positions in order to raise the cash to pay out the redemptions. This could impose capital gains tax liability on the remaining fund investors. In contrast, retail ETF investors sell their units for cash on the open market, which has no direct implications for the underlying fund.

ETFs can be redeemed for their underlying shares, but only institutional accounts would own a large enough position to form a redemption unit, and even for institutional accounts, selling an ETF is cheaper and easier than redeeming it. When redemptions do occur, they happen in weighty amounts of 50,000 units and more, and the fund surrenders the underlying securities in exchange for its own units. Canadian tax rules view this as a deemed disposition, a sale of sorts, which triggers capital gains reckoning. (Tax rules are different in the U.S. and a redemption there does not result in a deemed disposition.)

Although Canadian tax laws now permit the ETF to attribute the capital gains to the redeeming institution, the arrangement does not work perfectly. In 2004, the i60s distributed capital gains of nearly one whole dollar per unit. TD's ETFs don't have the same number of creation unit redemptions so with the exception of their Select Canadian Value Index Fund, their ETFs have distributed no capital gains since their inception. The TD Value ETF, though, has spit out gains in three out of its four years in existence, 2004 being by far the most notable with $1.29 of capital gains per unit. Index mutual funds had hugely lower capital gains distributions in 2004, many of them showing no capital gain distribution whatsoever, even index funds tracking the same index as the i60. To put this into perspective, even the relatively large capital gain distribution of the i60 represented less than 2% of net asset value of the unit, which was trading at more than $50.

You can surmise from looking at the difference between ETF capital gains distributions and index funds distributions just how much creation unit redeeming must be going on in the ETF. If an ETF and an index fund are tracking the same index, their portfolio readjustments will be nearly similar. This means the difference in the size of their capital gains distribution can come only from the ETF's institutional redemption activity.

U.S. ETFs are the very model of tax efficiency because fund level redemptions in the U.S. don't trigger any kind of capital gains liability. Minute capital gains distributions are the result. From 1993 to the end of 2005, Spiders distributed 16¢ a share of capital gains in total. From 1998 to the end of 2005, Diamonds distributed no capital gains at all. (Historical distribution information for all U.S. ETFs is available on *www.amex.com*.) As a species, U.S. ETFs are just about the most tax efficient pooled investment you can get. Canadian ETFs still have something to prove in this respect.

One more interesting tax related difference exists between index mutual funds and ETFs. With ETFs, capital gains are paid in units, not cash, so you don't actually receive this cash. It is automatically reinvested in the ETF. Of course, you still have to pay tax on this if you hold the ETF outside of a registered account. With index mutual funds, all the distributions are paid in cash whether dividends, interest or capital gains. You can elect to have this money automatically reinvested into the mutual fund, which is what most people do, but at least you have the comfort of knowing the cash would be available if you had to pay tax on those distributions.

Is It Easy to Sell?

The ability to buy and sell an investment at a competitive price, its "liquidity," should be a big consideration in any investment decision. All mutual funds score high on ease of buying and selling, but it's a little surprising that the mutual fund industry has grown so hugely successful with a product whose price cannot be determined when it is bought or sold. Investors buy and sell mutual funds without ever knowing beforehand at what price those trades are going to be executed. Imagine buying a car or a house, or doing your grocery shopping like that?

This strange arrangement stems from the way mutual funds are priced. At the end of each trading day, a mutual fund company tallies up the value of all the fund's constituents, establishes a net asset value (NAV), and transacts all the buy and sell orders that have come in that day at that NAV. The pricing process is completely controlled by the mutual fund company without any market scrutiny because, remember, the actual portfolio holdings are not known on a daily basis. Mutual funds have great liquidity because the mutual fund companies themselves buy and sell the units and are committed to ensuring the liquidity of their product and the integrity of their pricing. Nevertheless, this arrangement is in contrast to ETFs whose prices are posted in real time and subject to the scrutiny of the market as a whole.

Index mutual funds in Canada are almost exclusively no-load funds, which means they can be bought or sold without commission. To discourage short-term trading, however, a number of fund companies impose a minimum holding period or charge a short-term trading fee—as much as a 2% penalty on many funds held less than 90 days.

There is no such restriction on ETFs. If anything, the more ETFs trade, the better. The more trading, the better the apparent liquidity.

ETFs are as easy to buy and sell as a large and frequently traded stock, because that's what they are. ETFs such as Spiders, Diamonds, and Qubes are regularly among the most heavily traded securities on their respective exchanges. In fact, ETFs account for more than half of AMEX's total trading volume. In Canada, on a dollar volume basis, the i60s were the eleventh most actively traded security on the TSE in 2003 and the ninth in 2004. They have enormous liquidity. Even U.S. ETFs that have low trading volumes are perfectly liquid as long as their underlying securities are liquid.

As with all stocks, you have to have a brokerage account and pay brokerage commissions on an ETF transaction. This runs about $30 or less for an on-line order at a Canadian discount broker, $60 or less for a round trip buy and sell. Commission costs are trending down, too. At least one other discount brokerage charges $25. You don't have trading commission expenses with an index mutual fund, but a commission on a long-term hold is a small, fixed, non-recurring cost that is very quickly surpassed by a pricey MER. And if you do your ETF trading within a fee-based account, you may escape commission charges completely.

The virtue of stock trading is that it brings with it complete price transparency and prompt, if not nearly instant, order execution. All the normal stock trading mechanisms are available for ETF transactions, too. You can also buy ETFs on margin, trade them with stop loss or limit orders, and when available, even write options on them. In the United States, you can short sell ETFs without waiting for an uptick.

Prompt trading execution is more valuable than you might suspect. Remember that mutual funds are transacted only at the end of day after market close. The U.S. market as measured by the S&P 500 fluctuates on average 1.5% a day, which translates into a possible 1.5% average loss each time you have to wait a trading day to execute your order. Nasdaq's number is 2.2%, while the TSX's daily fluctuation is a more reassuring 1%. Those numbers represent the expected average risk you are taking each time you buy or sell an equity mutual fund.[6]

The Minimum Investment

Mutual funds have become hugely popular in good part because they require a very small minimum investment. You can buy a mutual fund for as little as $500 at one shot or for $25 a month with no fees or penalties. Many people invest regularly with a fund company by arranging a monthly pre-authorized payment plan, otherwise known as a PAC. Mutual funds make it easy to withdraw large or small amounts from mutual fund positions regularly or on demand. There are no trading fees imposed, and with no-load funds, there are no redemption fees unless you trigger a short-term trading penalty. It's also easy to automatically reinvest your dividends. Since almost all index mutual funds are no-loads, an index mutual fund investment is singularly flexible in letting you into the game with small bits of money.

ETFs, on the other hand, are generally bought in board lots of 100 units (shares). It is equally easy to buy less than 100 shares of an ETF, but the minimum trading commission still applies. If you intend to actively trade your ETFs, it's most cost effective to stick to board lots. For practical purposes, the minimum investment in an ETF can be relatively steep. One hundred shares of i60s in the spring of 2005 would run you about $5,200. One hundred Spiders would set you back more than $14,000 Canadian, and a number of popular ETFs like Diamonds and MidCap Spiders regularly trade around US$100 per share. The cheapest Canadian ETF in spring 2005 was iUnits' S&P/TSE Canadian Information Technology ETF trading around $7.00. Clearly, buying an ETF board lot will cost a whole lot more than the minimum $500 for a mutual fund purchase.

Any addition or withdrawal from an ETF position requires a buy or sell order and an associated trading commission. This makes reinvesting the quarterly dividends from equity ETFs or a fixed income ETFs interest payments a bit of a nuisance. Dividend reinvestment plans for ETFs, however, are beginning to be more broadly available. TD Waterhouse and the discount and full-service arms of RBC and CIBC offer dividend reinvestment plans on some iUnits and the more popular U.S. ETFs. Canadian ShareOwners' service allows reinvestments and PACs on all iUnits and some U.S. ETFs. With more requests, more institutions will provide this service on a larger selection of ETFs. Until you're able to enroll in a dividend reinvestment services plan, dividend cheques can be pumped into a money market fund—or treat them like birthday money from a kind aunt, taxable though it is. In 2004, i60s gave its unitholders $0.82 in cash for every unit.[7] With a board lot that's a generous aunt.

Short-Term or Long-Term Plays?

The mutual fund industry has gotten blue in the face advising clients that mutual funds are long-term investments. Not many investors seem to buy that when they buy their funds because the average holding period for fund investors keeps declining and is now around 2.5 to 2.9 years.[8] But investor behaviour aside, the longer you hold a mutual fund, the longer the MER compounds to corrode your returns. For the long term, there's no question the index product with the lowest MER is preferable.

For one or two years and an investment of around $10,000 or less, an index mutual fund is probably your better bet, says Steve Geist, President, TD Mutual Funds. The calculation goes something like this:

Cost Comparison: ETFs vs. Index Fund (fig. 21)

Investment	$6,000		$10,000		$10,000	
Horizon	2 Years		1 Year		2 Years	
	ETF	**Index Fund**	**ETF**	**Index Fund**	**ETF**	**Index Fund**
Commission (in and out)	$58	$0	$58	$0	$58	$0
MER Cost	$42	$96	$35	$80	$70	$160
Total Cost	$100	$96	$93	$80	$128	$160

Assumes ETF MER of 0.35% and index fund MER of 0.8%, trading commission at $29.

Over the short-term there may not always be a cost advantage to an ETF over an index mutual fund, but in the longer-term the cost efficiency of an ETF shines, and the comparison with a conventional (load) mutual fund is unequivocal.

RRSP Eligibility

Another attraction of index mutual funds is the selection they offer of fully RRSP eligible foreign indices. This allows investors to build a diversified indexing strategy completely within their RRSPs without having to compromise on foreign exposure due to foreign content restrictions. These index mutual funds are usually distinguished from their counterparts by "RRSP" in their name, like CIBC's International Index RRSP, which is linked to the MSCI EAFE Index.

So far there are only two ETFs linked to foreign indices that are fully RRSP eligible. These track the S&P 500 index (iUnits S&P 500 Index RSP Fund) and the MSCI EAFE Index (iUnits MSCI International Equity Index RSP Fund). With the proposed elimination of the RRSP foreign content restrictions, this selection shortcoming will become irrelevant.

Choice of Indices

Mutual funds can't match the extraordinarily broad range of indices that ETFs track. You can find an ETF for just about any index you can think of. The breadth of U.S. ETF offerings makes it easy to gain exposure to just about any geographical area, economic sector, market segment, country, or major investment style. This diversity proves very useful in portfolio construction, as we'll see when we put together some model portfolios.

Paradoxically, with 145 index mutual funds at last count, Canadians still don't have a huge selection of foreign indices to select from—and that's with all the major banks, insurance companies, and no-load fund companies falling over themselves to bring you an index product. It's not hard to find a TSX fund or one using the S&P 500, Nasdaq, the Dow, MSCI EAFE, and the Wilshire 5000. But the huge selection of style and capitalization indices available in the U.S., like the Russell value/growth indices, and the large, mid, and small cap indices, have not spilled over into the Canadian mutual fund industry. This can be a problem for those wishing to use index mutual funds to add, for instance, a small cap index to their overall index strategy, or a value index to capture the growth of a whole investment style.

Frustrated Canadian investors can only press their faces to the glass and look longingly at the tantalizing selection of low cost index funds sponsored by Vanguard Group, the second largest mutual fund company in the U.S. Canadians are prohibited from buying U.S. mutual funds, but the whole universe of 171 U.S. ETFs and HOLDRS (and counting) is open to us.

Index-Linked GICs

Index-linked GICs are designed for those taking their first timid steps towards indexing. These products are offered by banks and credit unions typically in 3- or 5-year maturities to appeal to regular GIC investors who are disappointed with low interest rates but who aren't ready to take the plunge into index mutual funds. The GIC's principal is fully guaranteed, but its return is linked to the performance of an index or set of indices. This sounds like an easy enough concept, but its implementation can be complicated.

All index-linked GICs have either a cap or a participation rate that affects your gains. The longer the time to maturity, the higher the cap or participation rate. A 3-year GIC, for example, might be capped at a 25% return depending on what index is involved; whereas a 5-year product might have a 50% cap. Capping limits how much you can earn on your GIC. A 25% cap means that your GIC will not earn more than 25% of the market gains over the maturity of the GIC no matter how well the index does over that period. Participation rates are generally higher than caps for the same term of investment, but may result in giving you lower returns than a cap. A participation rate of 55% or 65% means that the investor gets only 55-65% of the index's gain over the investment period.

If the market goes up just 25%, a 25% cap would probably give you more of that return than a 65% participation rate, which will give you just 65% of that 25% growth. Why doesn't the 25% cap in this example certainly give you more? Your return depends not only on the cap or participation rate, but also on how the market growth is calculated.

A few years back, these products used to be horrifically complicated because the growth on the index would be averaged and each institution it seemed had their own way of doing that average. Some averaged the index's movement monthly from the first month; others averaged only the last twelve months or the last six months, or maybe did the averaging only quarterly in the last year to maturity. As the period of averaging increases, the index's gains will always decrease so averaging in a generally up market is disadvantageous. Remember, too, that the participation rate and the cap were both based on this average. Thankfully, averaging is getting less common with index-linked GICs and the product is becoming far more straightforward.

Index-linked GICs are fully RRSP eligible—even the ones linked to foreign indices—and they can be bought in $500 to $1000 minimums. Your principal is fully guaranteed, and if you hit the market at the right time you can make considerably more than the ordinary GIC interest rate. Of course, you can also make nothing if markets are miserable and there are no dividend payments. You're also locked into these things until they mature. You cannot cash in these GICs (except for death and hardship) and all the gains are taxed as interest income at your highest marginal tax rate.

Moshe Milevsky, a finance professor at York University and author of *Money Logic: Financial Strategies for the Smart Investor*, says that the insurance on a 5-year GIC (in the form of a principal guarantee) probably isn't worth putting up with the cap. Markets tend to go up, especially over five years, so he'd buy a 3-year product on the most volatile market he could find and that way get the biggest advantage from the product's insurance.

He doesn't like averaging and always looks for the highest cap available, but fundamentally he'd rather buy an ETF with a put option. A "put" is a contract that allows you to sell the index at a prearranged price some time in the future. That automatically limits your downside risk while giving you full scope to soar with the index. Not exactly a simple strategy you can buy at the bank, but for folks with $10,000 or more to invest in index-linked

GICs, a better overall approach—logically, though perhaps a big psychological stretch for habitual GIC investors.

Equity-Linked Notes

Linked notes have suddenly given rise to an impressively large market. A recent study by Investor Economics says the overall size of the market-linked instruments universe is now C$21 billion.[9] This giant number includes index-linked GICs and principal-protected hedge funds, but notes are playing an increasingly important part.

All major banks and mutual fund companies offer a wide sweep of guaranteed principal notes with returns linked to any one or an assortment of securities, indices, mutual funds, and/or futures products. Term to maturity for these offerings is usually longer than that for an index-linked GIC, somewhere around six to eight years. Unlike GICs, though, these notes can often be sold on a secondary market.

Returns are not guaranteed, of course, and the calculation to arrive at the return can also involve participation rates and other limiting factors. Phillips, Hager & North Investment Management Ltd. did a survey of these products and concluded that many products use "innovative methods of calculating the interest payable (or return) ... Close examination of these calculations often leads to a disturbing conclusion: potential returns can be severely limited, especially in a robust stock market environment. Furthermore, the fees on these products tend to be ignored or downplayed..."[10]

In other words, as currently structured, these products are complicated, not necessarily cost effective and tie up your money for a long time with certainty that you will not be getting a market return. The PH&N survey concluded that investors are better off buying the underlying investment the notes are linked to because the principal guarantee diminishes in value the longer an investment is held.

The problem with equity-linked notes is not the concept itself, but that they have been used to offer a feature, principal protection, which is appealing but not worth a lot. Their sponsors have surrounded this feature with complexity and high fees.

Futures

Instead of buying your target index through a mutual fund or an ETF, you can get the same benefit by buying a futures contract on your index of choice. It takes some sophistication, serious assets, and a special trading account, but for those determined to squeeze the last nickel out of their investment costs, it shouldn't be overlooked.

A futures contract is a legal obligation to buy or sell a specific commodity or financial instrument at a specific price at a specific time in the future. These contracts are traded on a futures exchange which sets all the terms of the contract except for the price. Each day the accounts of the two parties to the contract—the one who must sell and the other who must buy—are marked to market. That means the exchange tallies up the (symmetrical) loss or gain on both sides. When one party makes money, the other party loses exactly the same amount.

Marking to market is one of the things that distinguishes futures from options. Buying an option gives you the right but not the obligation to buy or sell at a fixed price in the future. You can exercise an option or let it expire, and there is no daily marking of profits and loses. (Options are asymmetrical.)

Suppose you figure the S&P 500 is going to go up in the next few months. (Future contracts can go out as far as a year but one-month contracts are the most heavily traded.) You can buy one contract (expiring on the third Thursday in your target month) for 250 times the current value of the index. On 2002 May 18, 2005 the S&P 500 was at 1186. One August contract would cost 250 x .$1186 = $296,500 (US). Before you faint, know that you will have to come up with only a fraction of that amount to buy the future. One of the big attractions of futures is that they can be done on margin. For 10% or less of the contract price down, you execute your trade on margin and watch your account daily for profits—or margin calls if you're losing money. You pay commission only when you get out of the contract. In RBC's case, that commission is US$90. A discount broker might charge as little as US$35.

E-Mini Futures

Few investors like dealing with the intimidating capital requirements of full-blown futures contracts, so the Chicago Mercantile Exchange has come up with something more retail user-friendly—"E-mini futures." E-mini contracts are one-fifth the size of a conventional futures contract, but with similar features of their larger counterparts, including being bought on margin. The E-minis come in monthly and quarterly contracts and are available on the S&P 500, the Nasdaq 100, S&P Midcap 400, and the Russell 2000. Options on the E-mini S&P 500 are also offered. (To learn more about these inventive Mini Me's, see *www.cme.com*.)

ETF Futures

The popularity of E-minis may have something to do with yet another exciting ETF advance. The Chicago Mercantile Exchange has introduced futures on ETFs. As of mid-2005, they had contracts on Qubes, SPDRs, and the iShares Russell 2000. If you're stifling a yawn right now, you've missed the best part of this news. These futures will be one-fifth the size of the E-mini contracts, which are themselves one-fifth the size of standard futures. Investing in three major ETFs just got incredibly cheap.

In a somewhat related event, early 2005 also saw the introduction of options on SPDRs. Since the SPDR is one-tenth the value of the index, an option of SPDRs is much lower than an option on the S&P 500 Index itself. Although options are available on many U.S. ETFs, options were not available on SPDRs because of licensing issues.

The Canadian Options

Canadian futures contracts exist on the S&P/TSX 60 Index and on four S&P/TSX sector indices: Information Technology, Financials, Energy, and Gold. You can also buy an option on the on the S&P/TSX 60 Index or the i60 ETF itself.

What Index Future?

The most commonly used equity financial futures contracts in Canada are contracts on the S&P/TSX 60 Index. On U.S. exchanges the most popular are futures contracts on the S&P 500, Nasdaq 100, the Dow Jones Industrial Average Index, the Russell 2000 and the S&P MidCap 400. For the more ambitious, other contracts can be arranged but the selection of indices is nowhere near as great as that offered by ETFs. There are less than 20 indices available with standard futures contracts, and there's virtually no representation for sector indices.[11]

Tracking and Management Fees

Futures track an index as smoothly as the Montreal Metro hugs its rails from day to day, though intraday the contracts can anticipate the market and trade rich or cheap. Marking to market generally means your contract's value will go up and down in daily synch with the index and in exact proportion, too. There are no management fees and transaction costs are limited to the small brokerage commission for the contract. Since you sell or reverse contracts before they mature, little of your money is consumed by the actual cost of the contracts, which further improves your tracking. And don't forget that these contracts are done on margin. You get enormous exposure to a market index with proportionately little of your own money tied up.

You do have to foot money to open a futures/margin account, which requires some capitalization, but the nice thing is that T-bills are acceptable. You're not even losing money on the money tied up to support the margin account.

Taxes

Profits from futures contracts are taxed fully as income. (You cannot elect to have them treated as on capital account—see Chapter Six.) Losses from futures contracts are fully deductible from income. You cannot hold futures in your RRSP.

Short-Term or Long-Term Plays?

A study by an analyst at Salomon Smith Barney in New York concluded that futures are a cheaper way to get short-term exposure to financial markets but that long-term, ETFs are better. That analyst believed the "roll costs" of contracts over time had more of an effect on costs than the MER on Spiders. The analyst pointed out further that the minimum investment for futures trading was much higher than 100 shares of an ETF, and that ETFs are often linked to sectors where no futures contracts are available.

It's a matter of debate it seems. One other analyst, Jon Maier, who has looked at this question, doesn't agree. He thinks ETFs are always cheaper, short or long term, when you take into account mispricing risk and market impact of the futures contract itself. Maier's UBS Warburg report on exchange traded funds calculates all costs of an ETF purchase at 23.16 bps (0.23%). An identical calculation for a 3-month futures contract would cost 60.14 bps (0.60%) by his calculation. The longer the hold, the better ETFs look, according to the New York–based analyst.[12] The biggest advantage he reports with futures is the ease with which they can be leveraged. ETFs can be margined but you can borrow only up to 50% of their value (70% if they're optionable). Futures will let you get away with margining up to 90% of the contracts' value.

Leverage, of course, is a very sharp double-edged sword. Most investors would rather not. Hillary Clinton is said to have made a tidy sum on cattle futures. Maybe by the time she's running for president there will be a livestock ETF. Until then, it's likely most of us will content ourselves with relatively simple ETFs and leave futures to those who don't mind margin calls.

Index-linked GICs, equity-linked notes, index mutual funds, ETFs, or some variation of a futures contract; you've got to decide which product best suits your situation, and part of that depends on how much money you want to give over to passive investing and for how long. The longer the holding period, the more you should favour ETFs for their parsimonious MERs. As you'll see in the next chapter, there's a wealth of investment strategies suited for ETFs, some of which would not be possible to replicate with index funds because the index selection is nowhere near as broad as the buffet offered by ETFs. And of course, index funds are hard pressed to come anywhere close to matching ETFs in rock-bottom cover charge.

You might be surprised to discover that the American pioneer and outspoken advocate for low-cost index investing has kind words to say about ETFs, without actually liking them.

ETFs or Index Mutual Funds?
An Interview with John Bogle

John Bogle is founder of the Vanguard Group, the largest index mutual fund company in the world and the second largest mutual fund company in the United States. He's an active advocate of low-cost mutual funds, but not a great fan of ETFs despite the fact that Vanguard is the first U.S. mutual fund company to come out with an ETF, the VIPERs series. Mr. Bogle is retired from the day-to-day management of Vanguard.

As you read this, keep in mind that Mr. Bogle is speaking from a U.S. perspective where the difference in annual costs between his hugely popular index funds and ETFs is quite small. The MER on Vanguard's S&P index fund is 0.12% vs. the S&P 500 ETF, the Spider, with an MER of 0.10%. In Canada, the disparity between index fund MERs and comparable ETFs can be much wider.*

John Bogle: ETFs are a truly great product badly used. There's no reason not to use an ETF for long-term holdings. I'd call it a flip of the coin for long-term investors. That says they're a very, very good product because the index fund is the killer app[lication]. There's no way to improve on it for the market as a whole. It gives you virtually 100% of the market's return, and in the long run probably 1% of all managers can give you 100% of the market's returns over fifty years. That's just not very good odds. Why would somebody take a 1% chance when they're guaranteed to get the market's return in an index fund?

Now, what is the reality with ETFs? The turnover rate of all stocks in the U.S. is about 100% a year. Spider's is 1800%. The average holding is 12 days. That's a misuse of a big aggregated index. Turnover for QQQQ's is 3500% a year. It's a speculative medium [in which] shares are held for 2.2 days on average. It's a great way to trade the Nasdaq, but why would anybody in their right mind think they can make any money trading the Nasdaq? Trading is a loser's game.

I contrast it with a great Purdey shotgun. It's a perfect instrument for hunting and for suicide. I think many more investors are using these ETFs to commit financial suicide than they are to hunt for long-term returns. Anything that persuades people to trade more is against their best long-term investing interest.

We came out with VIPERs because we want to be competitive in the marketplace. If everybody else is doing it we want to do it too. There are some potential tax advantages for our existing shareholders [because] we can move very low cost stocks into the VIPER class without a tax impact to the fund. [VIPERs will also be helpful in] getting traders now in our funds out of our funds into the trading shares.

I'm not madly in love with it. People have argued that we should not let people trade our funds: slap 'em down. We've tried to be fairly good at that. [We allow] one round trip every six months—very tough trading restrictions. Maybe we could do that a little bit better, but in any event, we've elected to go the other way. It may not be a decision I would have made, but it's not a decision that's unrespectable.

An ETF is an index fund. If you buy and hold it for your investment lifetime of 50 years, it's completely indifferent as to whether you've owned a mutual fund or an ETF if it's a broad index. It's a distinction without a difference. What matters is how these funds get used. The evidence is overpowering that they're both marketed to traders and used by traders. All market mutual funds are boredom personified. ETFs are excitement personified. It's like sailing: hours of complete boredom punctuated by moments of sheer terror.

The ETF is great with the right long-term perspective because they keep costs and taxes low and those are crucial things. And that's good, but if they're used for trading, they're just another stock, maybe a little less risky one because of their diversification.

June 19, 2001

*The lowest-cost Canadian index ETF is the i60 with an MER of 0.17%. Contrast that with the lowest-cost publicly available Canadian equity index fund, TD's Canadian index e-fund, with an MER at 0.31% covering the S&P/TSX Composite Index. (MERs from www.globe-fund.com as of May 2005.)

A Note about HOLDRS

Somewhere between a whole index and a hand-picked portfolio of your own making lie HOLDRS (pronounced 'holders'.) HOLDRS are exchange traded baskets of securities, each typically containing 20 different stocks related by industry sector. These elect stocks remain in the portfolio unchanged for the life of the trust unless corporate events cause changes to the stock itself like reconstitution, delisting, etc. Though HOLDRS are usually included in ETF discussions, they fall short of being full-blown ETFs because some of their distinguishing characteristics make them more like a passive closed-end fund than an ETF.

HOLDRS stands for "HOLding Company Depositary Receipts." For the cost of a stock trade and few other expenses, they provide an instant portfolio with a very focused sector concentration. HOLDRS cover specialized sectors like business-to-business internet companies, internet-architecture firms, and more diversified, established sectors like telecommunications, utilities, and pharmaceuticals.

HOLDRS is a signature product designed and offered by Merrill Lynch & Co., Inc. in the United States and Canada. They've been popular. First introduced in 1999, there are now 17 HOLDRS trading on AMEX with US$7.7 billion in assets.[13] Merrill Lynch had an unfortunate habit of launching their highly specialized internet and technology plays at very close to the market peak. Many early HOLDRS investors saw their high-tech portfolios plummet—some by as much as 95%. But dismal timing aside, these products have a number of attractive features and a few worrisome drawbacks, too.

On the attractive side, HOLDRS have no MER or any other ongoing fees or costs apart from a small annual trustee fee ($8 per 100 shares of HOLDRS) that is paid out of dividends and other distributions. If the portfolio doesn't generate enough income to pay the trustee fee—not a far-fetched scenario when dealing with internet companies—the trustee fee is waived to the extent it can't be paid from distributions.

Because they do not have to comply with the concentration limits that apply to mutual funds and ETFs (in the U.S.), your HOLDRS portfolio will never be forced to sell a winning stock. This will spare you the sting of unwanted capital gains and the disadvantage of a smaller holding in a good investment. With HOLDRS, as with an individual stock holding, you can ride a winner as long as it runs and you decide when to sell it and trigger your gains.

HOLDRS also bring that wonderful creation/redemption process pioneered by ETFs into the clutches of retail investors. You can easily redeem HOLDRS for all its underlying securities. This gives you the freedom to sell the shares you don't want on the open market and keep the rest. The trustee charges a $10 fee per round lot of 100 HOLDRS shares for this service. Less likely, but also possible, you can create 100 HOLDRS by surrendering the requisite number of shares of the underlying portfolio to the trustee who, for $10, will issue you HOLDRS in exchange. ETFs like Spiders and i60s permit this creation/redemption only with huge share volumes of 50,000 or more, which means in practice that only institutional investors and arbitrageurs can take advantage of this feature.

HOLDRS are bought, sold, created, and redeemed in multiples of 100 shares and only in lots of 100. (ETFs, you'll remember, do come in odd lots.) Of course, because you can't buy anything less than a round lot of 100 HOLDRS, the investor buying these keepers had better have enough money for 100 shares. In May 2005, that would have meant forking over as much as US$16,300 for Biotech HOLDRS, or as little as $217 for the beat-up B2B HOLDRS.

In addition to their accessible redemption feature, HOLDRS are retail-friendly in another way. You get the voting rights associated with all the underlying shares. This is in contrast to other baskets of securities such as mutual funds and ETFs. With mutual funds, the beneficial owners do not get voting rights to the underlying securities. ETFs give voting rights only to those investors who hold a creation/redemption unit, typically about 50,000 shares or units of the ETF. The vast majority of retail ETF investors, then, would not have voting rights on the underlying securities. Social investors, eager to influence corporate behaviour through their voting rights will appreciate the voting feature of HOLDRS—and the flexibility to divest themselves of companies within the portfolio that don't cut the mustard ethically.

Along with these voting rights you'd better get yourself a bigger mailbox because you receive all the investor relations mailings from the twenty or so underlying companies, too. The two non-sector HOLDRS, "Market 2000" and "Europe 2001," have around 50 companies in each of their baskets. If you take pity on your mail carrier's back and your recycling box, you can elect to receive most of these corporate mailings electronically.

Cheaper to hold and more flexible than ETFs, HOLDRS as a structure have a lot going for them. The actual execution, however, could use some work. With just a few exceptions, HOLDRS' portfolios are highly sector specific. As such, they expose you to a lot more risk than a broad market index or even a sector mutual fund with a greater number of holdings. The risk hasn't been academic either. As a group, their losses from inception have been breathtaking.

The B2B Internet HOLDRS has been the most spectacular. It

launched in February 2000 at US$95.09 and in May 2005, it rested at a stomach wrenching $2.17, up a bit from $1.80 in 2002. Biotech and utilities have been good plays for investors, but apart from those most HOLDRS are down from inception or slightly better than flat.

One winner has been the only Canadian-based HOLDRS, CP HOLDRS. This was designed around the spinoffs of Canadian Pacific Railway and was launched in 2001 at C$50. As of May 2005, it was chugging right along at around $114 a share.

Leaving performance issues aside, HOLDRS have a structural feature that is not all that desirable. The portfolio is a snapshot in time. What goes in at the beginning stays in unchanged unless there's a spinoff, merger, consolidation, or other corporate event that would cause any of the underlying securities to be withdrawn from AMEX. This means the number of holdings in the fund could shrink and the corresponding concentration of the remaining stocks would increase. Gradually, your investment would become less diversified. An amendment to the rules governing HOLDRS now permits them to retain stocks resulting from some of these stock rending corporate events, but this doesn't entirely ameliorate the structural problem.

Suppose a private biotech company discovers a cure for cancer; they go public, and their stock immediately rockets skyward. A biotech HOLDRS put together before that company went public would miss out entirely on the biggest biotech shooting star in history. An index continually refreshes its holdings to keep up with market activity, so any index-based product like an ETF will not miss out on the next Viagra. The static portfolio construction will haunt any HOLDRS, but especially those in a rapid growth sector—the very sectors these products have chosen to exploit.

Market appreciation and losses will, over time, change the balance of the HOLDRS underlying securities relative to each other. The longer you keep a HOLDRS, the more risky and less representative the portfolio may become. Internet HOLDRS is a good example of the danger. This HOLDRS was launched with AOL at 19.6% of the original portfolio. Time Warner swallowed AOL, which resulted in AOL Time Warner Inc. stock taking up 47% of the portfolio at a point when only 20% of Time Warner's revenue was coming from internet-related businesses.

Lest you worry that the absence of an ongoing management fee will make HOLDRS a fleeting product, take heart. Merrill Lynch has not turned altruistic. HOLDRS finance themselves by charging a 2% underwriting fee at the initial offering (for 10,000 HOLDRS or more the underwriting fee is 1%), a charge that is paid only once and does not spill over into the secondary market.

Before grasping a brand new HOLDRS for your own, if there are any more introduced, take a good look at the costs. Although a 2% underwriting fee may not seem unreasonable, keep in mind that the upside potential of a HOLDRS initial public offering (IPO) is not like the promise of a new stock IPO. HOLDRS are baskets of securities that have each already had their own public debuts. Just repackaging them into a HOLDRS and launching that as an IPO doesn't automatically create any new upside potential. In fact, the very act of gathering them up to repackage could in itself push the shares' prices up. You may find an underwriting fee palatable for a stock IPO with great expectations, but where's a similar excitement with a HOLDRS IPO?

Short Selling Exemption

All ETFs in the U.S. are exempt from the short selling uptick rule. Regulators feel that because ETFs represent a diversified basket of stocks and not a single security, there is little danger of them doing major damage if they are sold short into a falling market. HOLDRS used to have the same exemption, but eight of them have lost this exemption either because the number of their underlying shares falls below 15, or because they no longer meet certain "actively traded" requirements. (Appendix C indicates which HOLDRS no longer have the uptick exemption.)

All U.S.-based HOLDRS trade on AMEX, and all have options associated with them. (For more information on HOLDRS go to *www.holdrs.com*, an extensive site with prospectuses. Also see the Appendix.)

Notes

1) Salomon Smith Barney research report on exchange traded funds, Feb. 6, 2001, p.16. The S&P 500 change occurred in late 2000.

2) ibid.

3) As of May 18, 2005, *www.globefund.com*, index fund universe. Note that segregated funds guarantee investors' capital, which is one reason segregated funds have higher MERs than other funds.

4) This point is made graphically at *www.bylo.org* in an article entitled "Performance of Indexed vs. Actively Managed Portfolios (CARs for the 15 years ending 31Dec'00)," March 14, 2001. The article compares the returns of median mutual funds to median index funds over 15 years and calculates how profoundly the MER differential affects long-term returns. Also see *www.iunits.com* "Investor Tools and Data" for an MER impact calculator, and Norman Rothery, "Active Funds vs. Indexing," viewed September 28, 2002, *www.ndir.com/SI/articles/mutual.vs.tips.shtml*.

5) Donna Green, "Ask MoneySense," October 2000, for a more detailed discussion of the MER calculation and what it leaves out.

6) Fifty-two week standard deviations from Phillip Witter, CFA, CIM, Product Analyst, Barclays Canada.

7) Unlike dividends, capital gains are paid in units, not cash. Total distributions for the i60 per unit were $1.766 in 2004.

8) The author was not able to find Canadian data on holding periods, but there's no reason to think the Canadian holding period is that much different from that in the U.S. Two and a half year U.S. holding information from John Bogle, President of Bogle Financial Markets Research Center, founder and past chairman of The Vanguard Group, "Mutual Fund Directors: The Dog that Didn't Bark," Jan. 29, 2001 speech. Available on *www.vanguard.com* Bogle's Speeches, (*http://www.vanguard.com/bogle_site/january282001.html*) Also see Gavin Quill, "Investors Behaving Badly: An Analysis of Investor Trading Patterns in Mutual Funds, Journal of Financial Planning, November 2001, article 11, *www.journalfp.net/jfp1101-art11.cfm*. This article states the 2.9 year holding period and the 5.5 year holding period in 1997.

9) Investor Economics report, "Market-linked Instruments," Toronto, May 2005.

10) "Structured Investment Products: A Closer Look at Index-Linked GICs and Mutual Fund-linked Deposit Notes" by Phillips, Hager & North Investment Management Ltd., February 2004, p. 3. *www.phn.com/pdfs/structured_investment_products.pdf*

11) Kevin McNally, "ETFs versus Futures," Salomon Smith Barney research report, February 11, 2002, p. 4.

12) Salomon Smith Barney research report on exchange traded funds, Feb. 6, 2001, p.18, and UBS Warburg report by Jon Maier, March 13, 2001.

13) Morgan Stanley, "ETF Global Summary Report," March 2005 by Deborah Fuhr, p. 11.

Part Two

Making ETFs Work for You

Chapter Four

Investment Strategies Using ETFs

Staking your money on an index among the countless ones out there seems to require either strong opinions or impressive self-confidence. With nearly 200 ETFs available in North America, where do you begin? Well, in truth, the choices get narrowed down remarkably quickly because you want to establish two main goals in your overall portfolio: prudent diversification and intelligent asset allocation.

Diversification is the uncomplicated essence of a good portfolio management. Part of good diversification is asset allocation. You've likely heard more times than you care to remember that asset allocation is responsible for 93.6% of your portfolio returns. That is possibly the most widely quoted false statistic in personal finance. The study, done by Gary Brinson in 1986, actually says, "Data from 91 large U.S. pension plans indicate that investment policy dominates investment strategy (market timing and security selection), explaining on average 93.6% of the variation in total plan return."[1] In other words, asset allocation explained, on average, 93.6% of the *variation* in the portfolios studied. Variation, or variance, is a measure of the risk of an asset or an entire portfolio. So what the study is actually saying is that asset allocation is the predominant factor in controlling the riskiness of the portfolio. Perhaps not the profound conclusion of the misquotes, but an important observation anyway. Evening the peaks and valleys of your returns will give you a better opportunity to put compounding to good long-term benefit. Compounding works more quickly on consistent gains rather than an equivalent return spread over years of losses and gold strikes.

Because the Brinson study has been wildly misunderstood, it has been revisited a number of times. A more recent paper looks at this study, adds some more empirical evidence, and wrings a more meaningful conclusion from it all. Roger G. Ibbotson and Paul D. Kaplan, in their article, "Does Asset Allocation Policy Explain 40, 90, or 100 Percent of Performance?" say:

In summary, the impact of asset allocation on returns depends on an individual's investing style. For the long-term, passive investor, the asset allocation decision is by far the most important. For the short-term investor who trades more frequently, invests in individual securities, and practices market timing, asset allocation has less of an impact on returns. The impact of asset allocation on performance is directly correlated with investment style.[2]

So if you're going to be a buy-and-hold investor, your asset allocation should be your foremost consideration, and the key to an effective asset allocation is diversification.

Diversification means not putting all your eggs in one basket—not buying one stock when you can buy a number of different stocks to hedge your risk. Ditto for bonds and any other investment vehicle. Asset allocation is simply the process of extending the principle of diversification across asset classes. Holding 12 different stocks may mean you're diversified across equities (if you've selected stocks from different industries), but you're still exposed to the vagaries of the stock market without the backstop of bonds, cash, real estate, precious metals, etc.

Mutual funds made diversification and asset allocation easy. There's a mutual fund for any asset class you can think of, and because of the large sums mutual funds pool, they can offer instant and broad diversification to anyone with $25 a month. It's a wonderful thing.

But by now you know ETFs are a cheaper way to accomplish diversification and quality asset allocation. So, if you want to take a bite out of your investment costs and have more flexibility with your investments, this chapter contains some easy-to-emulate portfolio construction models and investment strategies using ETFs to help you build a solidly diversified portfolio with readily amendable asset allocation guidelines and excellent tax efficiency. There's enough information here to start you on the road to do-it-yourself freedom.

For those who prefer to work with an advisor, this chapter will give you a good understanding of the strategies your advisor will have at his or her disposal so that your investment portfolio will not be held back just in the interests of keeping it simple. Advisors can add value when they're free to use every tool in the arsenal to build your wealth. You'll notice, too, that there's still a role in these strategies for actively managed mutual funds for those asset classes not yet covered by ETFs, or for those sectors where you might believe active management can still exploit some inefficiencies.

Keep in mind that ETFs can be bought or sold only inside a brokerage account. If you don't already have a brokerage account, it may seem like an unwelcome complication, but once set up, the flexibility and convenience it provides make it hard to ever want to do without it. A brokerage account is useful because you can hold just about everything but the junk in your basement in it. This means you can consolidate all your investments in one account if you like—with the exception of bank GICs which can't be transferred to another institution. You can easily open an account at no charge with a full-service broker or an on-line discount broker.

Time to put theory aside and put ETFs to their practical use.

Core and Satellite

Core and Satellite is a popular portfolio construction method, especially for the equity side. It starts by allocating the largest chunk of money to the least risky equity holding. I think this should be a broad-based equity ETF, but any low-cost, reliable broad-based fund can be used. Surrounding that core like electrons are smaller investments in industry sectors, management style, market capitalization, and individual stock selection. This method is also known by the trademarked name, "Core and Explore," propounded by Charles Schwab & Co., Inc. in the U.S., but it has been done in Canada since the very early 1990s by the brokerage firm Lévesque Beaubien, and subsequently expounded in a book by Duff Young called *Core and Explore: The Investment Rush without the Ruin.*

I recommend the core of the portfolio be passively managed, but the exploratory parts can be either passively or actively managed. An important consideration for the electrons is their maneuverability. They're the ones you may wish to use to dart in and out in anticipation of changing market conditions or hold longer term as a secular play. They're the ones the money manager is counting on to boost returns above the index benchmark.

As the savvy investor knows, the asset allocation sets the return expectations. A good allocation finds a balance between what you need to earn on your portfolio and your risk tolerance. A solid, personalized asset allocation is the foundation of good portfolio management. Mutual fund companies have had fairly sophisticated, proprietary asset allocation programs for years. Let's look at how an investment advisor might implement the Core and Satellite approach.

Core/Satellite Equity Allocation Strategy (fig. 22)

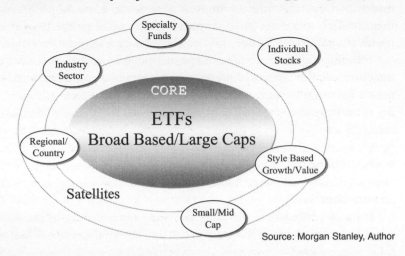

Source: Morgan Stanley, Author

The Asset Allocation Decision

After your initial asset allocation is determined, your advisor might recommend that you put half of each asset class in a passive vehicle such as an ETF, to form the stable nucleus. The other half of each asset class could be actively managed by selecting individual stocks or by over-weighting sectors with sector ETFs. This approach works especially well with a sector like technology in which individual stocks can be risky. A diversified portfolio with a broad selection of technology companies mitigates the business risk of individual stocks while still giving the chance to capture the potential of the whole sector. This Core and Satellite approach provides lots of room for tactical portfolio changes, letting advisors overweight sectors without throwing off the structural asset allocation.

The Fixed Income Component

It is also possible to "core" the fixed income portion of your portfolio with ETFs. A combination of Barclays Canada's iG5 and iBond funds could form the passive nucleus. You could then "satellite" with actively managed corporate or high-yield bond mutual funds, income trusts and preferred shares. This strategy gives the flexibility to trade bonds in anticipation of interest rate changes and changes in credit quality—the two major ways active bond fund managers make money.

If Canadian bonds don't seem diversified enough for you, there are also six fixed income ETFs in the U.S., among them one for corporate bonds and one for government inflation-protected bonds. Dividend generating ETFs are well used in the U.S, also, to supplement a fixed income stream.

Canadian investors, though, have to note that U.S. dividend income is taxed at the same rate as interest income in Canada. Additional fixed income ETF offerings are expected on both sides of the border and with them, added flexibility for the fixed income side of your holdings.

You may not realize it, but there are more benefits to bond ETFs than may immediately appear. Individual investors like you and me have to buy bonds through brokerages that hold them in inventory. Although there is no commission charge on a bond purchase, there is an invisible charge taken by the house on the sale of a bond that is factored into the yield your bond delivers. A bond that might cost $900 per $1,000 face value will be sold to you for the purposes of example at $910 per $1,000. That extra $10 over wholesale cost is the brokerages' built-in (and most often undisclosed) commission.

Until recently, you and I were not privy to the wholesale cost of bonds. Investors had no accurate way to tell how large a cut the bond desk was taking on a bond transaction because the bond market prices were veiled from us. With the advent of on-line bond trading information services like E-Bond Inc., that has changed. However, for those of us not yet familiar with the on-line bond services now in Canada, or whose bond trading doesn't justify an on-line subscription to one of these services, you can get a feel for current interest rate levels from looking at the yields of other bonds of a similar nature, if you can get current quotes of those bonds and use this to judge the fairness of the yield on your particular bond purchase. That's about as close as you can come to figuring out whether you got a good price on your purchase.

With bond ETFs all you have to worry about is the brokerage commission to buy the fund and the annual MER. You can bet the ETF is getting a better yield on their bonds than you would be able to get simply because of the size of their purchase. You can also bet that a $29 commission is a lot less than the money you lose in yield on an individual bond purchase. The real question is if the 0.25% or so MER is also less than the yield hit you'd take on an individual bond buy. Twenty-five basis points is dramatically less than the MER on a conventional bond fund, which can easily run you 0.74% for an index bond fund to 1.86% for the AGF Canadian Bond Fund, hardly the most costly bond fund either.

Building Blocks

Very similar to the Core and Satellite approach is the Building Blocks method of portfolio construction. In this model, decreasing amounts of money are allocated to increasingly risky equity groups. The base of the pyramid starts with a very broad-based passive investment such as TD Asset Management's S&P/TSX Composite ETF or iShares Russell 3000. Then, in decreasing weight, might come a value and/or a growth ETF or mutual fund, then perhaps a mid-cap ETF, followed by a sector ETF say in healthcare, and then finally the smallest block of all, individual stocks.

Equity Building Blocks (fig. 23)

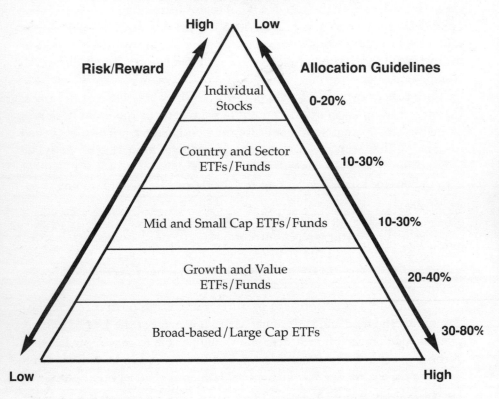

Allocation guidelines: Author   Source: Morgan Stanley Equity Research

One of the many beauties of this approach is that your portfolio's return will probably stay fairly close to the return of its main holding, in this case, the S&P/TSX Composite ETF. The approach also gives a disciplined framework so you shrink your exposure as the riskiness of the investment increases. It's a big temptation to make sizable bets on hot industries. The Core and Satellite and the Building Block strategies let you have some exposure to a favoured sector, style, or stock, but in moderation and with due consideration for their inherent risk.

Naturally, not every possibility needs to be included in portfolios following this general core approach. Likely, you'll find it enough to tilt your passive core with a favoured sector or a promising stock, but if you're game to try all the flavours, the good news is that Canadians can use domestic ETFs for just about every block in the pyramid. There are Canadian ETFs for broad equity indices, a mid-cap ETF, a value and a growth ETF, and four industry sector ETFs. And of course, for a U.S. equity component there is a wealth of selection with U.S.-based ETFs in increasingly sophisticated combinations of style and capitalization.

For the foreign exposure, you could also invest the growth and value portion of the pyramid in international mutual funds with those style biases, swing in a U.S. sector or a global sector ETF. (See Core and Satellite components below for more ideas.) There are a limitless number of ways to utilize this strategy.

Core Components: Broad Market/Large Cap Base (fig. 24)

Step 1: Select one ETF from each desired **exposure** (one from broad OR one from large cap) and weight appropriately.

Equity Exposure	Type	Canadian Listed	U.S. Listed
Canada	Broad	TTF, TCF	
	Large Cap	XIU, XIC	
United States	Broad		IYY, IWY, VTI
	Large Cap	XSP*	IVV, SPY, IWB, DIA
International	Broad	XIN*	EFA

* These ETFs are not considered foreign content, as they use futures contracts and other derivatives to track their target indices. Should the foreign content restrictions be lifted by the Canadian government, the sponsor of these ETFs, Barclays Canada, proposes changing their structure while keeping their underlying target indices the same. Instead of futures contracts and other derivatives, the funds would invest in iShares tracking the same target indices. iShares are U.S.-based ETFs managed by Barclays U.S. In addition, Barclays Canada proposes using currency hedging strategies within these funds to reduce the risk of exchange rate fluctuations.

Fixed Income Components (fig. 25)

Step 2: For fixed income allocations, select appropriate ETFs to match **credit** and **term** exposure.

Fixed Income Exposure	Credit & Maturity Term	Canadian Listed	U.S. Listed
Canada	Short (Gov't)	XGV	
	Broad	XBB	
United States	Aggregate		AGG
	Government		
	(short, mid, long)		SHY, IEF, TLT
	Corporate		LQD
	Inflation Protected		TIP

Satellite/Tilt Components (fig. 26)

Step 3: Layer on to the core, one ETF for each desired exposure to strategically **tilt** the portfolio.

Strategy	Exposure	Canadian Listed	U.S. Listed
Style/Cap	Growth	TAG	IWZ
	Value	TAV	IWW
	Mid Cap	XMD	MDY, IJH, IWR, VO
	Small Cap		IJR, IWM, VB
Industry Sector	Energy	XEG	XLE, IYE, OIH, IXC
	Financials	XFN	XLF, IYF, IYG, RKH, IGX
	Healthcare Broad		XLV, IYH, PPH, IXJ
	Healthcare Biotech		BBH, IBB
	Tech. Broad	XIT	XLK, IYW, IGM, IXN, VGT
	Tech. Telecom		IYZ, TTH, WMH, VOX
	Real Estate	XRE	IYR, ICF, RWR
	Gold	XGD	GLD, IAU
Country/Regional	Europe Broad		IEV, EZU, EKH
	Asia Pacific		
	Japan		EWJ
	Asia Ex.-Japan		EPP
	China		FXI, PGJ
	Emerging Markets		EEM, VWO, ADRE

Sample ETF Portfolios

Building traditional portfolios is as easy as snapping Lego pieces together when you combine the Core and Satellite/Tilt components together. The following four portfolios showcase just how flexible ETFs are in helping you achieve your investment objectives. The number of possible portfolios is virtually limitless. There is a suitability section at the bottom of each portfolio to help you consider the fit with your overall investment plan. Treat these sample portfolios as starting points to be adjusted based upon personal circumstances and investment objectives.

Don't hesitate to make portfolio substitutions based on personal preferences or current holdings. Almost all of the ETFs have a near twin or two, making them quite interchangeable. This also makes them useful for tax loss harvesting, a strategy we'll delve into in Chapter Six. In addition, substitutions to the model may be made with virtually any active investment vehicle. For example, you may prefer a fixed income ladder of strip coupons inside your RRSP for some, or all, of your fixed income component. You will probably want to hold onto actively managed mutual funds that are performing well or that still have a punitive DSC penalty attached to a redemption. Individual stock selection, in certain sectors, may help round out a unique core and satellite portfolio.

Sample RSP Portfolio (fig. 27)

ETF	Symbol	Sector/Market	% of Portfolio	MER
Fixed Income				
Canadian Bond	XBB	Cdn Fixed Income	30%	0.30%
iShares Lehman Aggregate	AGG	U.S. Fixed Income	10%	0.20%
Equity				
S&P/TSX 60 Index	XIU	Cdn Equity	20%	0.17%
iShares Russell 3000	IWV	U.S. Equity	20%	0.20%
IShares MSCI EAFE	EFA	Int'l Equity	20%	0.35%
		TOTAL	100%	0.25%

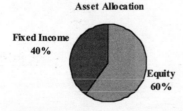

Asset Allocation

Fixed Income 40%

Equity 60%

Geographic Breakdown

Canada 50%

U.S. 30%

International 20%

Suitability

Account Type:	RRSP
Asset Mix:	Balanced
Investment Strategy:	Buy and Hold, Periodic Rebalancing
Risk Tolerance:	Low to Moderate
Portfolio Content:	Core or Complete Portfolio

ETFs "With Options"* Portfolio (fig. 28)

ETF	Symbol	Sector/Market	% of Portfolio	MER
Canada				
iUnits S&P/TSX 60 Canada Index	XIU	Cdn LargeCap	20%	0.17%
United States				
S&P 500	SPY	U.S. LargeCap	30%	0.10%
iShares MidCap 400	IJH	U.S. MidCap	10%	0.20%
iShares Russell 2000	IWM	U.S. SmallCap	10%	0.20%
International				
iShares MSCI EAFE	EFA	Int'l Equity	30%	0.35%
* All these ETFs have listed options.		TOTAL	100%	0.20%

Capitalization Breakdown

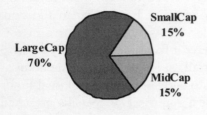

LargeCap 70%
SmallCap 15%
MidCap 15%

Geographic Breakdown

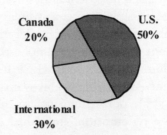

Canada 20%
U.S. 50%
International 30%

Suitability

Account Type:	Open
Asset Mix:	All Equity
Investment Strategy:	Hedging with Covered Call Writing/Put Buying Available
Risk Tolerance:	Low to Moderate
Portfolio Content:	Complete Equity or Core

Value Tilt Portfolio (fig. 29)

ETF	Symbol	Sector/Market	% of Portfolio	MER
Canada				
S&P/TSX 60 Canada Index	XIU	Large Cap	15%	.17%
TD Select Canadian Value	TAV	Cdn Value	10%	.55%
United States				
iShares S&P 500	IVV	Large Cap	20%	.09%
iShares S&P 500/Barra Value	IVE	Large Cap Value	10%	.18%
iShares S&P MidCap 400	IJH	MidCap	15%	.20%
iShares S&P 400/Barra Value	IJJ	MidCap Value	5%	.25%
iShares S&P 600/Barra Growth	IJT	SmallCap Growth	5%	.25%
iShares S&P 600/Barra Value	IJS	SmallCap Value	5%	.25%
International				
iShares MSCI EAFE	EFA	International *	15%	.25%
		TOTAL	100%	.18%

* Int'l style ETFs likely available in late 2005 or early 2006

Style Allocation

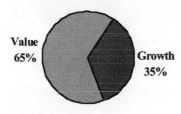

Value 65%

Growth 35%

Geographic Breakdown

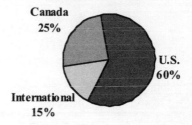

Canada 25%

U.S. 60%

International 15%

Suitability

Account Type:	Open
Asset Mix:	All Equity
Investment Strategy:	Value Style Bias
Risk Tolerance:	Moderate
Portfolio Content:	Equity Core

Income Portfolio* (fig. 30)

ETF	Symbol	Sector/Market	% of Portfolio	MER	Yield
Canada					
iUnits Canadian Bond	XBB	Cdn Bonds	30%	.30%	3.9%
iUnits Canadian Financials	XFN	Financial	25%	.55%	2.3%
iUnits Canadian REITs	XRE	Cdn REITs	15%	.55%	5.7%
United States					
iShares Lehman Aggregate	AGG	U.S. Bonds	15%	.20%	4.0%
iShares DJ Select Dividend	DVY	U.S. Equity	15%	.40%	2.8%
		TOTAL	100%	.40%	3.7%

*Additional Canadian and International income oriented funds expected in 2005 -2006
As of June 2005.

Asset Class Breakdown

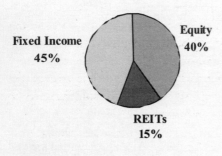

Fixed Income
45%

Equity
40%

REITs
15%

Geographic Breakdown

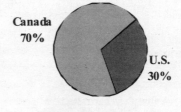

Canada
70%

U.S.
30%

Suitability

Asset Mix:	Balanced
Investment Strategy:	Income and Growth
Risk Tolerance:	Low to Moderate
Portfolio Content:	Total Return Portfolio

The Building Block method and the Core/Satellite approach anchor your portfolio in a passive index while giving you quite a bit of room to do some tactical maneuvering with a portion of your portfolio. You can adjust from value to growth when the economy starts heating up, or back to value as a more defensive play. You can tilt from sector to sector as you anticipate action and of course you can still enjoy your individual stock picks. Hard to imagine an easier to maintain portfolio that'll let you have so much fun.

Working out how much you should allocate to core and how much to satellite does take some thought. As a rule of thumb, the more risk averse you are, the greater the percentage of your portfolio should be put in the core—even up to 100%. Your portfolio will then perform in line with the asset classes you've chosen. No better. No worse. It's a trade-off. You've given up the possibility of outperforming the market for the promise of not underperforming it (except by the amount of the small MER).

At the other extreme would be the 100% satellite portfolio—the swing for the fences approach. But as in baseball, when you focus on the home runs, you all too often strike out. Most investors will find comfort in a core position ranging from 50 to 70% of their portfolio, with the conservative crowd approaching 100%. As always, your investment decisions have to be in line with your financial goals and risk tolerance.

Rebalancing

The success of any asset allocation investment strategy depends on disciplined rebalancing. Over time, your carefully allotted percentages are going to come unstuck. Not all the assets will grow in proportion to one another. What started off as a 10% position may have grown to 20%, and your core may look a little gnawed in comparison. Rebalancing is the process of bringing your portfolio's asset classes back in line with an optimal allocation.

As anyone knows who has sold a winner to buy more losers, this takes intestinal fortitude. The big temptation is to continue to let winners run. That's when greed overtakes reason. It is always best to leave something for the next guy. By rebalancing you capture your gains and plow them into asset classes that have yet to make their move. You lose out a little on the high end, but chances are you capture the full movement from off the bottom of the next hot asset class. Rebalancing at least once a year has a smoothing effect on returns, which increases the benefits of compounding.

Unfortunately, rebalancing an ETF portfolio comes with commission costs and probably a tax bill (outside a registered account). This means you have to decide how religiously you want to keep to your ideal asset allocation. Rebalancing to adjust for a 5% deviation isn't worth it in a small portfolio, but it could be in a large portfolio. These are judgments you have to make, perhaps in consultation with a financial advisor or accountant. Don't let the tax tail wag the investment dog. Rebalancing has to be done to get the full benefit of these strategies, an important part of which is their defensiveness.

Sector Rotation

Sector rotation is a fairly aggressive investment strategy that ETFs make very easy to execute, but unfortunately, not any easier to get right. Sector rotation managers invest in industry sectors they believe are poised for significant advances. Strategies vary greatly, but generally they fall into two camps based upon the expected holding period. Intermediate sector rotation is usually measured in months and attempts to capture cyclical moves. Secular strategies are based on multi-year trends.

The aim is to buy into a sector when it is still out of favour and to sell when it has peaked. Trouble is, nobody has a reliable crystal ball. Analysts have spent lots of time tracking historical sector performance in hopes of discovering some pattern or predictability to the ascendant sectors. Let's just say it's still an art, but one that plenty of managers think they can exploit. Plenty of ordinary investors unknowingly do sector rotation when they buy and sell industry-specialized mutual funds such as internet and technology, health sciences funds, precious metals, and funds with a preponderance of financial stocks like AIC's Advantage Fund. Sectors go in and out of favour, but with a little cunning and some luck most everyone thinks they can pick the next hot sector. As the technology stock crash has shown, a big part of sector betting is knowing when to leave something for the next guy or sit through some gut-wrenching downturns. Exiting a sector before its decline can be as important as jumping onto it before its rise.

To give you some idea of how volatile sector investing can be, on the opposite page is a chart courtesy of Morgan Stanley Equity Research on the historical performance of major sectors.

The current crop of ETFs make sector investing easy. Not only that, but ETFs bring an efficiency to sector investing that is hard to emulate because of the broad index approach they take. Instead of relying on a manager to make good representative picks in the sector at hand, an ETF simply snaps up the sector index and is done with it. There's no active manager risk and you can be assured that you're going to be along for the ride, though

Historical S&P/MSCI Sector Performance (fig. 31)

	1995	1996	1997	1998	1999	2000	2001	2002	2003	2004	2005YTD
Best	Health 58.2%	Info. Tech. 44.8%	Financial 49.0%	Info. Tech. 78.5%	Info. Tech. 79.7%	Utilities 57.1%	Consum. Discret. 2.0%	Consum. Staples -4.4%	Info. Tech. 46.6%	Energy 31.5%	Energy 11.5%
	Financial 53.7%	Financial 35.5%	Health 42.3%	Telecom Services 53.1%	Materials 25.6%	Health 25.6%	Materials 1.0%	Materials -7.2%	Consum. Discret. 38.1%	Utilities 24.3%	Utilities 7.6%
	Telecom Services 41.8%	Consum. Staples 26.6%	Telecom Services 41.1%	Health 43.5%	Consum. Discret 24.8%	Financial 24.8%	Industrial -7.3%	Energy -11.0%	Materials 34.8%	Telecom Services 19.8%	Health 3.8%-
	Consum. Staples 40.2%	Energy 25.9%	Consum. Staples 34.4%	Consum. Discret 41.2%	Industrial 19.8%	Consum. Staples 19.8%	Consum. Staples -8.3%	Financial -14.3%	Industrial 29.7%	Industrial 18.0%	Consum. Staples 1.0%
Performance	Info. Tech. 39.1%	Industrial 24.9%	Consum. Discret. 33.3%	Consum. Staples 15.5%	Telecom Services 18.9%	Energy 15.5%	Financial -10.7%	Health -19.0%	Financial 27.9%	Consum. Discret. 13.3%	Materials -3.3%
	Industrial 38.8%	Health 21.6%	Info. Tech. 27.8%	Utilities 14.9%	Energy 18.2%	Industrial 4.9%	Energy -12.3%	Consum. Discret. -23.4%	Energy 22.4%	Materials 13.2%	Industrial -4.3%
	Utilities 32.7%	Materials 15.4%	Industrial 27.0%	Industrial 11.5%	Financial 3.8%	Materials -14.4%	Health -12.4%	Industrial -25.7	Utilities 21.1%	Financial 10.9%	Financial -5.1%
	Energy 31.0%	Consum. Discret. 13.6%	Energy 25.2%	Financial 11.4%	Health -10.3%	Consum. Discret. -20.0%	Telecom Services -13.7%	Utilities -30.1%	Health 13.3%	Consum. Staples 8.2%	Telecom Services -9.2%
	Materials 20.8%	Utilities 5.7%	Utilities 24.8%	Energy 0.8%	Utilities -9.3%	Telecom Services -38.8%	Info. Tech. -25.9%	Telecom Services -34.2%	Consum Staples 9.2%	Info. Tech. 2.6%	Consum. Discret. -9.4%
Worst	Consum. Discret. 20.3%	Telecom Services 0.2%	Materials 8.1%	Materials 6.6%	Consum. Staples -15.5%	Info. Tech. -40.6%	Utilities -32.5%	Info. Tech. -37.6%	Telecom Services 3.3%	Health 1.7%	Info. Tech. -9.6%

Source: Morgan Stanley

Year to date through May 5, 2005. Performance for all cited indices is calculated on a total return basis with dividends reinvested. Categories are based upon S&P 500 GICS Sectors.

Historical S&P/MSCI Style Performance (fig. 32)

Performance	1995	1996	1997	1998	1999	2000	2001	2002	2003	2004	2005 YTD
Best ↑	Value 38.3%	Large Cap 23.2%	Value 38.3%	Growth 38.7%	Growth 33.2%	Bonds 11.6%	Bonds 8.4%	Bonds 10.3%	Small Cap 47.3%	Internat 20.7%	Bond 0.9%
	Large Cap 37.5%	Growth 23.1%	Growth 37.2%	Large Cap 28.7%	Internat. 25.3%	Mid Cap 8.2%	Small Cap 1.0%	Value -15.5%	Mid Cap 40.1%	Mid Cap 20.2%	Value -0.2%
	Growth 37.2%	Value 21.6%	Mid Cap 34.5%	Internat. 18.2%	Small Cap 21.3%	Value 7.0%	Mid Cap -7.0%	Internat -15.9%	Internat 39.2%	Small Cap 18.3%	Mid Cap -1.8%
Performance	Mid Cap 34.5%	Mid Cap 19.0%	Large Cap 33.3%	Value 15.6%	Large Cap 21.0%	Small Cap -3.0%	Value -7.4%	Mid Cap -16.2%	Value 30.0%	Value 16.5%	Internat -2.3%
	Small Cap 28.4%	Small Cap 16.5%	Small Cap 28.4%	Mid Cap 10.1%	Mid Cap 18.2%	Large Cap -9.1%	Large Cap -13.0%	Small Cap -20.5%	Growth 29.8%	Large Cap 10.9%	Large Cap -3.0%
	Bonds 18.5%	Internat. 4.4%	Bonds 9.7%	Bonds 8.7%	Value 7.3%	Internat. -15.2%	Growth -20.9%	Large Cap -22.1%	Large Cap 26.4%	Bonds 6.8%	Growth -4.2%
Worst ↓	Internat. 9.4%	Bonds 3.6%	Internat. 0.2%	Small Cap -2.5%	Bonds -0.8	Growth -22.4%	Internat. -22.6%	Growth -27.9%	Bonds 4.1%	Growth 6.3%	Small Cap -8.3%

Source: Morgan Stanley

Year to date through May 4, 2005. Performance for all cited indices is calculated on a total return basis with dividends reinvested. Indices used for categories include: MSCI EAFE for International, Russell 1000 Growth for Growth, S&P 500 for Large Cap, Russell 1000 Value for Value, Russell Midcap for Midcap, and Russell 2000 for Small Cap.

because of concentration restrictions, perhaps not always the entire ride.

There are five sector ETF offerings in Canada, all by Barclays Global Investors Canada Limited. These iUnits are in energy, information technology, gold, financials, and REITS (real estate investment trusts). More sector ETFs are expected in the future. In the U.S., there's an astonishing 57 sector ETFs, including 15 sector HOLDRS out of 17 HOLDRS in total.

These are the domestic sector ETFs and HOLDRS in the U.S.:

Consumer Discretionary
Consumer Discretionary Select Sector SPDR
iShares Dow Jones U.S. Consumer Services
Consumer Discretionary VIPERs

Consumer Staples
Consumer Staples Select Sector SPDR
iShares Dow Jones U.S. Consumer Goods
Consumer Staples VIPERs

Energy
Energy Select Sector SPDR
iShares Dow Jones U.S. Energy
Energy VIPERs

Financial
Financial Select Sector SPDR
iShares Dow Jones U.S. Financial
Financials VIPERs
iShares Dow Jones U.S. Financial Services

Health Care
Health Care Select Sector SPDR
iShares Dow Jones U.S. Healthcare
Health Care VIPERs
iShares Nasdaq Biotechnology

Industrials
Industrial Select Sector SPDR
iShares Dow Jones U.S. Industrial
Industrials VIPERs
iShares Dow Jones Transportation Average

Information Technology
Technology Select Sector SPDR
iShares Dow Jones U.S. Technology
iShares Goldman Sachs Technology
iShares Goldman Sachs Networking
iShares Goldman Sachs Semiconductor
streetTRACKS Morgan Stanley Technology
Information Technology VIPERs
iShares Goldman Sachs Software

Materials

- Materials Select Sector SPDR
- iShares Dow Jones U.S. Basic Materials
- Material VIPERs

Natural Resources

- iShares Goldman Sachs Natural Resources

Real Estate

- iShares Dow Jones U.S. Real Estate
- iShares Cohen & Steers Realty Majors
- REIT VIPERs
- StreetTRACKS Wilshire REIT

Telecommunications

- iShares Dow Jones U.S. Telecommunications
- Telecommunication Services VIPERs

Utilities

- Utilities Select Sector SPDR
- iShares Dow Jones U.S. Utilities
- Utilities VIPERs

HOLDRS

- B2B Internet
- Biotech
- Broadband
- Internet
- Internet Architecture
- Internet Infrastructure
- Oil Services
- Pharmaceutical
- Regional Bank
- Retail
- Semiconductor
- Software
- Telecommunications
- Utilities
- Wireless

HOLDRS

HOLDRS are fixed baskets of securities that trade on a stock exchange. (To learn more about them, see the end of Chapter Three.) HOLDRS have no concentration limitations. They're permitted to hold an unlimited amount of any constituent. This makes them different from ETFs. U.S.-based ETFs, including sector ETFs, must abide by some concentration rules: no more than 25% of a fund's assets can be invested in a single security and the sum of all individual securities in the fund making up more than 5% of the fund cannot collectively exceed 50% of the fund's assets. This diversification requirement is most likely to impinge on sector ETFs because of their relatively narrow focus. There is no similar concentration restriction imposed by regulators on ETFs in Canada, but Barclays Canada's iUnits sector ETFs have a 25% cap on the weighting of any one company in its Canadian sector funds—in keeping with the 25% cap the S&P folks have imposed on their own index. Such restrictions ensure a diversified portfolio but they can affect the tracking of an uncapped index, and will when highly weighted companies become market favorites as Nortel Networks did in early 2000, and took over more than a third of the TSE 300's weighting.

Some Sector Strategies

Jumping in and out of sectors is for the self-confident, active investor, or an investor with an investment advisor of similar qualities; if you get it right it can give you spectacular returns. One very capital-intensive way to play the sectors involves buying up all the Sector Spiders in weights that you judge to be most opportune. Since all nine Sector Spiders equal the entire S&P 500 Index, you would have large cap exposure with your own customized sector weightings. Not only that, but you are then free to trade the sectors individually. Ideally, you'd be selling the falling sectors and riding the winning sectors and using the tax loss on the non-performing sectors to offset the capital gains on the ascendant sectors. You can do this, too, with the iShares Dow Jones sector ETFs, which together make up all of the Dow Jones U.S. Total Market Index.

For those with smaller investment stakes, there are more modest ways of sector investing. Analysts have found some basic sector rotation patterns to be fairly consistent across market cycles based on the reaction of sectors to interest rate movements.

Morgan Stanley has honed sector interest rate sensitivity to a fine point. They studied six business cycles to the end of 2000 and found that equity returns averaged 15.7% for the first 6 months following a second U.S. Federal Reserve interest rate cut, and 18.4% for the 12 months following the second rate cut. In an Equity Research Report called "Using ETFs to Capitalize on Sectors Favored for Recovery," the Morgan Stanley equity team says, "As soon as investors became convinced that the Fed was committed to promoting recovery, as evidenced by its second interest rate cut, aggressive sectors started to outperform defensive ones. After the second rate cut, investors began to focus on sectors that were positioned to benefit from economic and earnings recovery."[3]

Sector Rotation Strategy Model (fig. 33)

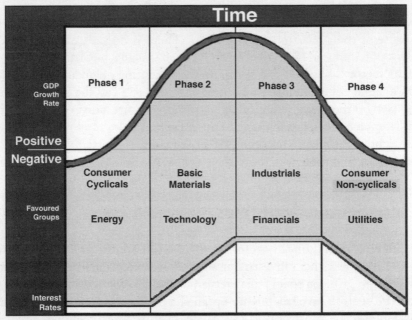

Average S&P Sector Returns During Fed Easing Cycles Since 1981 (fig. 34)

6-month period following the second Fed Easing

	Average Return (%)
Financials	19.0
Consumer Discretionary	18.5
Health Care	16.7
Information Technology	13.9
Consumer Staples	13.7
Industrials	13.0
Telecom Services	11.6
Materials	10.9
Energy	10.3
Utilities	8.5

12-month period following the second Fed easing	Average Return (%)
Information Technology	20.9
Consumer Discretionary	19.9
Health care	19.0
Financials	16.7
Industrials	16.5
Consumer Staples	15.7
Materials	13.8
Telecom Services	10.9
Energy	9.6
Utilities	6.7

Source: Morgan Stanley Equity Research, Jan. 20, 2001

Most sector rotation strategies are correlated to interest rate movements, but there are any number of other factors that might serve a similar purpose with enough cleverness and research. Some sophisticated quantitative analysts are beginning to apply their trade to ETFs. This work makes ETFs all the more interesting to brokers and investors who want to employ ETFs in active trading strategies using sector and/or regional tilts. The fact that the target investments are diversified portfolios rather than individual stocks does mitigate risk, too.

Fundamental Analysis, Macro Calls, and Sector ETFs

If you're a numbers kind of person, or you have access to current fundamental analysis data, you could determine the price to earnings ratio (P/E) and the expected earnings growth of each individual company within a sector ETF. Do some averaging and you could determine if the sector as a whole is trading below its historical norms. That's a buy signal.

You can also play sectors defensively with a macro economic outlook. Should you be concerned about an economic slowdown you can shift into defensive, stable companies like Gillette, Proctor & Gamble, or Safeway, or you can buy a consumer staples ETF—especially if the sector is cheap.

Want to protect yourself against an overvalued U.S. dollar? Think gold. There's a strong correlation between a falling dollar and rising gold prices. Gold tends to do well in periods of close to negative short-term interest rates, too. That's all well and good until you have to decide what gold stock to buy to execute your plan. There's a lot going on in a gold company—price hedging programs, international properties, and so on. Some gold companies stand to profit well from price increases in gold and others not so dramatically. Barclays' iGold ETF is a portfolio of 19 gold companies (as of May 2005).

A staunch contrarian will like the value and growth styles tilt strategy. Growth and value investing styles rotate in and out of favour. When one style has vastly outperformed the other a courageous person might tilt their portfolio towards the out-of-favour style in hopes that they would not be too terribly early in their call. U.S. mid cap style ETFs would probably give the best returns should you get this strategy right. Being really aggressive, you could short the in-vogue style and go long the out-of-favour style.

To try these sector strategies for yourself, you'll need access to data and number crunching. There are a number of companies who sell the kind of fundamental analysis required, The Bank Credit Analyst in Montreal being one of them. (*www.bankcreditanalyst.com*)

Seasonality

Seasonality is a popular topic for quantitative analysts. Hidden among the barrage of market data, they look for and sometimes find odd regularities or associations. Perhaps the most well-known of these is the correlation between the U.S. markets and the presidential cycle. Usually, the fourth year of an administration finds the market booming. Markets will continue going higher after the election of a new president and during his legislative honeymoon. Into the second year, markets start coughing with the worst of it around October of second year—midterm. After that, the cycle starts again and markets begin moving up.

One seasonal pattern with the S&P/TSX has led to the saying "Buy when it snows. Sell when it goes." According to technical analyst Don Vialoux, buying the broad Canadian market at the end of October and selling at the end of March would have returned an average of 6.7% to the end of March 2005, realizing 87% of the market's gain over those ten years. The strategy has been profitable in nine of the past ten years. The same pattern exists with broadly based U.S. indices, though the sweet spot for that market continues to the end of April. Buying the S&P 500 at the end of October and selling at the end of April would have been profitable in nine of the past ten years and averaged 100.2% of the market's overall return for those ten years. The sweet spots yielded an average of 6.3% while the entire period averaged 6.28%. Vialoux believes his work has at least one important lesson for Canadian investors: those who sock their money into RRSPs near the end of October have "consistently realized higher returns than investors who contributed near the end of February."[4] He expects the trend to continue.

Sectors show seasonality, too. Here's Vialoux's examination of Canadian and U.S. sectors.

Canadian Sector Seasonality (fig. 35)

S&P/TSX Sector	Period of Strength*	Average Return (%) Last 10 Periods	# of Profitable Trades out of 10
Energy **	Jan – May	11.7	9
Information Technology **	Oct – Jan	15.6	7
Consumer Staples	Aug – Dec	8.4	8
	Mar – Jun	8.5	10
Health Care	Nov – Feb	7.6	6
Consumer Discretion	Sep – Apr	10.7	8
Financials **	Sep – Dec	10.0	10
	Feb – May	5.1	9
Industrials	Sep – May	13.1	10
Telecom †	Sep – Jan	19.4	10
Utilities	Aug – Dec	5.5	8
S&P/TSX Composite Index **	Oct – Mar	6.7	9

*   Measured from month end to month end.
**   Canadian Sector ETFs available as at the end of May 2005
†   Heavily influenced by BCE's interest in Nortel in the 1990s

Source: Don Vialoux, www.dvtechtalk.com

U.S. Sector Seasonality (fig. 36)

S&P/TSX Sector	Period of Strength*	Average Return (%) Last 10 Periods	# of Profitable Trades out of 10
Energy	Jan – May	9.8	10
Industrials	Sep – Dec	8.3	8
Information Technology	Sep – Jan	13.1	7
Telecom	Aug – Jan	12.6	8
Consumer Discretion	Sep – Apr	14.2	9
Consumer Staples	Sep – Dec	8.9	10
Financials	Sep – Apr	14.3	9
Health Care	Aug – Nov	7.8	9
Materials	Sep – May	11.2	9
S&P 500	Oct – Apr	6.3	9

*   Measured from month end to month end.

Source: Don Vialoux, www.dvtechtalk.com

Another Market Timing Approach

Two Canadian investment advisors have formulated a very simple calendar investing strategy. Brooke Thackray and Bruce Lindsay have done extensive technical work that shows, they say, that the best time to enter the market is October 28th and the best time to exit the market is May 5th (conservatively) or July 19th (aggressively). They report that their method produced returns 50% higher than the TSE 300's return for the 15 years of the study. For the period historical data was available to them (1985-1999), they report that the TSE 300 returned 8.23% (without dividends) compared to their "Time In, Time Out" method with a 12.99% average return.[5] They've also had success beating the Nasdaq, S&P 500, and Dow Jones indices.

ETFs fit very well with a timing strategy like this as they allow you to get full market exposure while also making it very easy and inexpensive to enter and leave the market at precise times. And if Thackray and Lindsay, or Vialoux haven't convinced you to step entirely out of the market, you could consider selling covered calls on your ETFs during periods of seasonal weakness.

While recognizing that equity markets, sectors, and stocks do often have seasonal characteristics, investors should use a mix of technical, quantitative, and fundamental analysis before buying any investment. But when you're ready to pounce on a perceived upswing, ETFs are ready and waiting to spring.

Regional Tilts, or Not

ETFs are also well situated for regional rotation or tilts. When you think Japan is about to emerge from its decade and a half slumber, socking some money into iShares MSCI Japan might be for you. Foresee political unrest in Hong Kong? Short iShares MSCI Hong Kong. There are 24 country-specific ETFs, including two for China. If a single country is too narrow a bet for you, a large and growing clutch of geographically related country ETFs will serve, too. There's even an EMU iShare. Regional coverage is growing with ETFs for Europe, the Asia-Pacific area, Latin America, and emerging markets.

For the more conservative, you might just want to get more global exposure generally. Right now there are two ETFs and a HOLDRS that can give you that. SSgA's Global Titan has about 50 blue chip stocks from around the world. Barclays U.S.'s iShares S&P Global 100 holds 100 large global companies, and Merrill Lynch's Market 2000+ HOLDRs has about

58 large stocks from an assortment of countries. But these products are all currently considered foreign content for RRSP purposes. (See note with respect to proposed government changes in "How to Use This Book" on page 11.) Which brings us to an important point.

Global Sector Investing

Now that ETFs have made tactical sector and country investing devilishly easy, globalization may very well have diminished its usefulness. Take a deep breath. There's evidence that sector investing is most effectively done across global markets, at least in developed countries. Salomon Smith Barney research argues that globalization has meant many developed markets now move in close synchronization with each other, especially countries in the European Monetary Union. This change in correlations has led to a trend away from country-based investing in favour of global sector-based investing, at least in developed markets. In emerging markets, the country effect still seems strong.[6]

But take heart. There are now global sector ETFs to the rescue. A series of five ETFs based on S&P's ten global sector indices cover the energy, financial, healthcare, telecommunications, and technology sectors globally. This gives investors a totally new way to structure their asset allocation. Europeans have already caught on to this as the number of sector ETFs listed in Europe has grown dramatically. This is a trend worth heeding.

Style Weighting

The investment management world is divided into two halves—value managers and growth managers. You might say they're arch rivals, and they seldom thrive together. During the technology frenzy in the late 1990s, growth investing completely eclipsed value. There were even headlines about famous value investors like Warren Buffett and John Templeton being icons of times long gone. Technology was to so profoundly change our productivity that price to earnings ratios no longer had any significance and these old guys just couldn't accept the world had changed around them. Companies without earnings were exploding with promise, and their stock price rode along with the optimism. Then, POW! These companies exploded right in their investors' faces, and the bargain-hunting value style of investment management reasserted its dominion in the new century.

In a pure textbook sense, growth and value are opposing money management styles. In the realities of the marketplace, only a minority of money managers are extremists. Most subscribe to an approach that includes both camps to some extent, but let's lay out the camps. Staunch growth managers look for companies with faster than average gains in earnings over a specified period, usually a few years. They don't take much notice of price to earnings, or price to book ratios. During the tech bubble, some growth managers didn't even hold out for actual earnings growth. A company with the likely prospect of above average earnings growth was enough to ignite their buy buttons. Sometimes growth managers are really momentum investors in disguise, jumping on stocks whose price shows a lot of upward movement.

This would make pure value investors cringe in horror. These are the old-fashioned, bargain-minded folks who look for companies with good fundamentals but in an industry that's fallen out of favour. Value managers have to hold their noses to buy a stock with a price to earnings ratio over 20. Contrast that with all the growth managers who bought Nortel Networks when its P/E was over 100.

In some years, typically when the economy is contracting, value managers look very smart. In other years, growth managers get the glory. For the entire period between 1994 and 1999 large cap growth stocks delivered much higher returns than large cap value stocks, but from 1994 to 1997 value stocks led the pack for both mid and small caps.7 From 2001 on, value once again seems in ascendance. The prudent mutual fund investor should have a mix of both investment styles. With ETFs you can go one better and actually trade on anticipation of broad investment style changes, or tactically weight your portfolio with a growth or value bias. You might, for instance, want to go heavy on growth at the beginning of an economic expansion, and then tilt your portfolio in favour of value as the expansion slows.

Style-Based Exchange Traded Funds (fig. 37)

Broad Market Growth

iShares Russell 3000 Growth
TD Select Canadian Growth

Broad Market Value

iShares Russell 3000 Value
TD Select Canadian Value

Large Cap Growth

iShares S&P 500/Barra Growth
iShares Russell 1000 Growth
iShares Morningstar Large-Cap Growth
StreetTRACKS Dow Jones US LargeCap Growth
Growth VIPERs

Large Cap Value
iShares S&P 500/Barra Value
iShares Russell 1000 Value
iShares Morningstar Large-Cap Value
StreetTRACKS Dow Jones US LargeCap Value
Value VIPERs

Mid Cap Growth
iShares S&P MidCap/Barra Growth
iShares Russell Midcap Growth
iShares Morningstar Mid Growth

Mid Cap Value
iShares S&P MidCap 400/Barra Value
iShares Russell Midcap Value
iShares Morningstar Mid Value

Small Cap Growth
iShares S&P SmallCap 600/Barra Growth
iShares Russell 2000 Growth
iShares Morningstar Small Growth
StreetTRACKS Dow Jones U.S. SmallCap Growth
Small-Cap Growth VIPERs

Small Cap Value
iShares S&P SmallCap 600/Barra Value
iShares Russell 2000 Value
iShares Morningstar Small Value
StreetTRACKS Dow Jones U.S. SmallCap Value
Small-Cap Value VIPERs

Each index company has a different way of defining "value" and "growth." The S&P/Barra indices, for instance, define value as a certain price to book value range. Any stock that does not fit that definition of value automatically becomes a growth stock. No stocks are excluded and no stocks overlap their growth and value indices. MSCI style indices, on the other hand, have criteria for both value and growth; if a stock has both characteristics it is split between the two indices in proportion to its respective style affinities. Surprisingly, the different style indices have markedly different performances. MSCI US Prime Market Growth Index returned -10.7% for the five years ending Dec. 31, 2004, whereas S&P Barra Growth did -7.1%. For the same period, the S&P Barra Value Index did 2.5% when the MSCI US Market Prime Index returned 5.6%.[8] (See "Making Sense of the Indices" Appendix for more details about these indices and a chart contrasting the style methodologies of different ETF sponsors.) Before you buy a style index, make sure you know just what kind of value or growth you're getting into.

The Capitalization Curve

Market capitalization is a measure of a company's size, and size does matter. Large cap companies tend to move in tandem. Similar patterns are also seen with small and mid cap groupings. Smaller cap stocks have fewer research analysts following them and are subject to greater price swings. This makes them particularly ripe for a smart stock picker to exploit, though even at that, the majority fail to match their benchmark indices.

No matter what part of the capitalization curve you want to pursue, indexing is still the best way to do it. According to Standard & Poor's Indices Versus Active Funds Scorecard (SPIVA) for Canadian mutual funds, only 41.9% of active Canadian equity fund managers outperformed the S&P/TSX Composite Index in the five years ending Dec. 31, 2004. Fifty percent of small cap managers beat the S&P/TSX SmallCap Index and just 25% of Canadian U.S. Equity fund managers surpassed the S&P 500 (in Canadian dollars).

Fund managers in the United States had an even harder time looking themselves in the mirror in the morning. For the same 5-year period, the S&P 1500 Composite Index outperformed 56.4% of all U.S. equity funds; the S&P 500 beat 58.7% of U.S. large cap funds; the S&P MidCap 400 clobbered 84.2% of mid cap fund managers and the S&P 600 SmallCap Index trounced 72.4% of small cap fund managers.[9]

Analysts at Morgan Stanley believe mid and small cap stocks tend to do well during an economic recovery, especially when stock valuations are relatively low compared with large caps. Their research also leads them to conclude that mid caps "...offer the best risk/reward ratios over long periods of time...while their performance is highly correlated with small caps."[10]

A savvy investor could shift from mid caps to large caps and back again as the relative valuations and general economic conditions change. Add a style dimension to that and you could hedge your bets a little with ETFs in mid cap growth and large cap value.

You can ignore the capitalization factor completely by investing in very broad-based ETFs like the Wilshire 5000, but you could get more octane out of your investments by making the right call on the capitalization curve.

Using Options with ETFs

Options may conjure complicated, obscure trading strategies that only Nobel Prize winners can really understand and only their mothers can love. But in truth, there are some simple and conservative option strategies that can and should be used by more investors to minimize risk and increase returns. One of the great advantages of ETFs is that they can use all the same option strategies commonly used for single stock holdings as long as there are option contracts available on the ETF. So far, there are options on all the HOLDRS, all the Select Sector Spiders, and many of the larger, more popular ETFs.

Here's a list of the ETFs with options and where the options trade. Currently, all five Canadian-based ETF options trade on the Montreal Exchange.

ETFs and HOLDRS with Options (fig. 38)

Ticker Symbol	ETF	Options Exchange
Size and Style-based		
XIU	iUnits S&P/TSX 60	ME*
QQQQ	Nasdaq-100	A, C, P, PS*
DIA	Diamonds	C
MDY	S&P MidCap 400 SPDR	A
IJK	S&P MidCap 400/BARRA Growth	A
IJJ	S&P MidCap 400/BARRA Value	A
IJR	iShares S&P SmallCap 600	A
IWB	iShares Russell 1000	A, C
IWF	iShares Russell 1000 Growth	A, C
IWD	iShares Russell 1000 Value	A, C
IWM	iShares Russell 2000	A, C
IWO	iShares Russell 2000 Growth	A, C
IWN	iShares Russell 2000 Value	A, C
IWV	iShares Russell 3000	A, C
VTI	Total Stock Market Vipers	A
OEF	iShares S&P 100	A, C
FFF	Fortune 500 StreetTRACKS	A
Global		
DGT	StreetTRACKs DJ Global TITANS	A, C
EFA	iShares MSCI EAFE	C
Sectors		
XEG	S&P/TSX Capped Energy Index	ME
XFN	S&P/TSX Capped Financials Index	ME
XGD	S&P/TSX Capped Gold Index	ME
XIT	S&P/TSX Capped Information Technology Index	ME
XLB	Basic Industries SPDR	A, C
XLV	Consumer Services SPDR	A, C
XLP	Consumer Staples SPDR	A, C

XLY	Cyclical/Transportation SPDR	C
XLE	Energy SPDR	A, C
XLF	Financial SPDR	A, C
XLI	Industrial SPDR	A, C
XLK	Technology SPDR	A, C
XLU	Utilities SPDR	A, C
IYE	iShares DJ U.S. Energy	C
IYF	iShares DJ U.S. Financial Sector	A, C
IYH	iShares DJ U.S. Healthcare	C
IYW	iShares DJ U.S. Technology	A, C
IYZ	iShares DJ U.S.Telecom	A, C
IGN	iShares GS** Networking	C
IGW	iShares GS Semiconductor	C
IGV	iShares GS Software	C
IGM	iShares GS Technology	C
IBB	iShares Nasdaq Biotechnology Index	A, C

** Goldman Sachs

HOLDRS

BHH	B2B Internet	A
BBH	Biotech	A, C, PS
BDH	Broadband	A, C
EKH	Europe 2001	A
HHH	Internet	A, C, PS
IAH	Internet Architecture	A, C
IIH	Internet Infrastructure	A
MKH	Market 2000+	A
OIH	Oil Service	A, C, PS
PPH	Pharmaceutical	A, C
RKH	Regional Bank	A, C
RTH	Retail	A, C
SMH	Semiconductor	A, C
SWH	Software	A, C
TBH	Telebras	C
TTH	Telecom	A, C
UTH	Utilities	A, C
WMH	Wireless	A, C

*A= AMEX, C =CBOE (Chicago Board Options Exchange)
PS= Pacific Stock Exchange, P= Philadelphia Stock Exchange
ME= Montreal Exchange

Covered Call Writing

One of the most common and conservative option strategies is covered call writing. Writing a call on a stock or ETF is simply selling a contract that gives the contract buyer the right, but not the obligation, to buy the asset at a specific price some time before the expiration of the contract. You have the obligation to sell that asset at the agreed price if the contract is exercised. A call is "covered" when you own the asset you are writing the option on. If you didn't own it already, that would be in the street's vivid language, a naked call.

Suppose you own 200 160 units at a current market price of $54 and you believe the market is going to stay fairly flat for the next three months. You could write two call options on your 200 units to sell them at $54.00 any time during the next three months. You'll receive a premium for the sale of the option, say $1.50 per share to equal $300 (200 x $1.50). As long as the market does not go above $54.00, what's known as the strike price, you'll keep your units. If you end up having to sell your units, you've lost out on any appreciation of the units above $54.00, but you've pocketed the $300 premium. Options come in a wide variety of expiration dates. Conventional options can go as far out as nine months. Beyond that, there are LEAPS (Long-term Equity AnticiPation Securities) that go out as far as three years and are available on many U.S. ETFs.

Put Options

If you want to protect the value of your ETF position you can buy a put option at a strike price of, say, $49. Buying a put gives you the right, but again, not the obligation, to sell the ETF at a certain price before the expiration of the contract. You have to pay the premium but in return you get a guaranteed price for your current holding. The option premium in this case is just like paying an insurance premium, because you are essentially insuring your ETF's value for the period of the contract. If the market value goes below $49 dollars near the expiration of the contract, you could exercise the put and sell your ETF position for $49 per unit or sell the put and lower the effective cost of your ETF position.

Call Options

A call option gives you the right to buy a security at a specified price before the expiry of the contract. In exchange for paying a premium, you get the opportunity to capture future gains on an index without having to buy the index. You risk the option premium and that's all; whereas if you bought the ETF and it dropped in price you could be exposed to a much greater loss and you'd have a whole lot more money tied up.

As you can imagine, ETFs are suitable for all kinds of option strategies—limited only by the availability of options. If you're just starting with options, it's a good idea to enlist the help of an options licensed full-service broker who can help you direct your strategy, remind you of expirations, and generally lead you through the process. In the next chapter, we'll show you how one investment advisor uses covered calls to enhance his clients' returns.

Short Selling

ETFs can be sold short like any other stock. Short selling involves selling something you don't own in the anticipation that its price will go down. In order to do this your brokerage must borrow the stock which you must eventually return by buying on the open market. The short seller pays interest to the stock lender until the lender requires the shares returned or until the short seller voluntarily closes the position. To close the position, the short seller has to purchase the stock at the then-current market price and return it to the lender. If the price has gone down, the short seller has made a profit by selling high and buying low. If, on the other hand, the stock has gone up in price, he's lost money by selling high and buying back even higher. Perhaps it sounds like Russian Roulette, but short selling ETFs might be thought to be less risky than short selling individual stocks.

First of all, there's typically a huge bank of ETF shares available so you're unlikely to get something known as a short squeeze in which so many shares are loaned out that there are too few in circulation to comfortably buy back and close all the short positions. This causes the price of the shorted shares to go up, which ruins the strategy.

Secondly, it is arguably easier to forecast general index trends than it is to predict the future value of an individual stock. Suppose you think the U.S. market is going to decline because of threats of terrorism. You can short sell a Spider or a Diamond. If you've made the right prediction, you get to buy back the ETF you previously borrowed (and sold) for a lower price than you sold it for.

Most importantly, because of their diversified nature, ETFs are exempt from the uptick rule in the U.S. market. That rule says a short sale can occur only if the last sale was at a higher price than the sale before it (an uptick) or, if the last sale was flat, the previous sale to that must have been higher. ETFs can be shorted on the same price or on a downtick which is a tremendous advantage in a falling market.

In Canada, no stock can be sold short into a declining market but there is no uptick rule. A short sale must be done at a price no less than the price of the last board lot trade in that stock. Rules changed in Canada in late 2004, which made Canadian-based ETFs exempt from this restriction. This placed Canadian and U.S. ETFs on an equal footing so that both are able to be shorted in virtually any market environment. (Some HOLDRS excepted.)

You would want to short sell an ETF when you are confident the index is going to go down—or to hedge a long position in the same index, but buying a put option is a far less dangerous strategy to accomplish the same end.

A Word of Caution

Many of these ETF strategies involve some sort of market timing. Tilts, rotations, style weightings; all these require a bet on the shape of things to come in the market. That's why John Bogle, the founder of Vanguard Group and arch-advocate for index mutual funds, says that ETFs are like giving investors a loaded shotgun. ETFs are easy to trade. Therein lies their beauty, and their power to harm. Frequent trading most often results in poorer returns because the investment decisions are made in the heat of emotion and often disconnected from a long-term strategy. Market timing is a tool to be used in moderation, and is not recommended for novice investors who are best advised to hold a core broad index and perhaps, a small assortment of style/cap indices.

Technical Analysis and ETFs

Sophisticated investors with a penchant for technical analysis will welcome the ease ETFs bring to their strategic implementations.

The Sport of Kings (Who Cheat)

Technical analysis has been called the sport of kings (who cheat legally). By charting price movements and trading volume, technical analysts try to identify market trends as they emerge. Chip Anderson, the founder of stockcharts.com, likens it to betting on a horse race after the race has started. You'll have an advantage by being able to put your money on an early leader, but you won't win every time because leaders don't always finish first. Charts don't predict the future but, says Anderson, they will help you improve your odds of picking the winning horse.[11]

Interpreting charts to drive investment decisions may sound a little akin to palmistry unless you believe two things. First you must believe that price and volume action reflect all factors that can affect the future price of a stock. Then, you must also believe that the market is not random; trends are significant. With that foundation, seeing heads and shoulders in graphs and playing tick-tack-toe in point and figure charts will be the stuff dreams are made of.

Those dreams very likely include ETFs because they are singularly useful for those chartists who track broad market movements. For the price of a single trade, you can capture the movement of an entire market in the time it takes to place an order. The really confident can also short a market using ETFs.

Two excellent technical web sites have sections dedicated to ETFs. One site, *http://decisionpoint.com* tracks U.S. ETFs daily in a report they cleverly call the "Spider Web Daily." That subscriber-only service issues technical buy and sells on all U.S. ETFs. Another subscriber-only service at *http://dorseywright.com* provides an ETF iShares sector manager that builds portfolios using relative strengths. Their Conservative Sector ETF Portfolio and the Aggressive Sector ETF Portfolio are updated weekly and display the number of ETF shares to buy for any given portfolio size.

Fixed Income Meets ETFs

ETFs are too good an idea to restrict to equities. The broad diversification and transparency ETFs bring to other asset classes is an even bigger advantage in the fixed income area. Given the large minimum investment of a bond purchase ($10,000 or more), it is hard for investors to get a well diversified fixed income portfolio with good exposure to many maturity periods. That's why so many resort to bond mutual funds, but the drawback with those, of course, are their relatively high MERs, not to mention the tax inefficiency of active management.

Fixed income ETFs give you up-to-the-minute pricings, instant transactions, and modest management fees. They also allow you the freedom to tactically manage your fixed income investments in a way that wasn't feasible before. You can select a narrow maturity range or buy a broad bond market ETF for exposure to the full yield curve, and you can easily pop in and out as your interest rate forecasts change. Being able to buy 100 high quality corporate bonds of assorted maturities is also a huge convenience and cost saving. Professional bond managers have long used corporate bonds to boost returns in many conservative government bond portfolios and now you can do the same, only better, by mitigating your risk with buying a whole portfolio of corporate bonds in one fell swoop.

Fixed income ETFs are simple in conception. Almost all bond ETFs hold a portfolio of bonds. Canadians, though, have to be aware that one Canadian fixed income ETF stands out as unique. The iG5 holds only one 5-year Government of Canada bond at any one time. It is not linked to any index nor does it hold a portfolio of different bonds.

U.S. Based Fixed Income ETFs

There are currently six fixed income ETFs in the United States:

Fund	Ticker
iShares Lehman 1-3 Year Treasury	SHY
iShares Lehman 7-10 Year Treasury	IEF
iShares Lehman 20+ Year Treasury	TLT
iShares GS $ InvesTop™ Corporate	LQD
iShares Lehman Aggregate	AGG
iShares Lehman TIPS	TIP

As of May 2005

All of these ETFs are pegged to bond indices. The Lehman Treasury Bond indices are distinguished by the maturity duration of the underlying bonds: one short-term, one mid-term, and one long-term index. The GS $ InvesTop Corporate Bond Index contains 100 investment grade corporate bonds of assorted maturities. For the whole U.S. investment grade bond market, government and corporate, the Lehman Aggregate Bond Index is your product. Those worried about inflation will be interested in the Lehman U.S. Treasury Inflation Notes Index which encompasses U.S. Treasury inflation protected securities. (More information on these fixed income ETFs and their underlying indices can be found in Appendix B.) MERs on these funds are a slender 0.15% or 0.20%

With the exception of the $ InvesTop Corporate Bond Fund, none of these ETFs actually holds all the bonds in their respective indices. Barclays U.S., who manages the iShares, uses an approach called "stratified sampling" to select the bonds they believe are most representative of the overall index. The target index is broken down into groups of similar bonds, and only a few bonds in each group are purchased for the fund. This sampling keeps costs down while still enabling the fund to track the index closely.

Interest Payments

U.S. fixed income ETFs pay interest income monthly. Canadian investors are subject to withholding tax on these distributions. Capital gains are paid annually in the form of new shares that are subsequently consolidated. (See Chapter Seven for more information.)

Canadian Fixed Income ETFs

Canada currently has two fixed income ETFs:

Fund	Ticker
iUnits Government of Canada 5-year Bond Fund	XGV
iUnits Canadian Bond Broad Market Index Fund	XBB

As I noted before, the Government of Canada 5-year Bond Fund holds one Government of Canada bond at a time. About once a year the bond is sold to buy another government bond closer to the fund's target duration. This fund runs on a 0.25% MER. The Broad Market Fund holds about 120 bonds, another example of a representative sampling approach. This fund charges an MER of 0.30%.

Interest income for the government bond fund is paid semi-annually in cash while the broad bond fund pays its interest out quarterly. Capital gains in both funds are paid annually in new shares that are subsequently consolidated.

Managing Your Fixed Income Component

Bonds are an important component of any well diversified portfolio. That is not just a motherhood statement. Not always but commonly, bonds have a low correlation to the equity market which means that bonds generally do well when stocks suffer.[12]

Interest Rate Anticipation

Bond prices have an exact correlation with interest rate movements. As interest rates rise, bond prices go down. When interest rates drop, bond prices go up. It is an inverse relationship. Generally long-term bonds are affected more dramatically by interest rate swings than short-term bonds, simply because of their longer duration. Bond managers tend to stay with shorter maturities when they anticipate interest rate hikes, and favour longer maturities during periods of falling interest rates. ETFs allow you to do the very same thing. You can take defensive positions or opportunistic ones with the swiftness and ease of a single transaction and the cost of one brokerage fee, all the while knowing you are protected from individual credit risk by owning a diversified bond portfolio.

Credit Quality Plays

Professional bond managers often look to the corporate bond sector for undervalued bonds. The most attractive of these are bonds from solid companies in beat-up industries. Because the whole industry is unattractive, the bonds of any company within that industry will have to pay a premium interest rate to attract purchasers. Bond managers figure the likelihood of a solid company defaulting on its bonds is low and are happy to scoop up the interest premium.

This is an extremely difficult strategy for an individual investor to emulate. The analysis of credit risk is something best left to professionals, yet there are times of market turmoil and pessimistic earnings outlook when corporate bonds generally pay a much higher interest premium than the risk they represent.

Buying a basket of good quality corporates, like those in the iShares corporate bond fund, will mitigate the individual credit risk and will give you a chance to pump up your returns. Being able to jump in and out of the corporate market with your assessment of risk makes this an especially attractive opportunity especially when you need only one trade to accomplish this.

Principal Risk

There is one drawback to fixed income ETFs, but it is a fault they share with bond mutual funds. Unlike teenagers, bond portfolios never mature. The value of the fund is solely determined by market prices for the underlying securities. If, on the other hand, you held an individual bond to maturity, fluctuations in its value would be irrelevant to your return. Barring defaults, you will get the interest rate at which you bought the bond regardless of where interest rates go at any time, and your principal is fixed. In a portfolio with no maturity, this certainty does not exist and it is possible to lose principal with a bond fund or ETF. Extremely risk averse investors are probably better off sticking with individual bonds if they can tolerate no capital loss.

The Easiest Portfolio of All

After you've waded through complicated portfolio strategies you might be ready to settle into the couch, put your feet up and be paralyzed by indecision. That's when you call an investment advisor or manfully resolve to do the easiest thing possible without abdicating your responsibility altogether—employ the Couch Potato Strategy. This is a strategy formulated by Scott Burns, a U.S. personal finance journalist in 1991. It has the virtue of being dog simple, drop-dead easy and really cheap.

Simply put half your money in an S&P 500 index and the other in a U.S. government bond fund and put on your slippers. Rebalance to 50-50 once a year and guess what? The strategy would have returned an average of 10.3% from 1973 to 1990, outscoring 70% of managers in those 17 years.

MoneySense magazine has created a Canadianized version of this indolent strategy which they call The Classic Couch Potato Portfolio. They've divided the portfolio into thirds, one third in a Canadian bond index fund, a third in an S&P/TSX 60 index, and the last third in S&P 500 index fund. (For RRSP accounts concerned about foreign content, the S&P 500 fund could be a fully RRSP-eligible version.) Backtesting the portfolio to 1976, MoneySense has determined that the Classic Couch Potato Portfolio has on average a total annualized return of 11.8%, an advantage of more than a percentage point over Canadian stocks during that 25-year period. You can check on the Classic Couch Potato Portfolio's annual returns at *www.moneysense.ca*.

Of course, the costs of the portfolio would become positively miserly if instead of index mutual funds as the MoneySense folks did, you employed ETFs to do the heavy idling. There's an ETF for all three asset classes so you can afford a glass of wine while you're lounging on the couch. Realizing this, MoneySense launched the Global Couch Potato Portfolio made up of four Canadian ETFs. Check it out while you're at MoneySense's site; meanwhile, take a look at my ETF version of a couch potato portfolio.

Canadian Couch Potato ETF Portfolio (fig. 39)

Weighting	ETF	MER
30%	iBond (XBB)	0.30%
25%	TD300 or TD300C (TTF/TCF)	0.25%
30%	iRussell 3000 (IWV)	0.20%
15%	iIntR (XIN)	0.35%
100%	Portfolio Totals	0.28%

At a 0.28% MER for an ETF Couch Potato Portfolio, this strategy is as cheap as it is easy.

Resources

Some very helpful resources are waiting to be discovered on Barclays Global Investors U.S. web site, *www.ishares.com*. There's a customized portfolio tracker and a customized watch list service. You can find an ETF allocator and an index tracker to see how various industry groups are performing. Refer to a handy consolidated price and symbols sheet for iShares, determine the historical premium and discount for any iShare, and look at a tracking error chart for any index associated with an iShare.

Advisors have access to even more sophisticated on-line tools. There's an allocation calculator and an asset class illustrator for determining the historical risk/return of a hypothetical portfolio. Core/Satellite advocates will love the hypothetical portfolio tool to help you design satellite approaches.

What the Expert Says

An interview with Paul Mazzilli, Executive Director at Morgan Stanley in New York, and Director of Exchange Traded Fund Research.

You've written a lot about using investment strategies using ETFs, especially the Core/Satellite approach.

Paul Mazzilli: Yes, Core/Satellite sounds so simple, but it took a long time to get there. Now it's even in the CFA manual for chartered financial analysts' training and is broadly accepted. Currently as much as 30% of major pension plan assets are indexed. That's the core. It's hard to beat the markets in general, so why not have your portfolio in something that looks just like the market at a very low cost, well diversified way? That's the whole core strategy.

What should be the core?

We've written multiple research reports on the different cores. For a simple core position, S&P 500, Dow Jones, Russell 3000, Wilshire 5000, they all pretty much represent the broad market and move together.

We're now recommending people consider for core an allocation model with both growth and value ETFs in various market cap segments, and managing those to add tilt. For a broad-based international core, we like an EAFE ETF.

And outside the core?

On top of the core you can have sector allocations, real estate, gold, international countries and regions including emerging markets and Treasury Inflation-Protected Securities (TIPS). Traditionally, many smart pension plans would do it through outside managers. Now you can do it all with ETFs.

Finally, on top of the pyramid there's individual stock selection. We're not saying you should index everything. As a matter of fact, some of these very large pension plans with over $100 billion in assets have their own research analysts who probably focus on less than 150 stocks. And these are the most sophisticated plans in the world. They're saying, "We're going to minimize risk by having a core; we're going to add value by asset allocation decisions to different sectors or styles, international markets, and then we're going to really focus on stock picking where we can add value, but we've reduced our risk because it's a small part of our portfolio." In that section, if you can beat the market, your overall portfolio is going to beat the market, too. Individual investors can emulate this.

Is there anything ETFs are especially good for?

Diversified asset allocation. Six fixed income ETFs are now available in the U.S., which allows a total ETF solution to asset allocation—U.S. equities, international equities, and U.S. fixed income.

People tend to forget about overall asset allocation, growth vs. value, different sectors, bonds, foreign markets, which all the academic studies show make for the efficient frontier. If you want to get into sectors you have no exposure to, you can do it through ETFs.

If you wake up and have the idea you want to "go long" financial stocks because you think the Fed cutting rates is good for financials, how do you do it? You can get an idea, but it takes days to figure out which stocks in that sector to buy. You may buy two stocks and it turns out that one of them has an earnings disappointment. You may have made a great call on the sector, but been exposed too much to one stock. With an ETF, you decide you want to go long financials, the minute the market opens you can be long that sector, and more importantly you are long that sector in a very diversified way, so if one stock blows up but the sector does well you are protected.

Fees are much lower on ETFs, too. The average U.S. ETF [MER] is about 31 basis points. The average conventional mutual fund is about 152 basis points and the average [MER] for a U.S. index fund tracking the S&P 500 is 75 basis points. The iShares S&P 500 is 9 basis points. They're much more tax efficient, too. Index funds in their own right are very tax efficient, but what people don't realize is that other shareholder activity creates capital gains. We did a study that showed that for the last twelve years since SPDR existed it paid two very small capital gains distributions. The average open-end index fund has paid 1.75% per year in capital gains because of redemptions in an environment where the S&P itself has returned less than 10% per year.

2000 was an extremely difficult market in the United States and yet there was a record $345 billion paid out in capital gains distributions, and that came from portfolio turnover driven in part by redemptions. Some people had the misfortune of buying an internet fund in March and finding it worth 75% less at year end, but still got whacked with a capital gains distribution because throughout the year the fund was shrinking and selling assets it bought at lower prices in previous years and realizing gains. A big part of gains went to fewer investors at the end. In some extreme cases you could have got 90 cents of gains on your one dollar investment at year end. Since then, the distributions have not been that dramatic but can still have a significant impact on investors. The only way [U.S.] ETFs create capital gains is through index reconstitution, which would not happen to nearly this extent.

Any advice to investors now?

Some people have moved to the point of designing complete portfolios with ETFs. While this may be simple and efficient, it may oversimplify the investment process. In certain areas such as small cap growth, many active managers can still outperform while in areas like large cap value it is extremely difficult to outperform over the long run. I think ETFs are great but they are not the solution to everything. Investors should make sure to focus on those ETFs whose underlying index best meets their investment objectives and also consider fees, size and liquidity. You don't want to buy a $25 million ETF that trades once an hour.

May 13, 2005

At the 2005 Global ETF Awards, Morgan Stanley won for the most widely utilized ETF research by a bank or brokerage firm.

Notes

1) Gary P. Brinson, L. Randolph Hood and Gilbert L. Beebower, "Determinants of Portfolio Performance," Financial Analysts Journal, July/August 1986. pp. 39-44.

See *http://publish.uwo.ca/~jnuttall/asset.html* for an outstanding discussion of how the Brinson study has been widely misconstrued.

2) Roger G. Ibbotson and Paul Kaplan, "Does Asset Allocation Policy Explain 40, 90 or 100 Percent of Performance?" printed in the Jan/Feb 2000 issue of the Financial Analysts Journal. On-line at *www.ibbotson.com/download/research/Does_Asset_Allocation_Explain_Performance.pdf.* Thanks to Dan Hallett for this reference.

3) Paul J. Mazzilli, Dodd F. Kittsley, James P. McGowan, "Using ETFs to Capitalize on Sectors Favored for Recovery," Morgan Stanley Equity Research North America, January 29, 2001, p. 4.

4) This quote from "Buy When It Snows, Sell When It Goes," by Don Vialoux, April, 2005. This is updated monthly on Mr. Vialoux's web site where more of his work on seasonality and technical analysis can be found, *www.dvtechtalk.com*.

5) Brooke Thackray and Bruce Lindsay, *Time In, Time Out: Outsmarting the Market Using Calendar Investment Strategies*, (Oakville: Upwave Media Inc., 2000), pp. 100-101.

6) Salomon Smith Barney Equity Research Report, "The Global ETF Investor," May 2001.

7) Paul J. Mazzilli, Dodd F. Kittsley, James P. McGowan," Style Investing with ETFs: Growth and Value Plays," Morgan Stanley Equity Research North America, February 14, 2001, p.7.

8) Paul Mazzilli, Dodd F. Kittsley, Dominic Maister, "Choosing Among Growth, Value and Market Cap ETFs," Morgan Stanley Equity Research North America, February 28, 2005. et al, "ETF Quarterly: Index-linked Exchange Traded Funds," Morgan Stanley Equity Research, June 29, 2002.

9) Standard & Poor's press release, Toronto, February 2, 2005, " S&P Report Shows Canadian Active Funds Underperform Indices in 2004." Standard & Poor's press release, New York, January 18, 2005, "Indices Outperform Actively Managed Funds in 2004." Both releases can be found on *www.spiva.standardandpoors.com*. SPIVA reports are published in the U.S. and Canada quarterly and they are adjusted for survivorship bias.

10) As quoted by Paul Mazzilli and Lorraine Wang, "Exchange Traded Funds: Invest Down the Capitalization Curve with ETFs," Morgan Stanley Equity Research, May 28, 2002, p. 1.

11) Chip Anderson, "Predicting Future Human Behaviour is Hard—

Duh!" *stockcharts.com*'s Market Summary, September 21, 2002.

12) Adam Gebler and Kristin Bradbury, "Fixed Income iShares: Simple, Cost-Effective and Targeted Access to Bonds," Barclays Global Investors publication for advisors, Summer 2002, p. 3. From August 1998 to April 2002 Treasuries had a -29.88% correlation with the S&P 500. From June 1992 to April 2002, that correlation was 4.92%.

Chapter Five

Using ETFs with an Advisor

In the crowded financial services industry, you are a valuable asset. Brokerages, financial planning firms, mutual fund companies, banks, and insurance companies are struggling among the throngs to distinguish themselves in your eyes. They are all keenly aware that satisfying your needs efficiently is the key to their prosperity and ultimate survival. Part of the urgency motivating so much change in financial services is the growing commodification of basic financial services. Just as you're likely to buy gasoline based solely on price, so increasingly sophisticated investors are likely to shop for financial services with a sharp eye to fees. The internet has empowered investors not just through the wealth of low-cost choices available for stock trading, but mostly through the explosion in the breadth and depth of investment information available at the click of a mouse. Brokerage firms used to have something of a monopoly on respected analysts and technical specialists. Today, these same analysts are fighting for credibility, undermined in fact or in perception by their firms' corporate underwriting activity.

If you're like most, you'd like the help of a trusted and competent financial advisor to help you coordinate all your financial needs: investing, insurance, tax planning, and estate planning. Trouble is, most of us feel we've got too little money to be of interest to any advisor with those kinds of skills, or we're afraid of paying too much for more promise than delivery in an industry notorious for its inherent conflicts of interest. We end up continuing to buy the mutual funds *du jour* through our familiar mutual fund salesperson or stockbroker and promise ourselves to get thoroughly organized at some point. In many cases, that probably means deciding to completely revamp your portfolio yourself and sign up with an on-line discount broker. (You may even have bought this book in anticipation of doing just that.)

There's nothing wrong with such a do-it-yourself ambition except that every year it's put off may be taking you another year further from your goals. It's also unnecessarily complicating your life, because the industry has grown sensitive to the worry about corrosive costs and the conflicts of interest between advice and commissions. The industry's response has been the development of a burgeoning variety of programs to provide all inclusive service in fee-based programs. Advisors paid by fee and freed from commission can steward your assets within any number of different fee-based arrangements.

Fees, however, have a nasty way of pushing up your costs. Adding a fee to a portfolio of conventional mutual funds with MERS of 2.30% for instance, may mean an overall cost to you of 3.30% annually. As a result, fee-based programs have turned to ETFs and other low cost investments to keep overall costs down.

If your financial advisor can't recommend ETFs or fee-based programs using ETFs because of licensing restrictions, there are other ways for your advisor to take advantage of ETFs. Innovative programs that put ETFs inside mutual funds are giving many advisors access to ETFs that they've never had before, but more on that after we've explored the more direct way of using ETFs with an advisor.

Fee-Based Programs Can Save You Money Over a Portfolio of Mutual Funds

Fee-based programs have become the fastest growing programs in the financial services industry, and for good reason. For one flat fee, based on a percentage of your assets, you get asset allocation planning, investment advice, ongoing contact with an advisor whose interests are perfectly aligned with your own, and a consolidated statement, usually with on-line access.

Any firm competing for your investment dollars will have some type of fee-based program. The larger firms will likely offer an assortment of programs, as do all the major brokerage firms. Minimum account size and fees vary with each program, but the higher the program's minimum asset requirement, the lower the fees.

Happily, ETFs and fee-based programs go together like soup and a sandwich. A fee-based advisor wants to justify his fee by saving you money over a mutual fund portfolio with an average MER of 2.5%, so he's motivated to get you the best products with the lowest costs. No conflict there, and investors are voting with their feet. For the year ended December 31, 2004, assets in all fee-based accounts were up 14.6% from 2003, with a very respectable $719 billion.[1]

Fee-based arrangements represent a different business model—a new way of structuring your relationship with a financial specialist. It's a relationship in which the costs are spelled out explicitly, unbundled from the investment products and left open to scrutiny—and, for larger accounts, negotiation. That's a big departure from the conventional arrangement with mutual funds.

"People don't have any idea how much they're paying in fees [with mutual funds]," observes John Hood, a fee-based investment counsellor running his own firm in Toronto. "I was looking at a portfolio referred to me that was full of mutual funds. The client was paying $50,000 a year in management fees, which was ridiculous."

That's not so extraordinary either. A $2 million portfolio with an average MER of 2.3% will cost $46,000 a year in management fees, $10,000 to $20,000 of which goes to the advisor as a trailer fee. A million dollar portfolio, something most of us aspire to upon retirement, costs $23,000[2] a year if fully invested in mutual funds with average MERs. As Hood points out, the damage to your retirement capital isn't just the expense of fees—it's also the foregone returns had those fees been invested.

Hood charges a flat 1% of assets for his services on $200,000 minimum accounts: all-in costs, including MERs and transactions costs, total 1.2%. On a million dollar account that's $12,000 in fees—a far cry from $23,000. On accounts over one million, Hood reduces fees or absorbs transaction costs in restructuring clients' portfolios. Often you'll find fee-based advisors reduce their fee with increasing account size.

Going from $23,000 in MER charges to $12,000 in fees is great but it is not a clear-cut savings of $11,000. Sometimes the investments themselves have costs, even within a fee-based program. Bonds have commissions built into their prices. ETFs and low cost, no-load mutual funds have MERs, too. And as is the case with all mutual funds, the MER does not include the trading commissions on trades done within the fund. However, investment management fees in a fee-based program usually do include stock trading commission costs. Always ask your advisor the total costs of your investments, including MERs and what expenses there are within the investments over and above the MER. In a fee-based environment, you want to be sure you're in an arrangement that is genuinely better (and cheaper).

ETFs Are a Perfect Fit for Fee-Based Programs

Because of this drive to keep fees competitive and total costs low, Hood uses ETFs extensively in his client portfolios. But not just because of their razor-thin costs. "ETFs allow me to compete [with the big firms] simply because of their performance. I know ETFs are going to outperform 80% of the broad market mutual funds because there is so much congruence between their largest share holdings and their respective ETFs, but with a much lower cost structure," he says.

"Another advantage of ETFs is that they clarify things," Hood notes. "Clients know roughly where they are just by knowing how the indexes are doing."

The simplicity has other strengths. "A lot of planners," continues Hood, "have a client meeting every year, get the maximum RRSP contribution, and dribble it in bits and pieces into the latest hot funds. In ten years, the client's going to have 40 funds. It's nuts. Their portfolios aren't diversified; they're splattered!" These fund *du jour* folks can very well end up with an inefficient, high-cost portfolio that dramatically underperforms.

But then Hood has also seen advisors convert a mutual fund portfolio with 30 funds into a portfolio with 40 ETFs. "That doesn't make any sense either," he says.

On a typical $300,000 to $700,000 portfolio, Hood recommends no more than 5 to 8 ETFs because he believes that clients approaching retirement should have their investments in the currency of the country in which they'll be retiring. Canadians staying in Canada should have Canadian investments. "This is more important than global diversification," he says, "especially after witnessing the decline in U.S. dollar assets over the past two years." He is eagerly anticipating a Canadian ETF on the U.S. market that is hedged against currency fluctuations.

Hood employs ETFs on the equity side of his portfolios. For fixed income he uses bonds or a bond index ETF combined with a covered call-writing strategy. "I buy stocks that pay a dividend and sell long-term options against them." He also writes covered calls on ETFs that pay dividends like the i60s. "That lets me significantly boost the yield on the income portfolio," he says, to the tune of 7-8% in tax-advantaged capital gains and dividends. He calls his method "index, hedge, and grab the cash." So between ETFs and his covered call-writing strategy on the fixed income side, he says he's able to effectively compete with big brokerage houses and their research facilities.

Unlike mutual funds, Hood notes that ETFs can also be used as part of a portfolio hedging strategy; further, put options can be purchased on ETFs as part of a risk management strategy.

Hood is far from alone in understanding the advantages of ETFs in fee-based programs. Keith Matthews is another fee-based advisor with a passion for ETFs. Matthews is a partner and associate portfolio manager with PWL Capital Inc. in Montréal. PWL Capital uses ETFs and DFA asset class funds widely in the equity components of their client portfolios.

"For 0.50%-1.50%, we will build you the best portfolio possible. I am now going to go out into the universe of all possible products for the best after-fee portfolio. When we look at the thousands of different mutual funds out there—dealing with management drift, management change, I get surprises. They're not tax efficient. I can't control the inflows or the outflows of cash into the portfolios that impact my client. When you look at all these different aspects, you can't ignore the power of exchange traded funds.

"Studies show clients are better off working with investment advisors. The no-load mutual funds have given better rates of return than load mutual funds on paper, but the actual returns captured by clients has been much higher in load portfolios. Having an advisor pays dividends in the long-term world. Staying the course, fee for discipline, for long-term asset rebalancing, these have been proven to be of tremendous value to clients. PWL's minimum account size is $500,000.

"A fee-based manager is trying to maximize your after-tax return. It's all about after-tax. Over a 10-year period, managing in a buy and hold environment, making slight modifications, using ETFs and a variety of other securities, you will get a better after-tax return relative to the other alternatives available out there. Period," Matthews says unequivocally.

Four investment principles drive PWL's approach. 1) Diversify and capture the return of an entire asset class. 2) Returns come from three factors, market, price, and size: stocks outperform bonds; value stocks outperform growth stocks; small company stocks outperform large company stocks. 3) Design tax-efficient portfolios and minimize trading. 4) Use transparent institutional-type investment tools.

Noting that ETFs are pure asset pools, unlike equity mutual funds that will hold cash and foreign equities, Matthews says, "ETFs empower investment advisors to do very exact asset allocation. There's nothing passive in that. Handing the investment decision off to a fund manager is really being passive. Where's the accountability in that?"

Passion for the fee-based approach runs deep in many advisors who have set themselves apart in this way. Matthews is a case in point. "Fee-based is about how I can best grow your portfolio over ten years—after costs, after taxes—not how can I generate the most amount of commissions from you."

A Cost Survey of Different Fee-Based Arrangements

As a consumer you do have to be cautious about the kind of program you choose with a fee-based advisor because fee-based doesn't always mean rock-bottom pricing. There's an assortment of programs and arrangements a fee-based advisor can recommend and some are more expensive than a portfolio of conventional mutual funds.

Generally, the most expensive fee-based accounts are a kind of wrap program that pools investors' assets in some way—either with mutual funds or with proprietary pooled funds. Wraps are accounts that provide ongoing monitoring and asset allocation rebalancing for a fee based on a percentage of invested assets. Typically, they are sold by one party but managed by another. This distinguishes them from fee-based investment counsellors like Hood and Matthews who actually execute the investment decisions themselves. Pooled wrap programs are offered by mutual fund companies, brokerages, banks, and trust companies.

Mutual Fund Wraps

Wrap programs can use an assortment of retail mutual funds as a sort of fund of funds approach. These are mutual fund wrap programs and generally have the highest costs. Examples of these programs include Mackenzie's STAR program and CIBC's "All-In-One Fund Solution," and CI Portfolio Series among others. Programs like these have very low minimum investments—from $25 a month through a pre-authorization chequing program to as much as $20,000. CIBC's, for example, requires just $500. A 2005 report by Toronto-based Investor Economics says MERs on the funds within these kinds of programs range from 0.86% to 4.95% with the typical asset-weighted cost to the investor being 2.56%.

Pooled Wraps

Wrap programs can also use proprietary in-house mutual funds known as "pools." These pools usually have lower MERs than conventional load funds, but your advisor will probably charge you an annual fee to place you in these programs, or collect a trailer through the fund company. Minimum account sizes typically range from $10,000 to $250,000. Mackenzie's Symmetry Portfolio Service, AGF Harmony, CI Insight, and Frank Russell Canada's Sovereign programs (distributed by RBC Dominion Securities, TD Waterhouse, Richardson Partners, and ScotiaMcLeod) are examples of pooled wraps.

Before advisor compensation and without adjustment for large purchase MER discounts, a pool management fee might be around 1% or higher.

Some pooled wraps used to have fees to execute asset allocation which were over and above the pools' MERs. When advisor compensation was taken into account, some of these products could have fees considerably in excess of conventional mutual funds. Investor awareness and competition have generally moderated these fees.

Segregated Wraps

A third kind of wrap program that might be offered by a brokerage is a "segregated wrap." These programs use an investment manager or a number of different managers who invest your money directly in individual securities. These programs are often customizable to take into account your current holdings, but have high minimum investments, from $250,000 to $1,000,000. Fees are quite variable from company to company and often negotiable to some extent. Typically, a company might give the advisor a 25-basis-point bargaining window, half of which comes from the advisors' remuneration, but anything greater than a 25-basis-point discount on fees usually comes completely out of the advisor's cut. Program fees range from as much as 2.63% to as low as 0.40% for a $2,000,000 portfolio mostly in fixed income; though Investor Economics' 2005 report says the asset-weighted MER is typically about 2.03%. Most of these accounts come with a fixed number of free trades per year.

Are Wraps Cheaper?

Pooled programs are often touted by investment advisors as being tax efficient for a few reasons. The investment service fee on non-registered accounts (only) is tax deductible, and some pooled funds calculate and assign the capital gains tax liability of each investor as they exit the pool so that the remaining investors don't get stuck paying the tax for the clever investor who bailed out before a distribution. These features won't come anywhere near compensating for the cost of the programs themselves if you get a pricey one. Before going into any of these programs you have to be certain you're getting off cheaper than simply holding load mutual funds and getting your advisor to do an annual rebalancing to an asset allocation you determined together.

"...[A] hybrid approach that uses regular mutual funds and other low-cost products (i.e. exchange traded funds, bonds, etc.) can provide investors with a very well-diversified, tax-efficient, and low-cost portfolio and provide ample compensation for your advisor," says Dan Hallett in his study of pooled wrap programs in an article in *Canadian MoneySaver*.[3] Hallett is president of Dan Hallett & Associates Inc., an independent investment research firm and licensed investment counsel in Windsor, Ontario. His conclusion: stay away from these wrap programs and find a better way.

The better way is to work with an advisor to find the best and lowest cost investments around. That mandate becomes less complicated when it is in the context of a transparent fee-based relationship.

Fee-Based without Wraps

Just as you have to be careful of institutional fee-based programs, so do you have to exercise some discrimination with the portfolios of fee-based advisors. Not all portfolios are equal—especially when it comes to costs. Two advisors may both charge 1% in fees, but their portfolios could end up being significantly different in total costs after the embedded costs on the recommended investments are taken into account.

A fee-based advisor has the same tools at his or her disposal that any other advisor does, but has the freedom of choosing even those that don't pay a commission. The most cost-effective portfolio would be composed of individual bonds, stocks, and ETFs in an account with an unlimited number of free trades. The least cost-efficient portfolio would be one entirely of load funds with a fee on top, which, believe it or not, is still available in the marketplace.

Somewhere in the middle is a fee-based account holding 0% commission front-end load funds, but watch out for this. Front-end equity funds generally pay 1% a year in trailers to the advisor. This fee is discreetly charged to you through a plump MER. Fee-based advisors should be making their money on your fee, not on your embedded costs. Sometimes, though, advisors can't find the right type of investment in a no-load fund or with an ETF and must resort to a front-end fund at zero commission. Your advisor may want, for instance, an actively managed fund for emerging markets or Latin America. There's nothing wrong with this so long as you understand the advisor is, in effect, double-dipping—getting a fee and if not a commission, then a trailer fee funded through the higher MER you are paying on that fund. Scrutinize the asset allocation in these cases especially. Plenty of advisors believe you don't need exotic asset classes and that they add only volatility.

To better accommodate fee-based advisors, fund companies have come out with different classes of funds that are essentially no-load with reduced MERs. These funds have no DSC penalties because they don't pay the advisor a commission on the sale of the fund, and they sport lower MERs. "F" class units ("F" stands for "fee-based") have stripped the commission and trailer costs out of the MER leaving only the fund company's cost of running the fund. Another reduced MER class is called "I" class, standing for "institutional." "I" class units have MERs slightly higher than "F" units because they still pay an advisor a small trailer fee. They are designed for clients with high minimum investments. Mackenzie Financial Corp.'s "I" class, for instance, is exclusively for those with $500,000 invested in

Mackenzie funds—and possibly in the context of a fee-based arrangement with an advisor.

But again, exercise caution. These reduced MER classes are not all the same. "The vast majority of clients don't know that "I" class units pay the advisor more than is disclosed up front in the fee-based arrangement," observes John De Goey, a financial advisor in Toronto and author of *The Professional Financial Advisor*. "Clients don't ask about trailers or read the fine print. The net effect is that the client thinks 1% is fair, and the advisor thinks 1.25% is fair so they both feel they've struck a good bargain, but it's likely the client won't understand just what the advisor is being paid. How much is fair compensation is open for debate, but the disclosure of this compensation is not debatable. It should be absolutely transparent."

The Ontario Securities Commission (OSC) seems to agree. Under their "Fair Dealing Model," the OSC has proposed increased disclosure on trailer fees. How ever this comes to pass, the moral is to be sure you know exactly what and how your advisor is being compensated. Fee-based accounts can hold more within them for your advisor than you might think.

How One Advisor Uses ETFs with His Clients

As is evident from his comments above, De Goey is outspoken about the right of clients to know how much they are paying and for what. He uses an assortment of relationship models with his own clients but he prefers the fee-based approach he has designed. As he likes to put it, he sells parts and service separately. His approach has broad-based ETFs at its core with "F" class mutual funds added where clients request active management.

Here are two sample portfolios De Goey might recommend for his clients:

Agressive RRSP (80% equity, 20% fixed income) (fig. 40)		%
Fixed Income:	iUnits 5-Year Government of Canada Bond	10.0
	DFA 5-Year Global Fixed Class	10.0
Canadian Equity:	iUnits S&P/TSX 60 Capped	
	DFA Canadian Applied Core Equity (ACE)	10.0
U.S. Equity:	iUnits S&P 500 RSP	10.0
	DFA U.S. Equity Applied Core Equity	15.0
International Equity:	DFA International Equity ACE	15.0
	C.I. Signature Global Small Companies	5.0
	iUnits MSCI International Equity RSP	5.0
Alternative (tangibles):	iShares Emerging Markets	10.0
	iREIT	10.0
	Total	100

Conservative, Non-RRSP (50% fixed income, 50% equity) (fig. 41) %

		%
Fixed Income:	iShares Real Return Bond	10.0
	iUnits 5-Year Government of Canada Bond	20.0
	DFA International 5 Year	20.0
Canadian Equity:	DFA Canadian ACE	5.0
	iUnits S&P/TSX 60 Capped Index	5.0
U.S. Equity:	DFA U.S. Equity ACE	7.5
	iUnits S&P 500	7.5
International Equity:	iUnits MSCI International Equity RSP	7.5
	DFA International ACE	7.5
Tangibles:	iREIT	10.0
	Total	100

De Goey has a tiered fee structure, or as he calls it, a marginal fee rate. He charges 1.40% on the first $250,000; 0.70% on additional assets between $250,000 and $2 million, and 0.35% on anything over $2 million. This is his fee before GST. It does not include transaction costs nor does it include MERs on the investments. At $600,000, De Goey's fee is 0.99% plus GST. The total cost of this model is the sum of the investments' MERs, De Goey's fee and any transaction costs.

You may not think taking the MERs into account adds much, but watch what it does to the all-in costs. With MERs the cost goes to about 1.66%. Here are the total costs to De Goey's clients as he calculates them.

One Advisor's Cost Comparison and Fee Schedule* (fig. 42)

Asset Level	<$250,000	$600,000
Approach/Mix:		
Pre-existing Wrap Account	2.75% to 3.25 %	1.60 % to 3.00%
Traditional Mutual Funds**	2.40%	2.40%
De Goey Conservative	1.90%	1.47%
De Goey Aggressive	2.00%	1.57%

* Assumes an all equity portfolio.

** This does not include trading commissions to buy ETF positions.

De Goey's aggressive portfolio of $250,000 would have an all-in cost of 2.00%, a savings of around 40 basis points over the average MER for a Canadian equity fund, but as De Goey sees it, he is offering his clients advice, better tax efficiency, tax deductibility of fees on non-registered accounts, and a personalized investment policy statement. And as assets climb, total costs diminish.

For a while, De Goey could not offer his clients "F" class funds for technical reasons beyond his control. This highlights another issue you should be on the look out for: Firms, by their organization, licensing, and back office systems, limit the product universe available to their representatives. Furthermore, plenty of financial planners can't sell bonds, individual stocks, or ETFs because they're not licensed to do so. These financial products require a securities license. Mutual fund salespeople are required to have nothing more than a mutual funds license, which does not equip them to sell or even administer individual securities, including ETFs. These advisors are restricted to mutual funds because they have not undertaken to obtain a securities license or because their firm has not structured itself so as to be permitted by regulators to hold securities licenses on behalf of employees, a necessary condition of having securities-licensed personnel.

If you hire a fee-based advisor, first make sure the firm is able to transact securities like stocks, bonds, and ETFs, and that the advisor herself is securities licensed. Paying a fee to someone to simply select mutual funds is a little like golfing with one arm tied behind your back. It's better than being in the office but not terribly effective. Then make sure your advisor has no other restrictions in acting on your mandate: "Build me the best possible portfolio." Too many times the actual portfolio falls short of the ideal because of avoidable practical obstacles. Don't tolerate the obstacles. Find a firm and an advisor who can give you the universe—of investment products anyway. Why limit your range of investment possibilities and your chance at better returns?

For an investor, the draw to fee-based is the independence of the advice. Since a fee-based investor pays a flat fee based on the size of the account, the advisor should be free to recommend the very best investments for your situation without heed to how well the product will help their monthly commission numbers. As you'll see, your advisor will likely welcome the suggestion of a fee-based relationship.

Why Advisors Have an Interest in Going Fee-Based

This may surprise you, but advisors have a powerful motivation to be transitioning to fee-based arrangements. For one thing, a fee-based advisory practice is worth about twice what a traditional transactional business can fetch on the resale market.4 When advisors retire or change careers, they typically sell their "book of business" to another advisor for some multiple of annual revenue. Fee-based practices attract a high price because their income stream is more steady and reliable, and the business is easier to transfer into another's care.

Fee-based arrangements also attract higher net worth clients and permit the advisor to position himself as a money coach or consultant rather than a salesman. All in all, your advisor has got plenty of incentive to give you the most efficient portfolio possible, for a fee.

Something more subtle is at play, too. A fee-based business, if done wisely, can give brokers and advisors a freedom from their companies that they've never had before.

Dean Alexander, CFA, is an independent portfolio manager in Vancouver, managing over $250 million in assets. He uses ETFs for his U.S. and international exposure, and he's a big fan. "I think they're one of the best investment ideas I've seen come along in the 32 years I've been in the business," he says. Alexander believes they are superior to actively managed large cap mutual funds particularly in U.S. and international markets. "The larger cap market is very efficient," he says, "and it's difficult for an active manager to beat the returns that can be earned on a well-constructed ETF." He believes investors looking for better returns from active management are best to focus on small caps where managers can uncover good companies before they become widely followed.

"Any broker must question why they are putting their clients into the typical mutual fund with high fees and back-end charges," Alexander continues. "By using mutual funds, the broker restricts the clients' options and is giving control of the client to somebody else," he says. A broker would be much better off charging a 1% fee and using an ETF portfolio. It is better for the client and it is better for the broker. The broker retains control of the client and the clients get the benefits of mutual funds at a fraction of their cost."

"You can run a very viable business on 1%," he asserts, with some credibility. He's been doing it for 15 years. (His fees are 1% or less.) Alexander breaks down the math by assuming most veteran brokers control on average about $50 to $100 million in assets. One percent of $100 million is a cool million. Even after the company takes its share, Alexander says, "If he can't have a comfortable life on that income, there's something wrong."

"The smart brokers," he says, "are going to start building portfolios with ETFs and charging 1%." If the broker's company decides to change the rules of the game, the broker is free to walk with his clients, who are tied to no other product than the broker's skill. The broker can then set up his own firm or transfer to a more welcoming company. "To the competent, ethical people in the business, ETFs give them the opportunity to get out of the midst of big institutions."

So you see, your advisor does have many reasons for transitioning to a fee-based arrangement, and even better reasons for using ETFs to do so.

What's a Fair Fee?

Just how much that fee should be is up to you to decide. For accounts under $100,000 the best strategy is almost certainly to do it yourself with a simple Core and Satellite strategy or the Couch Potato Portfolio. (See Chapter Four.) For accounts from $100,000 to $250,000, a 1% fee is getting off easy as most fee-based advisors reserve the magical 1% charge for larger portfolios. After $250,000 you're in a good position to negotiate the fee—especially with the fixed income portion of your portfolio.

Remember, your advisor has as much interest in adopting a fee-based arrangement as you have. You can't get what you don't ask for, so bargain hard for the best deal you can get. Your advisor, if she's enlightened, will appreciate that bargaining because in the end, if you're both satisfied with the arrangement, you'll be a loyal client and she'll have a steadier cash flow. Then again, recognize you'll be writing a cheque every quarter or authorizing a monthly automatic debit to your investment or chequing account to pay these investment advisory fees. But don't kid yourself. Lower, transparent investment costs are certainly in your best interest. Higher, hidden charges, while being out of sight and out of mind, are detrimental to your portfolio's long-term returns and your ultimate security.

John Bogle is a pioneer of low-cost investing in the United States. He founded the Vanguard Group, the largest index mutual fund company in the world and has spent most of his life urging the investment industry to "give investors a fair shake" with reasonable fees. In an interview for this book, the now retired Mr. Bogle shared his insights about fee-based advisors. Although Vanguard is a no-load company, he believes in the value of advisors for most people, with a caveat to the costs. "People have to think very carefully about how much that fee ought to be," he says. "I don't think 1% is unreasonable for $50,000. But when you get up to very large amounts, 1% is a huge amount. Get out a compound interest table. Take a look at the difference between 10% and 9% over an investment lifetime of 50 years. Just that little one percent: the difference is staggering. A dollar at 10% is going to be worth $117 in 50 years. A dollar at 9% is going to be worth $74. If you want to put $10,000 around that, it's $1,170,000 vs. $740,000 to the investor at a 1% difference. That's $377,000 to the croupier. Think of that. A third of the return is taken by the croupiers. The investor puts up 100% of the capital and takes 100% of the risk to get two-thirds of the returns. People have to focus on the long term and the impact of costs."

"Advisors should do their fishing in a low-cost pond," Bogle continues. "Of all the strategies that absolutely work, that's it. You can take any comparison of any mutual fund you've ever seen in your life and cut it any way you want. If you compare the high-cost quartile with the low-cost quartile over any reasonable period of time, the low cost quartile wins. That's as close to a certainty as you get in this world."

Of course, Mr. Bogle is not a big fan of ETFs because he believes they encourage too much trading and a short-term perspective. But that's an argument for another day. To my mind, anything that gives investors lower costs and greater flexibility is a good thing, and there's nothing preventing ETF investors from holding on to them indefinitely. If anything, it's cheaper to hold an ETF long-term than it is to hold an index mutual fund long-term.

ETFs Within Mutual Funds

There are over 100,000 financial advisors in Canada but fewer than 20,000 of them carry a securities license. Typically, financial planners and mutual fund sales professionals are licensed to sell only mutual funds. ETFs, being an exchange traded security, require a securities license.

For those advisors who aren't securities licensed and for the clients who are devoted to them, there are a growing number of ways of accessing ETFs and their benefits—through mutual funds.

Mackenzie, Talvest, and Elliott & Page all have at least one fund with a substantial ETF component.

Credit unions could soon be distributing mutual funds and portfolio programs using ETFs, too. Qtrade Canada is a company in Vancouver that provides financial services to financial institutions across the country, many credit unions among them. Qtrade has launched a family of mutual funds and portfolio and asset management services using ETFs extensively.

In a real breakaway innovation, Advisor Asset Management Group Inc, a Burlington, Ontario-based investment firm, has devised a program that works with financial advisors to construct a custom portfolio specific to their client base within a fund structure. Under their Blueprint Program, advisors, regardless of their licensing, work with Crystal Wealth Management System Ltd (ICPM) to design, develop, and provide ongoing recommendations for their custom-designed fund containing all types of assets.

The funds may hold individual stocks, bonds, hedge funds, ETFs, and other products that an advisor's clients may not have had access to before. For advisors, the advantages are even more striking. Imagine the administrative ease of having a whole client base in one fund. Rebalancing and adjustments formerly done one account at a time can now be done simultaneously for all clients through a single trade within the fund. The structure also allows the advisor's clients to hold a fully diversified portfolio, which may include alternative strategies, something that may not be currently available to clients with insufficient assets.

As utopian as that sounds, it is not entirely perfect. The custom Blueprint funds can be offered only to sophisticated clients with the minimum purchase varying by province, and to accredited investors. It's also a little on the expensive side. These funds charge about 2.0% to 3.0% in management fees and expenses, which includes a 1% advisor trailer fee. Advisors have input into the management fee and compensation structure for their custom-designed fund as the program has been designed to be flexible in that regard.

Like all other wrap or fund-of-fund programs, the overall cost of Blueprint's custom funds will vary by what is held by the fund. Advisors will likely avoid holding many mutual funds because that results in MERs on top of MERs. The best way to make the most of the Blueprint Program is to use individual stocks and bonds, ETFs, and a sprinkling of quality alternative strategy investments.

ETFolios

Years before these fund companies got interested, Guardian Capital Advisors LP. held the door wide open to ETFs for mutual fund licensed advisors with the introduction of their ETFolios program, a service that gives investors ETF portfolios customized to their individual risk tolerance and investment objectives, and rebalanced automatically. The program has a $50,000 minimum with a minimum 0.50% management fee. Add to that an average MER of about 0.25% for the ETFs themselves and the advisor's 0.50% to 1% optional trailer fee, and your all-in costs could be as low as 1.25%. The program also offers the option of some tactical management within the ETF portfolios for a management fee of 1.50%, but that applies only to the assets given over to tactical strategies which cannot exceed 50% of the invested assets.

Remember, on taxable accounts most of these fees are tax deductible, so this program is passing on to investors some of the cost efficiency of its underlying exchanged traded funds. As with all ETFs within the umbrella of a mutual fund, you have to be watchful that the combined fund management fee and the MER within the ETF is still reasonable and competitive for what it gives you.

Speaking of what it gives you, the ETFolios team has run 10-year back testing on many of their portfolios for a perspective on their risk/return profile. According to portfolio manager Sri Iyer, Director, Portfolio Engineering and VP Research at Guardian, individual ETFs "morph into something with different risk and return characteristics" when they are put together in a portfolio. The whole, in other words, is greater than the parts when it comes to risk management.

Iyer also notes that ETFolios are ideal for Individual Pension Plans and, because they break out management fees and commission within the program, it is "a core method to transition advisors' books from a commission to a fee-based practice."

For those who prefer to go it alone, ETFolios is also available through E*TRADE Canada or directly on *www.etfolios.com*.

Investment Counsel ETF Programs Available to Advisors

ETF portfolios can also be achieved through the services of an investment counselling firm that can accept mutual fund licensed advisors' clients in a sub-advisory arrangement. This is the novel idea behind the i-WRAP portfolio program belonging to Hahn Investment Stewards & Company Inc. Wilfred Hahn, the company's founder and former head of the Global Investment Group for the Royal Bank of Canada, has designed a program that partners with independent advisors who want to avail their clients of professional money management expertise with custom ETF portfolios.

i-WRAPS is a segregated wrap program in which clients hold a customized basket of ETFs that are actively managed to client objectives. Hahn's web site says they charge "amongst the lowest investment management fees in Canada's wealth management industry." Minimum account size is $100,000 with a management fee of 0.80% that declines with account size. The advisor can take as much as 1% on top of that, but Hahn says he would like to see the overall service come out at 1.65%. Over and above this are the MERs on the ETFs, but i-Wraps has an MER optimizing program that Hahn says gets the MER basis point cost on a global ETF portfolio down to the "low 20s." "Today we can manage a global account of $100,000 at substantially less cost than was possible for a $20 million account in the 80s," mostly attributable to the ETFs, says Hahn.

Once in charge of a global investment operation with more than $10 billion in client assets, Hahn says he became agnostic about individual security selection. "In 2000 I had an epiphany when I realized the day would come when a portfolio firm could build global portfolios exclusively with ETFs and offer enough strategy possibilities to do active management without security selection. We have come up with an innovative investment option that really aligns with the interests of the clients. What we are doing is such an obviously better way to do things. Everything is structured to get costs down." Their strategies include country mix, sector calls, style bets, and currency strategies. They are hoping to introduce a hedging component with leveraged and inverse return ETFs when those products become available.

"The best way of achieving one's retirement objectives," the steward continues, "is with a reasonable diversified investment policy and keeping costs down. We can't control the market, but we can control costs. Over 25 years, costs make a huge difference in retirement lifestyle."

Yet Hahn complains that advisors have been slow to recognize the superiority of this approach. "We're a threat to mutual fund advisors who see themselves as offering a mutual fund picking strategy. Not many advisors are willing to admit that wasn't the best. Perhaps they feel by introducing an ETF approach they are repudiating themselves. Some can't get over that."

Help your financial advisor get over the embarrassment. There really is a new kid on the block who plays a better game of ball. If you want to work with a financial advisor and reap the many benefits of exchange traded funds, there's really little stopping you now. Products and programs abound bringing these Bay Street tools to Main Street. You should have the same products and strategies to build your wealth as institutional money managers have had for years, and your advisor should be the first one helping you take advantage of them.

ETFs, Your Advisor, and You: An Interview with Kevin Ireland

Kevin Ireland is Vice President, ETF Marketing for AMEX where, according to their slogan, "ETFs were born, bred, and spend most of their quality time."

Do you think advisors are interested in selling ETFs?

Kevin Ireland: Advisors realize the transaction business has been commoditized. The only value added they have is truly as an advisor and that's a fee-based world. Being fee-based allows advisors for the first time to work in conjunction with their customers without a conflict of interest. If an advisor gets 1% on a customer with $100,000, he'll get twice as much when he turns that into $200,000 at 1%. And ETFs are really good parts of the tool box to do the asset allocation.

Do you see any trends in asset allocation?

Global allocation is exploding and I think it is going to continue to go that way.

You look at the [standard] asset allocation for global equities five years ago versus what it is today, it has more than tripled. The EAFE [Europe, Australasia, and the Far East] ETF is up to $14 billion and the emerging markets ETF is at $4 billion. I think we need to start fine-tuning global allocations, breaking it down more into regions and sectors. There's potential growth for ETFs in the fine tuning.

Gold has opened the door for having ETFs on basically any hard asset. From the public's perspective, they really haven't had that kind of access to the market before. Unlike buying stocks in a gold mine or an oil company, these are pure plays on the hard asset and very exciting.

What do you think of fixed income ETFs?

I think they really enhance the investor's ability to do asset allocation. I think it's even more important than on the equity side to be able to fill in the fixed income portion of your portfolio with a single purchase. You could buy a single treasury, but with an ETF you can get exposure to the entire yield curve. You want to buy corporate bonds? There's some risk right now, but now you can buy a 100 bond basket of high grade corporates all in one shot. These are strategies that only bond traders had before. Not only can you cover the entire yield curve with a single purchase, but you can take active views on which way the yield curve is going to go. You can do this in one or two purchases where you didn't have that kind of capability before.

Fixed income ETFs will be very important to advisors, but it's going to take a while.

There's still a lot of learning which will hamper the immediate growth of fixed income ETFs.

If you own a portfolio of 20 fixed income products and 20 stocks and you want to rebalance, effectively you've got to do 40 trades. With ETFs, though not as your entire portfolio, you can make that same adjustment in two, three, or four moves. It's simpler, cleaner, and you've lowered your risk with diversification.

Why should investors be excited about active ETFs?

Active ETFs will put more transparency on the active side. Even for the buy and hold guy, intraday price transparency is still an attractive benefit that lets you know where your fund is trading. They should be considerably cheaper, too, because you are doing away with the overhead. Unlike mutual funds, the transfer agent is not necessary. If you have several active ETFs competing, there will be downward pressure on fees. If you do a comparison of the passive ETFs vs. index mutual funds, ETFs are still cheaper. Sector Spiders average 25 basis points. A comparable mutual fund is a lot higher. I would think you'll see the actively managed ETFs be very competitively priced.

AMEX basically owns the ETF intellectual area. We have a full-time guy working on actively managed ETFs. We believe we're getting pretty close to seeing a fund company make a [securities commission] filing for an actively managed ETF but it's a coin toss on how long that will take to get through. Because there's no precedence, it will be reviewed very carefully.

We have patents on a couple of the processes that can mask the active portfolio [to prevent front running.] We have to look at the issuers, the fund companies, and the liquidity providers who will be using the blind portfolios. We have full acceptance on it. The process works and it offers a lot of benefits to the public. I think it is going to be a great product.

You could launch an active ETF as a share class of an existing mutual fund and from an economic stand point it is a lot more efficient to do it that way because of scale. The larger fund companies could do this. It is only a matter of time.

Have ETF assets peaked?

We hired a group to do a study on retail users. They came back to us and said while the number of people who know about ETFs is 10%, only about 3% of people are using them, so the growth potential is phenomenal. The 401k space is huge and right now mutual funds dominate that market. Only 1% of the 401k plans have brokerage windows. It is just a question of when, not if, the 401k plans open up. Once we crack that egg, we'll see real growth in the product, but it will grow anyway.

Unlike the mutual fund companies, there isn't a lot of money out there marketing ETFs.

Last year alone, we listed 22 new ETFs on AMEX and there are a whole lot more to come on board. Their incredible growth is due to their structure: it's simple, clean, cheap, and tax efficient, though you might not see as much tax efficiency in the active ETFs with a higher portfolio turnover. There's certainly a lot of room and the interest is growing.

June 1, 2005

Notes

1) Earl Bederman, Investor Economics provided this proprietary research.

2) A $23,000 management fee cost on a million dollar portfolio assumes an 80% equity, 20% fixed income asset allocation, with some above average MER equity funds like international specialty funds offsetting lower MER fixed income funds to average 2.3%.

3) Dan Hallett wrote an insightful and well-researched two-part article about pooled wrap programs in *Canadian MoneySaver Magazine*, "Pooled Wrap Programs: The Asset Management Maze," February 2001 and March 2001. Also see his "Unwrapping Wrap Accounts," in *Advisor's Edge*, November 2003, *www.advisor.ca/images/other/ae/ae_1103_unwrapping.pdf*.

4) "RIA Transitions, 2004 Transitions Report," by FPtransitions, available on-line at *www.FPtransitions.com*, p. 14. Thanks to Mark Yamada at Guardian Capital Advisors Inc. for that reference.

Chapter Six

Taxes: Implications and Strategies

An RRSP is a Canadian tax haven. Your retirement investments are as good as sunning themselves on a beach in the Cayman Islands while they're nestled in an RRSP account, but your investments outside an RRSP are battling the harshest Canadian element of all—taxes. Outside of a tax-sheltered account, taxes are the biggest expense most investors confront—bigger than commissions *and* management fees. This chapter will take you through the tax considerations of ETFs, both domestic and U.S.-based, and explore some tax strategies using ETFs. For the purposes of this discussion, we'll assume your investments are taking the full brunt of Canada Revenue Agency (CRA), outside a tax-sheltered account and held on capital account.[1]

Taxation of Canadian-Based ETFs

From a personal tax point of view, made-in-Canada ETFs are just like Canadian mutual funds. At the end of the tax year you get a T-3 detailing the nature and amount of income from your ETF. There will generally be some dividend income and some capital gains and possibly some interest and foreign income—just like a conventional mutual fund. (Mutual funds that are structured as corporations instead of trusts generate T-5s rather than T-3s.)

Just as with mutual funds, the income an ETF receives may come from capital gains on security trades, dividends from holdings, and interest. This income flows out of the fund to unitholders in the form of distributions that are taxable. It's hardly obvious, but having taxable distributions is actually an advantage because distributions minimize the total tax paid overall. This is why mutual funds and ETFs make distributions. Income kept within a fund is taxed at the highest tax rate. Passing the investment income to unitholders allows that income to be taxed at personal marginal tax rates, which may be lower than what the fund would otherwise have had to pay. That's why less total tax is paid when the fund's income is distributed to unitholders rather than being retained within the fund.

And again, like mutual funds, the tax character of a Canadian ETF's distributed income is retained when it is passed to unitholders. A Canadian dividend stays a dividend and a capital gain stays that way, too, giving unitholders the advantage of the dividend tax credit and the 50% break on capital gains.

With the exception of a few Canadian instances, ETFs generally distribute less income than most actively managed mutual funds. As we discussed in Chapter One, because ETFs do so little buying and selling within the fund, ETFs are remarkably good about keeping their gains to themselves and not troubling investors with large distributions.

Timing of Distributions

Equity ETFs listed in Canada distribute income quarterly and capital gains annually. One of Canada's two fixed income ETFs is the iBond which distributes interest income semi-annually. All Canadian ETFs—equity or bond—distribute capital gains at the end of the year in the form of reinvested, reconsolidated units. Cash is king, on the other hand, for all other distributions. Semi-annual and quarterly distributions are paid out in cash. Only capital gains distributions are paid out at the end of the year in additional units of the ETF. (See Chapter Seven for an explanation about reconsolidating reinvested units.)

Tax Records

Canadian distributions are recorded by the brokerage that holds your ETFs and it's the brokerage that issues the annual T-3 slips, not the ETF sponsor company. For those used to getting their tax slips from mutual fund companies, this is a bit of a departure and is a source of confusion to some ETF investors. Brokerages are responsible for issuing the tax slips for their clients' ETF distributions; whereas, mutual fund companies issue T-3 and T-5 slips for their unitholders.

Taxation of U.S.-Based ETFs

A small number of U.S. ETFs, including fixed income iShares, distribute income monthly.

Owning a U.S.-listed ETF is just like owning a U.S. stock. The income generated by the ETF is treated as ordinary income for Canadian tax purposes, just as is a U.S. stock dividend. Capital gains treatment applies on the sale of the ETF exactly as it does on the sale of any stock.

Dividends

U.S.-based ETFs are classified under U.S. tax rules as Regulated Investment Companies, or RICs for short. Distributions of dividends to Canadian residents from RICs are subject to a 15% withholding tax unless the distributions are being paid to a deferred income plan such as an RRSP or pension plan. A tax treaty between Canada and the U.S. exempts retirement accounts from withholding tax on RIC dividend distributions. As a result, U.S. ETFs held within an RRSP or RRIF receive their distributions free of withholding tax. Held outside of a tax deferred plan, U.S. ETF dividend distributions are subject to withholding tax. And remember, U.S. ETF dividend income is not eligible for the dividend tax credit, which is reserved only for the dividends of Canadian corporations.

Capital Gains

Distributions of capital gains from RICs don't incur withholding tax, but the bad news is that the capital gains portion of the distribution does not retain its character for Canadian tax purposes. You may not, however, be required to include all of the distribution from some U.S. ETFs in your income under a new Canadian tax rule, but people in the tax field believe that the new rule is so complicated that taking advantage of it is vastly impractical. (For those who really want to know how it works, follow the footnote.)[2]

Canadian holders of iShares may be fully taxable on iShares distributions but will be eligible for a foreign tax credit in respect of withholding tax paid. The same applies to any U.S.-based ETF, not just iShares. In other words, you won't be taxed twice on your U.S. ETF income. The foreign tax credit will apply to the money withheld by the U.S. government. Due to the practical difficulties in applying the Canadian tax rule about capital gains distributions from U.S.-based ETFs, your Canadian tax bill may very likely be calculated on every penny of U.S.-based ETF income without dividend tax credits, or an advantageous 50% inclusion rate for capital gains.

A Tax Advantage

From a tax perspective, you might think that it wouldn't make any difference whether you held a Canadian mutual fund that hold-owned a U.S. ETF or you held the ETF directly yourself. Either way, the dividends are subject to the 15% withholding tax (in non-tax-deferred accounts). Apart from being more cost-effective to hold the ETF directly, and thereby avoid the mutual fund's MER charge, it is also more tax efficient to hold the ETF directly.

The difference is in how CRA allows the foreign tax to be recouped. Canadian mutual fund unitholders get a foreign tax credit on the withholding tax their mutual fund paid. On the other hand, Canadian ETF owners have the choice of declaring a foreign tax credit or an outright tax deduction. This is an advantage because tax credits can be used only against taxes owing. A deduction lowers your taxable income and is more serviceable than a tax credit.

Adjusted Cost Base for ETFs

Distributions always bring to the wary investor's mind the Adjusted Cost Base calculation (ACB). The ACB of an investment is its average cost including acquisition costs (trading commissions) and reinvested distributions. You need the ACB to figure out the capital gains on an investment because it's the sale price minus the ACB that determines the capital gain (or loss). Fortunately, there are no special considerations in calculating the adjusted cost base of ETFs. It's pretty straightforward.

ACB = (total purchases + acquisition costs + reinvested distributions - return of capital) ÷ units purchased

Monthly and quarterly ETF distributions are paid out in cash (unless your brokerage has an arrangement to reinvest them) but the end-of-year capital gains distribution, if there is one, gets reinvested. That capital gain distribution becomes part of your ACB, so you or your broker must keep track of all the distributions you receive by keeping the T-3 slips issued from your brokerage. Your T-3 slip will also record any distribution that is considered a return of capital. (I'll explain how that can happen in Chapter Seven.) A return of capital is not taxed but it is included in your investment's total cost, which is why it has to be subtracted from your adjusted cost base. Your trading commissions to buy the ETF units are also included in the ACB.

Controlling Your Capital Gains

Apart from the capital gains embedded in an annual distribution, you can trigger a capital gain yourself by selling an ETF you own. Be it Canadian or U.S., you do get to avail yourself of the 50% capital gains inclusion rate when you make a profit on the sale of your ETF. That means that you are subject to tax at your marginal tax rate on only 50% of the realized gains. The other 50% is tax free. So if you are looking to maximize your after-tax returns with U.S. investments, you would favour U.S. investments with few distributions but with a good potential for capital gains upon the sale of the investment. That describes a number of U.S.-based ETFs.

SPDRs, for instance, are famously tax efficient even for a Canadian investor. Since their inception in 1993, SPDRs have distributed only 16¢ in fund-generated capital gains altogether. MidCap SPDRs haven't spun out a capital gain since 1999. You can learn the distribution history of all the AMEX-listed ETFs at *www.amextrader.com*. Click on "ETF Data," select an ETF, and then click on "distribution history." Be careful, though. A long history of minimal distributions doesn't always mean history will repeat itself. In 2000, some European iShares paid out hefty distributions after years of minimal income. The iShares MSCI Germany, for instance, paid out $2.53 altogether on a share trading in the teens.

In the case of the MSCI Germany ETF, a change in the concentration limits in the underlying index was responsible for the large distribution. Concentration reductions and index reconstitutions are the most common reasons for large distributions in an ETF that normally runs without so much smoke. Canadian ETFs have their distribution surprises, too. The iUnits MidCap Fund had a $2.57 capital gain distribution in 2004, which represented 3.9% of the unit's price. Blame Research In Motion for that. It graduated out of the mid cap index and so had to be sold out of the ETF for sizable gains. The best defense against surprise distributions is knowing what's in the underlying portfolio so you can be on the lookout for things that might pose a problem in the future.

If you're concerned that the Canadian taxation of a U.S.-based ETF will offset the ETF's fundamental tax efficiency, stick to the large and mid cap U.S. funds. They generally have low turnover within their portfolios and correspondingly lower distributions. Those with taxable accounts should be cautious with style-based ETFs and the small caps, as these regularly move companies in and out in keeping with the changes within the indices themselves, and thus throw out more distributions. For reasons we'll explain, U.S.-based ETFs are structurally more tax efficient than Canadian ETFs because they generate fewer capital gains; so, even if you have the *potential* to pay more tax on the distributions from a U.S.-based ETF, in most cases you're getting far fewer distributions than you would get with a Canadian ETF holding the same underlying assets.

In-Kind Redemptions at the Fund Level

At the personal tax level, there's a considerable difference between the tax treatment of U.S.- and Canadian-based ETFs. There's a big difference at the fund level, too, because of the way "in-kind redemptions" are taxed in the different countries.

An in-kind redemption happens when those giant creation/redemption units of 50,000 ETF shares or so are exchanged for the underlying securities in the fund. In the U.S., in-kind redemptions are non-taxable. This means the transaction is not treated as a disposition under U.S. tax law, so U.S.-based ETFs don't incur a capital gains tax liability from in-kind redemptions.

A Disposition

It doesn't work this way in Canada. Here, an in-kind redemption is viewed as a disposition by the fund, which results in the fund *and* the unitholder having a potential capital gains tax liability on the same gain. While a capital gains refund does exist at the fund level to address this potential double taxation of the capital gains, the mechanism does not work perfectly. An ETF can be liable to pay the capital gains tax resulting from a redemption, or distribute the capital gains to unitholders for them to subsequently pay the tax. This difference in tax treatment makes U.S.-based ETFs more tax efficient than Canadian ETFs and less likely to distribute capital gains than Canadian ETFs.

Canadian ETFs, however, are now able to designate capital gains realized on the redemption to the redeeming unitholder. The redeemer is able to reduce their proceeds of sale by the amount of the distribution (to avoid double taxation). This new mechanism worked well in 2004, but it will take a track record of a few years to see if this regime, and any subsequent changes to it, in fact makes Canadian ETFs as tax efficient as their U.S. counterparts. The nagging problem is suspended losses.

Suspended Losses

In-kind redemptions at the fund level don't always result in capital gains. Some times capital losses also result. Funds, like individuals, are permitted to use capital losses to offset capital gains but the rules are sticky.

Suppose a fund needs to shave down its weighting in XYZ stock. It sells a chunk of its holdings in XYZ at a loss. That loss could be applied to offset other capitals gains the fund has generated through other index adjustments. However, if within thirty days of XYZ's sale, a creation unit subscription is done, the fund must repurchase some of XYZ's shares it had previously sold at a loss. This repurchase immediately disqualifies the previous loss from being used to offset any capital gains. The capital loss becomes "suspended" in hope that it can be used to offset gains in the future. Gains are typically from corporation actions like acquisitions, spinoffs and income trust conversions which lead to index adjustments.

Because of the inkind subscription and redemption mechanism, ETFs can end up inadvertently triggering this suspended loss provision. Some funds, like the i60, have accumulated substantial suspended losses that the fund has not been able to tap in order to reduce some capital gains. Government finance officials are considering exempting index funds and ETFs from this suspended loss provision because the funds' losses result from non-discretionary trading. CRA's aim is to prevent the corporate equivalent of personal superficial losses (see below), but it has cast its net too broadly. Index products trade their portfolio simply to comply with a pre-established index. They may sometimes sell and buy the same security within 30 days, but the motivation in doing so has nothing to do with tax avoidance.

Distribution Tax Arbitrage

While the fund management itself is not selling or buying with a tax motivation, institutional unitholders may do in-kind purchases and redemptions with an eye to taxes.

Take a fund like the i60. Its monthly value increases as the dividends owing to it accumulate. Should an institution buy a creation unit at the beginning of a quarter and sell it just before the end of a quarter, it gains the net asset value appreciation due to the dividends without actually receiving the dividends. In essence, it converts what would have been dividend income into capital gains. (The same could be done with a fixed income fund's interest distributions.) This is called distribution tax arbitrage and it seems the i60 is vulnerable to this because of its holdings and its high liquidity. Again, due to suspended losses, the fund can be left with capital gains to distribute to all unitholders. Barclays Canada says they are looking at ways to discourage dividend arbitrage, but it won't be an easy fix. The ability to cash in an ETF quickly and easily is a hallmark of the product and what keeps ETFs trading so close to their net asset value. Too much of a good thing, perhaps.

Other institutional players, particularly financial institutions, may be doing another kind of tax motivated arbitrage. Some institutions may hold a large and active inventory to facilitate client orders or orderly trading in ETFs. In doing so, though, they prefer to receive the associated dividends tax free. Since eligible Canadian corporations pay out dividends in after-tax dollars, other Canadian corporations can receive these dividends tax free. But there is an important proviso for corporate investors: for the dividend to be tax free, the security must be held for a year or more or, if held for less than a year, it must be sold above cost. This tax rule results in more ETF trading than would arise without such a rule.

Superficial Loss Rule

Canadian investors may have one small tax break over their American counterparts when it comes to ETFs.

Both countries want to prevent what's known in Canada as superficial losses—trades that trigger a loss simply to offset some previously incurred capital gains. One of the hallmarks of a superficial loss, to CRA's mind anyway, is repurchasing the disposed investment within 30 days of having sold it.[3] This shows the purpose of the sale was to cash in on some tax losses—not to get rid of a dog. Suppose you sold SPDR for a loss but immediately bought an iShares S&P 500. Your underlying positions would be virtually identical. You simply sold one S&P 500 ETF and replaced it with another. In the U.S., most tax experts believe your capital loss would be disallowed.

In Canada, these kinds of tax loss switches between ETFs or index mutual funds were considered safe because you own different properties even though their constituents are the same (keeping in mind the provisions of the general anti-avoidance rule). However, in 2002, CRA issued a technical interpretation that dealt with the issue of identical properties and tax losses. Jamie Golombek, Vice President, Tax and Estate Planning, with AIM Trimark and head of the Investment Funds Institute of Canada's tax working group, says CRA seems to be changing this understanding: "Say you own a TSX Composite index fund from institution A and you sell it for a loss, then [within 30 days] you buy a different index fund on the same index from institution B, or an ETF on the same index. CRA is saying that's an identical property and the loss is denied."

Golombek goes on to say, "I think CRA is wrong from a legal point of view because these are different legal entities. They can't be identical."

Until this gets straightened out, the most prudent thing is to switch between similar but not identical indices when doing tax loss selling. You could, for instance, sell a TSX Composite fund or ETF and replace it with a TSX Capped ETF. A broad U.S. ETF like the Wilshire 5000 could be replaced with a Russell 3000. A Canadian growth ETF could be replaced with a Canadian mid cap ETF. There's no end to creative matchmaking.

U.S. Estate Tax Considerations

U.S.-based ETFs are attractive investments for Canadians looking for U.S. index exposure, so it's important to understand the consequences to your estate if you should die with a significant position in U.S. investments.

Canadian residents who are not U.S. citizens are subject to U.S. estate tax on the value of their U.S. assets owned at death. U.S.-based ETFs are U.S. assets so they get included in the tally. Whereas Canada taxes only the increase in value of assets owned at death, the U.S. system taxes the entire value at death. If you're a Canadian resident who is not a U.S. citizen and your worldwide estate is less than US$1.5 million, there is nothing to worry about with respect to your U.S.-based ETFs. They won't be subject to U.S. estate tax. If, however, your worldwide estate is greater than US$1.5 million, your U.S.-based ETFs will be taxed. The good news is that your ETFs are eligible for an estate tax exemption equal to the greater of US$60,000 or the enhanced exemption provided under the Canada/U.S. treaty. Under this treaty, U.S. assets are eligible for an exemption equal to a standard exemption of US$1,500,000 (in 2005) multiplied by a formula that divides the U.S. assets by the value of the estate's worldwide assets. The standard (but prorated) exemption of $1,500,000 will go up to US$3.5 million by 2009.

The U.S has repealed the U.S. estate tax for 2010. It is fully expected this repeal will last for 2010 only and that thereafter some standard exemption amount will be reinstated. Keep in mind that Canada gives foreign tax credits for U.S. estate tax to minimize the chance of double taxation. In the best case, the investor pays the higher of the two taxes, but quite likely the payment is split between the U.S. and Canadian tax collector. Canadian residents with large U.S. holdings, including ETFs, should consider obtaining estate planning advice to deal with the issue of U.S. estate taxes.

Foreign Reporting Requirements

CRA, ever vigilant, doesn't want Canadians investing abroad without the knowledge of the government lest someone avoid paying their fair share of tax. Canadian residents who own specified foreign property that at any time of the year exceeds $100,000 in total value, must file a Foreign Income Verification Statement (T1135) with their personal income return. The "specified foreign property" includes shares of foreign corporations and interests in trusts, which includes ETFs. Foreign-based ETFs would have to be reported if your total specified foreign property is greater than CDN$100,000.

Tax Saving Strategies

We're all happy to pay for a kinder, gentler society but few of us are happy to pay more than the law requires. Here are some tax planning suggestions that ETFs can help facilitate.

Avoiding Mutual Fund Distributions

At the end of a mutual fund's fiscal year, the fund distributes its income if it has any. Sometimes these distributions can be large and trigger a proportionately large tax liability. This is especially painful when your distributions are automatically reinvested in new units of the fund. You don't see any cash from the distribution but nevertheless have to pay CRA to cover the tax liability. In a money-losing year, that adds insult to injury. There is a way to avoid this: sell the fund before the record date for the distribution and avoid the distribution altogether. This may, however, trigger capital gains and unbalance your asset allocation. There's not much you can do about the capital gains, but you can keep your assets covered by buying an ETF that is comparable to your fund's holdings. This judicious mutual fund sale might save you some taxes if the tax on the fund distribution is greater than the tax on half your capital gain. Replacing the fund with a similar ETF will mitigate the asset allocation damage that selling a strategic mutual fund could have on your portfolio's overall balance. Just be careful not to walk into a distribution on the ETF side. Also watch out for changes in the distribution policy of some mutual funds. A call to the ETF sponsor for a distribution estimate would be a good idea.

Tax Swaps and Tax Loss Harvesting

Selling one security for tax purposes and immediately purchasing a similar investment is called a "tax swap." It is done not only to escape mutual fund distributions, but often also with the intention of crystallizing a capital loss to offset a capital gain now or in the future.

Crystallizing a loss for tax purposes, otherwise known as "tax loss harvesting," is done because of the tax rules regulating the relationship between capital gains and capital losses. Capital losses can be claimed against capital gains to offset the tax liability arising from the gains. The rules allow you some choice as to when you apply your capital losses. You must first claim your loss in the year you triggered it, but then you can apply it to a gain claimed any previous year back to three years, or carry the capital losses forward indefinitely into the future.

Swaps allow investors to maintain or alter their market exposure and asset allocation when they take a loss. You could, for instance, dump a Canadian tech mutual fund and buy an iUnits S&P/TSE Canadian Information Technology ETF. You'd gain the tax loss on the mutual fund but still have similar technology exposure and no worries about the superficial loss rules, as long as the tech fund was not an index fund with the same index as your ETF. Swaps work well between mutual funds and ETFs, be they sector plays or broad indices. And with the growing number of ETFs, it's now even possible to swap between different ETFs in the same sector or asset class. This is an especially appropriate strategy if you feel your targeted market sector is bottoming.

You gain some tax management flexibility and, as your ETF is fully invested, you get to ride the sector's full upswing when it happens. And if you want to repurchase your original loser, ETFs can help you maintain asset exposure while you wait out the 30 day superficial loss rule. You can sell your original holding, declare a capital loss to offset some capital gain liability, and then buy a sector ETF in the industry you still want to cover. After 30 days, you can sell the sector ETF and repurchase your original languishing investment. In this way, you will have avoided a superficial loss but still have kept your industry exposure. With any luck, you might also pick up your original stock at no more than you sold it for.

Equitizing Cash

Pension funds and other big institutional investors use ETFs widely for something called "equitizing cash." The name doesn't sound appealing, but the technique is popular. Equitizing cash simply involves taking cash and quickly turning it into equities—usually an extremely liquid, broad-based equity ETF. This enables managers to be in the market just in case one of those big up days hits—the kind of days pundits say make up only 1% of the time but account for half your returns. (Of course, you also have the risk of hitting a day everyone would rather forget.) For taxable accounts, this has the happy result of avoiding interest income, which is taxed heavily, in return for potential capital gains and dividend income.

Individual investors can also equitize their cash. ETFs provide a way to turn the interest income of cash into less punitively taxed income with little loss of liquidity and the benefit of market exposure, though with some added risk. Of course, this has to be done in the context of your entire portfolio because taxation shouldn't be the only investment consideration, though it's one that is too often neglected—it's only the after-tax return that pays for those trips to Hawaii.

With the introduction of fixed income ETFs, cash can now be easily "bondized," too.

Micromanaging Tax Liability in an Index

Broad indices like the S&P 500 and the Dow Jones Total Market are made up of a number of industry sectors. In the U.S., all these sectors are represented by ETFs, so it's possible to own a whole index by buying all of its component sectors in the right proportions via ETFs. The nine select sector SPDRs, for instance, fully replicate the S&P 500. Naturally, your total costs will be higher using this strategy as you'll have higher MERs and incur many more commission charges, but the advantage is in being able to micromanage each sector's losses and gains. As one sector slumps you can sell it to use that loss to offset the surge in another sector.

You can even try to enhance your returns by custom weighting the various sectors rather than keeping them in synch with the broader index. If you already own a lot of technology or financial stocks, you might want to underweight those sectors. Got a hankering for consumer staples? Here's the chance to easily overweight that sector. It's not a strategy for a couch potato, that's for sure.[4] The ETF Allocator on *www.ishares.com* will certainly help with this strategy.

Taxation of Option Strategies

Option strategies can be taxed in two different ways depending on whether the options are treated for tax purposes on capital account or on income account. The general rule of thumb is that an option strategy is speculative and thereby on an income account and fully taxed. If, however, an option is used to hedge an investment you already own, this is not considered speculative and the option will be treated as on capital account.[5] The following discussion will assume you are using options on capital account. (You can refer back to Chapter Four for an explanation of the option strategies discussed below.)

Call Options

The purchaser of a "call option" has paid a premium for the opportunity to buy a security—like an ETF—at a certain price by a certain date in the future. Should the option expire without being exercised, the premium paid becomes a capital loss in the taxation year in which the option expires. If, instead, the option is exercised, the option premium is added to the cost base of the ETF. A call option holder has one other course of action open to her. She can sell the option on the secondary market before its expiry. The net gain or loss that results from that sale is a capital gain or loss in the year the option is sold.

The premium paid to the writer of a call option is considered a capital gain. (A call writer is the person who promises to sell a security at a certain price by a certain date in the future.) Should the option be exercised, though, the option premium is instead added to the proceeds of the security sale. That way it becomes part of either a capital gain or a capital loss.

Put Options

Similarly, the premium paid to the writer of a put option is treated as a capital gain. If, however, the option is exercised, the premium is subtracted from the cost of buying the ETF units. This means the adjusted cost base of the ETF will be lower than it would be otherwise, leading to higher capital gains when those ETF units are sold. (Someone who writes a put promises to buy at a certain price up to some specified time in the future. Someone who buys a put is buying the right to sell at a certain price some time in the future.)

If a put option expires unexercised, the buyer of that put can claim the premium he paid for it as a capital loss in the year the put expired. If instead, he sells the put on the secondary market, the net gain or loss is taxed as a capital gain or loss in the year it is sold. Should the put be exercised, the premium paid to buy the put is deducted from the proceeds of the ETFs sold. This reduces the resulting capital gain, if there is one. Alternatively, it increases the capital loss.

When the writer of either a put or a call buys an offsetting option to protect his position, the cost of acquiring that offsetting position is treated as a capital loss.

Knowing how your option strategy will be taxed should be a factor in determining its viability as a strategy.

Short Selling

Short selling, the practice of selling shares you don't own, is speculative, so the proceeds are generally taxed as on income account. This means the profits are fully taxed. Taxpayers can, however, make a 39(4) election with respect to their Canadian securities that will have the effect of treating all their Canadian stock transactions as on capital account. (Unfortunately, there is no similar election for options or foreign securities.) This is a once-in-a-lifetime declaration and there's no going back once you've made it. (This election is not available to traders and dealers.)

Taxes are a can of worms. Short selling trust units, of which ETFs are a kind, results in somewhat different tax treatment than short selling a conventional stock. The party loaning a stock or an ETF to a short seller receives payment to compensate for any lost dividends. With a conventional stock, that payment is taxed as dividend income. With trust units however, that income is taxed as regular income. This may not seem completely reasonable, but not so long ago tax rules were a lot more unbalanced when it came to loaning ETFs. It used to be that the party loaning ETF units was considered to have made a disposition for tax purposes upon making the loan, immediately triggering capital gains or loses. Thankfully, that unfair situation has been rectified.

Tax-Efficient ETFs Ideal for Retirement Compensation Arrangements (RCAs)

"ETFs make absolutely excellent RCA investments," says Gordon Lang, President and CEO with Gordon B. Lang and Associates Inc. RCAs are supplemental pension arrangements for professionals with professional corporations, senior executives, or successful entrepreneurs. They have unusual rules that require 50% of all contributions to be deposited with Ottawa in a "refundable tax account." The other half of the contribution stays in the RCA in investments. All investment income in the RCA account, including realized capital gains, is subject to refundable tax. "Many large companies have all their RCA money invested in T-bills or other short-term assets which are exactly the worst kind of investments to have in one of these accounts," he says. Most RCA assets are held in the plan for a long time and over a 10- to 15-year span he says, "short-term assets are the lowest yielding asset group and the highest taxed."

"I've always looked at the twin objectives of RCA investing to minimize the amount of money in the refundable tax account and to maximize money in the RCA invested account," continues Lang. That would suggest RCA investments should favour assets that do not generate very much taxable income or realized gains. A buy-and-hold style equity mutual fund fits that description as does an equity ETF, but Lang thinks the ETF is by far the preferred investment. "For fairly large amounts, the beauty of ETFs is that they are inexpensive to manage. The management fee is low and the cost of buying them isn't high. And you have a lot less rebalancing or selling of securities." Based upon research conducted by Barclays Canada, U.S.-based ETFs can make a difference of up to 50 basis points in after-tax returns within an RCA.

Few RCA managers, according to Lang, have thought through the implications of short-term fixed income vehicles. "The level of expertise in the RCA market is abysmal," he says. "Most of the liabilities are essentially with respect to final average salary pension plans. The risk there is salary inflation and the best way of meeting that risk is equities. Short-term investment returns bear very little relationship to long-term salary increases and to the liabilities associated with them."

The tax efficiency of many ETFs makes them a good investment for you, too, with or without an RCA.

A Tax Expert Talks about Common Tax Mistakes

Jamie Golombek, Vice President, Tax and Estate Planning with AIM Trimark Investments generously provided this interview. I had the luxury of inserting my own comments after his.

Jamie Golombek: A lot of people overlook constructive tax loss selling. In October and November, investors should look at their portfolio for tax losses, but don't sell an investment just for tax purposes. You should look for something that has not met your target and which you are planning to sell anyway. Think about selling it towards the end of the year instead of selling it a few months later so you can take those losses and apply them against other gains that year, and in particular against any potential capital gains distributions from funds.

This often comes up right at the end of the year, but it's too late to do it at the end of December because you have to start worrying about cut-off dates and settlement dates. We tell investors in October and November to sit down with their advisor, review their entire portfolio, and make a decision as to whether this is the right time to sell something that's under water.

Howard Atkinson: It's best not to leave tax loss selling to the very end of the year for another reason, too. The November to April span is a seasonally strong period in the market, so tax loss selling should generally be done in October.

JG: To help in tax planning, AIM Trimark generally provides financial advisors with a list of estimated distributions four to six weeks in advance of fund distributions. We even post them on our web site so advisors can help their clients plan for them.

HA: That's a valuable service for investors and helps in their tax planning. ETF providers also generate capital gains distribution estimates well ahead of the distribution date. And for those who might want to manage their tax bill by trading around fund distributions, ETFs allow this more easily than mutual funds because the trades occur in real time with real time prices.

If you are a conscientious asset allocator, the last thing you want to do is sell to avoid a distribution or for the tax loss and be without that asset exposure. Like Murphy's Law, that's the time the class will go up in value. In 2001, Nortel scooted up 90% from its low in September to its high in December. If you'd sold it for a tax loss, you'd have missed out on that bounce or had to buy it back 31 days later at a higher price.

I suggest keeping asset class exposure in these cases, so the Canadian Information Technology Index Fund ETF (XIT) would have been a good proxy. Of course, if an investment no longer fits your objectives then you don't need to replace it, but if you do replace it, do so right away because of seasonality considerations.

Switching into an ETF allows you to keep your asset class exposure without running afoul of the superficial loss rules provided you sit it out for 31 days, and so long as the original security doesn't hold the same index as the ETF.

JG: A lot of people try to save money by doing their tax returns themselves. I don't think that's a bad idea so people can learn how taxes work. Nevertheless, it's a good idea every few years to pay an accountant to review your tax return. Unless you work in the area, you may be missing opportunities, simple things.

Suppose you've sold some stock this year and you have a lot of gains, and you're also making large charitable donations. An accountant would say, "Wait a minute, shouldn't we be donating stock to the charity? You'll save yourself half the capital gains tax."

HA: That's a very good point. I believe accountants' fees are low as a percentage of what they can save you. You've only got three years to carry back capital losses and if you lose out on claiming them then, you've lost recouping capital gains tax paid in the past. (Losses can be carried forward indefinitely, however.)

JG: Investors are getting a big refund every year because of their RRSP contributions. An accountant would likely suggest you reduce your withholding tax from your paycheque instead.

HA: You get a reduction in tax withholdings when you show CRA you are contributing the money to an RRSP. Unfortunately, ETFs aren't a good vehicle for periodic investments. For that, mutual funds are better.

JG: On seeing both a husband and wife's tax returns, an accountant might have a few suggestions, too. Suppose the wife is working full time and the husband is at home looking after the kids. What a great opportunity for an income-splitting spousal loan. These are very simple ideas that can be introduced with a review of investors' tax returns.

HA: I once heard an accountant say that for most investors, the only thing you can do legally to mitigate taxes is to deduct, divide, and defer. The three "Ds" he called them. Deduct the maximum allowable expenses, divide the income by income splitting as best you can, and defer paying taxes for as long as possible. One of the ways to defer tax is to avoid realizing your capital gains every year. ETFs are particularly good at letting you control your capital gains.

JG: A lot of people are using the tax planning guise "Oh, They'll Never Find Out," when it comes to foreign holdings. That's not tax planning, that's tax evasion. And the CRA has innocent ways to find out. All Canadians have to report and pay tax on their worldwide income and the penalties are very severe if you don't.

HA: That's something investors holding U.S.-based ETFs may not be completely aware of. Canadians must report specified foreign assets with a total cost over C$100,000 at any time during the year. This includes shares of foreign corporations, including U.S.-based ETFs.

April 29, 2005

Notes

1) Being held on capital account is opposed to being on income account. It means that only 50% of capital gains would be taxed and 50% of losses would be deductible. When investments are held on income account there is no break for capital gains.

2) The Canadian rules on capital gains distributions from RICs say an investor who receives a distribution from a U.S. trust will be taxed on the amount of the distribution that represents income of the trust, as calculated under Canadian tax rules. Since some U.S. ETFs are trusts, this might have you thinking you can ignore 50% of the capital gains income from a U.S.-based ETF trust. Problem is, as an investor you can't know how the ETF's capital gain was calculated in the first place and so can't know positively how much of that distribution to include in your income. The two countries have different ways of calculating capital gains. The practical upshot of this is that ETF investors in Canada are not safe in assuming they can discount the U.S. capital gain by 50%. If you do and get questioned by CRA, the burden of proof is on you and since there's no way to determine how the U.S. gain was arrived at, CRA wins by default. Furthermore, this rule doesn't apply to ETFs that are corporations, in which case all the distributions are included fully in income anyway. (All the MSCI iShares series are structured as corporations.)

3) Superficial loss rules are a little more complicated than just the 30-day rule. Neither you, your spouse, your corporation, nor other affiliated people can buy the asset, or an identical asset, within 30 days before or after your sale of it. This turns out to be a big problem for mutual funds that sell parts of their holdings at a loss but, because they still retain part of the (larger) position, cannot claim the capital loss.

4) Thanks to Paul Mazzilli, Executive Director and Director of Exchange Traded Funds Research at Morgan Stanley in New York, who wrote about this strategy in "ETF Strategy Guide," July 2001 put out by Morgan Stanley Equity Research Department.

5) For a full discussion of income vs. capital accounts, see CRA's Interpretation Bulletin IT479R. You can find this at *www.gov.ca*. Go to CRA and search on "Transactions in Securities."

Part Three

Where ETFs Came from and
Where They Are Going

Chapter Seven

Lifting the Hood: How ETFs Work

Remember when Japanese cars suddenly made North American cars look like gas-sucking tanks? ETFs are revving up to do the same thing to the mutual fund industry—but don't anticipate a rollicking demolition derby because fund companies will respond with innovations of their own. To have the best chance of understanding future new fund products, it's a good idea to know the inner workings of today's innovations. Here we'll lift the hood to look at some detailed issues affecting ETFs. They're not inherently complicated, but you do have to get close to the oil to understand their finer points. We'll show you how you can know you are getting a fair price for an ETF, how distributions are treated, how dividend payments and other sources of cash work inside an ETF, and the differences between American and Canadian ETFs. We'll also discuss what happens when an ETF is closed down, a circumstance that has befallen a few unpopular ETFs. Finally, we'll explore the interesting but little-known hazards of index construction as it affects ETFs. For those not mechanically inclined, feel free to skip to the next chapter.

Are You Getting a Fair Price?

The value of an ETF unit is initially set as a fixed percentage of the underlying index. For i60 units, it's one-tenth the S&P/TSX 60 index. (For iUnits sector funds, it's one-quarter the index value; TD's Composite and Capped Composite ETFs are one-three-hundredth.) Thus, when the 60 index is at 520, an i60 should be around $52. Of course, that would be way too easy. Dividends and other sources of cash (which do not get reinvested) also have to be factored into the unit price.

Barclays Canada's web site says, "The trading price of an ETF is approximately equal to the trading value of the underlying securities held in the fund plus any undistributed net income." This is correct as far as it goes, but unless you know what that undistributed net income is, you can't calculate the net asset value (NAV) for yourself. And it's important that you know this, otherwise you can't determine if you are buying an ETF at a fair price, which means one that is close to NAV. (The price of most ETFs track their respective NAVs well most of the time, but it's prudent to check.)

Undistributed net income is made up of the estimated cash amount per unit and something known as a "distribution price adjustment." The estimated cash amount is a tally of dividends received by the fund but not yet declared as distributions. The distribution price adjustment reflects an amount per unit declared as distributions (and therefore deducted from the NAV) but not yet paid to unitholders. Usually the distribution price adjustment will be zero since there are just a few days every quarter between the declaration of distributions with ETFs and their payout to unitholders.

To figure out how much you should be paying for an ETF, here's a formula you can use to get a close approximation:[1]

Current index value + estimated cash amount per unit + distribution price adjustment = NAV
   (divisor)

The divisor is the ETF's fraction of the index. In the i60's case, the divisor would be one-tenth. Canadian ETF sponsors publish what's called "the core asset value per unit," which is the first part of the NAV equation; i.e. the current index value divided by the index divisor. This number is calculated based on the previous trading day closing value and is not to be mistaken for a current value.

The estimated cash amount is also published at the end of each trading day by the ETF sponsor and so is an estimate done one day in advance. The distribution price adjustment per unit is also provided by the ETF sponsor.

For iUnits, you can find these numbers on Barclays Canada's web site, *www.iunits.com*; click "Broker/Dealer" for daily fund values/baskets. Barclays Canada, the sponsor of the iUnits, updates the NAV for all their Canadian ETFs daily on their site so you don't have to do the calculation yourself. TD Asset Management's site, *www.tdassetmanagement.com*, also gives a NAV value per unit as of the close of the previous day's market and how that changed from the last daily close. They also report an estimated cash amount and a distribution price adjustment.

Things are a lot easier for savvy ETF investors in the United States. The American Stock Exchange, where the majority of ETFs trade, broadcasts every scintilla of information you would ever want to know about their listed ETF through seven ticker symbols per ETF. (To find these ticker symbols go to *www.amextrader.com*, "ETF data," click on the desired ETF and then its tear sheet.)

These are the seven ticker symbols for S&P Depositary Receipts (SPDRs):

Ticker Symbols for SPDRs (fig. 43)

SPY	Trading Symbol	SPX	Underlying Index Trading Symbol
SXV	Intraday Value	SXV.SO	Shares Outstanding
SXV.NV	Net Asset Value	SXV.EU	Estimated Cash Amount
		SXV.TC	Total Cash Component

Source: www.amextrader.com

Two of these symbols reflect real time values, but most of them reflect one-day-old values. The market value for SPY is quoted in real time, and is the trading price for one Spider share. The "intraday value" is more fully known as the "intraday indicative value" and is the estimated value of the underlying portfolio calculated every 15 seconds. With this and the estimated cash its amount for the entire portfolio divided by the index divisor, it's easy to see how much of a premium or discount the market price represents per share.

The "net asset value" (SXV.NV) is as of the close of the previous trading day and is computed per share. It includes the value of the underlying securities plus portfolio, cash, accrued dividends but minus accumulated expenses. The figure for "shares outstanding" (SXV.SO) is also as of the end of the previous day. The "estimated cash amount" (SXV.EU) is, as its name implies, an estimate for the current day based on the actual cash holdings in the fund at the close of the previous day.

Ticker Symbols for DIAMONDS (fig. 44)

DIA	Trading Symbol	INDU	Underlying Index Trading Symbol
DXV	Intraday Value	DXV.SO	Shares Outstanding
DXV.NV	Net Asset Value	DXV.EU	Estimated Cash Amount
		DXV.TC	Total Cash Component

Source: www.amextrader.com

Ticker Symbols for Qubes (fig. 45)

QQQQ	Trading Symbol	IXNDX	Underlying Index Trading Symbol
QXV	Intraday Value	QQQQS	Shares Outstanding
QQQQN	Net Asset Value	QQQQM	Estimated Cash Amount
		QQQQT	Total Cash Amount Per Creation Unit

Source: www.nasdaq.com

All ETFs listed on AMEX have a similar but not necessarily identical symbol scheme. Check out AMEX's ETF screener and a total return calculator on their web site, *www.amex.com*.

Having this information available by ticker symbol makes it easy and straightforward to get timely information about the financial underpinnings of an ETF. You can find all seven ticker symbols associated with the 100-plus ETFs listed on AMEX *www.amextrader.com*.

Shockingly, many Canadian brokers don't have access to these ancillary ETF ticker quotes because it is an election on their data service which costs money. Don't be surprised if even your full service fellow charging you $50 a trade doesn't get these tickers without going through the same steps as you.

The values for the ticker symbols calculated daily are cranked out Monday through Friday around 4 p.m. in New York. As it happens, a number of ETFs trade until 4:15 p.m. New York time, but rather than getting a sharper price at the end of the trading day, the spread between bid and ask widens at the end of the day and at the beginning of the morning until the most recent numbers are digested. If you're going to buy an ETF, it's often best to avoid those periods.

Some ETFs Trade Later in the Day Than Others

Many U.S.-based ETFs trade 15 minutes after the close of the regular market.

Here's a list of the ETFs that have extended trading from 9:30 to 4:15 p.m. New York time:

• All broad-market ETFs (except streetTRACKS DJ funds)
• iShares Sector Index Funds
• iShares MSCI EAFE, S&P Latin America 40, Europe 350, TOPIX 150.

All other ETFs stop trading at 4:00 p.m. Eastern Standard Time.

Liquidity

Liquidity is the ease with which an investment can be bought and sold without substantially affecting the market price of the investment. Trading volume is a good indication of liquidity. The more a stock trades, the more liquid it is. Typically, the more liquid an investment, the narrower the spread between the bid and ask price. ETFs with big assets are highly liquid—like the i60s, Qubes, Diamonds, SPDRs, the S&P 500 iShares, the Russell iShares series, and the S&P mid and small cap series. In general, broad market ETFs trade swiftly and frequently and are widely held.

Liquidity might appear to be a concern with lightly traded ETFs such as streetTRACKS Dow Jones STOXX50, with an average daily trading volume of less than 6,000 shares. Some country iShares also have low volumes like the iShares MSCI Netherlands ETF with $45 million in assets and only 19,000 shares traded on average a day.[2] Normally, such thin trading volumes would pose a problem for an institution wanting, say, to move 10,000 or more shares. Spreads can widen in these circumstances but remember that ETF prices are ultimately tied to the value of the underlying securities. As long as these securities are liquid and the arbitrage mechanism is not impeded, the price of even a thinly traded ETF should stay fairly resonant with the NAV. Even if the ETF itself is not a model of liquidity, the liquidity of the underlying portfolio should prevent excessive price discrepancies. According to an ETF report put out by Goldman Sachs Derivative & Trading Research "the dollar volume of the trading activity in the underlying stocks is more significant in assessing liquidity than the dollar volume of the ETF."[3]

How Is Cash Handled?

You might wonder how cash can get so plentiful in an ETF portfolio that you must take it into account in order to make sense of an ETF's price. After all, isn't one of the reasons ETFs are superior to mutual funds because they have so little cash? Well, yes, ETFs still have a lot less cash proportionally than most mutual funds because they don't have to deal with redemptions in cash or cash influxes waiting to be invested. ETFs strive to be investment rich but cash poor—and try as they may, they still have some pesky cash hanging around.

ETFs get cash from a few sources. First, their underlying stocks generate dividends. Most ETFs pay out their dividends quarterly and their capital gains annually, but between payouts, the dividend income must be mopped up somehow. Canadian equity ETFs don't reinvest the dividend income they receive into the underlying securities. Instead, they put that money into a separate account. That account generates interest income which helps to pay the fund's expenses. As a result, Canadian equity ETFs don't generally distribute interest income—only dividend income and capital gains which are taxed more lightly than interest income.

Cash can sometimes arise from the creation of new ETF units between dividend quarters. The creation of new ETF units requires three things:

the basket of securities to make up the ETF; cash for dividends already received on those securities; and cash equal to the value of any accrued dividends. The cash received in this process gives rise to a return of capital at a future distribution.

Fixed income ETFs will have regular interest income. Cash within the Canadian bond ETF, the iG5, is distributed semi-annually as interest income when it is received. (That ETF holds only one Government of Canada bond at any one time.) The other Canadian bond ETF, the iBond Fund, pays out interest quarterly. Interest income received by the fully RRSP eligible i500Rs, on the other hand, is reinvested into the fund.

Because these are pretty street-wise critters, ETFs also scarf a few dollars from lending their securities to short sellers. This was a source of income for TIPS, the i60's predecessor, and TIPS' exemption from the general prohibition for funds against lending securities was passed on to the i60s. In early 2001, regulators changed the rules to permit all mutual fund trusts to lend their securities. Now all Canadian ETFs, and mutual funds that are structured as trusts, can lend out their own securities and charge a fee for doing so.

Canadian vs. U.S. ETF Structure

The legal structure of investments may seem like a pretty arcane thing, but these legal differences can make a difference to your costs and ultimate returns. All ETFs in Canada are now structured as mutual fund trusts, so they all must conform to the same rules and labour under the same restrictions. Their U.S. counterparts, however, come in a few legal varieties and this structure makes a difference in how they treat their dividend income, whether or not they can lend securities, and how they are permitted to track the index.

Exchange Traded Unit Investment Trusts

The oldest ETFs, SPDRs, Diamonds, Qubes, and the S&P 400 Mid-Cap Spiders, are exchange traded unit investment trusts (UITs). With the UIT structure, dividends and income are not reinvested, the underlying securities cannot be lent, and the index must be replicated. Optimization is not permitted. BLDRs, the NYSE's basket of ADRs, is also of this structure.

Exchange Traded Open-End Index Mutual Fund

This more contemporary structure permits the funds to reinvest dividend income the moment it is received, and it gives the funds the flexibility to optimize their index strategy if they so desire. Lending securities is also permitted, so this is by far a more flexible structure for ETFs. Sector Select Spiders, all iShares (except Gold), StreetTRACKS ETFs (except Gold), VIPERs, Powershares ETFs, Rydex ETFs, and Fidelity ETFs are exchange traded, open-end index mutual funds.

Both ETF structures distribute dividends and capital gains, so there is no tax treatment difference between the different legal structures for a U.S. resident. There's no difference in tax treatment between these structures for Canadian residents either; unfortunately, all U.S. ETF distributions are treated as ordinary income by Canadian tax collectors, unless you can provide a capital gains distribution breakdown acceptable to CRA.

Exchange Traded Grantor Trust

This is a restrictive legal structure that does not permit dividend reinvestment, securities lending, or the use of derivatives. This structure is used by the two ETFs that hold actual, physical gold. It is likely that any future ETFs that hold actual commodities will also be grantor trusts. HOLDRS are also grantor trusts. (See the end of this chapter for an explanation and discussion of HOLDRS). In this structure, all income is paid directly to shareholders.

Structure Comparison of ETFs (fig. 46)

Characteristics	Exchange Traded Open-End Index Mutual Fund (U.S.)	Exchange Traded Unit Investment Trust (U.S.)	Exchange Traded Grantor Trust (U.S.)	Exchange Traded Mutual Fund Trust (Cdn.)
Dividends	reinvested until quarterly distribution	not reinvested	paid directly	not reinvested when received
Index strategy	may optimize	replication only	cap-weighted basket	may optimize
Loan securities	yes	no	no	yes
Derivatives	may use	may not use	may not use	may use
Funds	iShares, StreetTRACKS, Sector SPDRS Rydex, VIPERs Powershares Fidelity ETFs	SPDRS 400 SPDRS, Diamonds, Qubes BLDRs	HOLDRS streetTRACKS Gold iShares Gold	iUnits, TD ETFs

Source: Morgan Stanley Equity Research for U.S. ETFs, author for Canadian ETFs.

The Canadian ETF Structure

ETFs in Canada are structured as mutual fund trusts. A trust preserves the tax characteristics of its income and passes it on to the unitholders. So when a Canadian ETF issues a distribution, it lands in investors' hands as dividend, interest or capital gains with their respective tax treatments. This structure permits the manager to optimize an index if desired. Mutual fund trusts are permitted to loan securities

Dividends and Capital Gains Distributions

The current crop of Canadian-based equity ETFs distribute their dividends quarterly and their capital gains annually in December. The iUnits 5-year government bond fund (iG5) distributes interest income semi-annually and capital gains income annually in December. The iUnits bond fund that tracks the Scotia Capital Universe Bond Index (iBond) distributes income quarterly and capital gains in December.

ETF quarterly distributions are made in cash to unitholders. If you find those quarterly cheques a nuisance, ask your brokerage about a dividend re-investment plan. TD Waterhouse and the full-service and discount arms of RBC and CIBC offer dividend reinvestment plans for some iUnits and the more popular U.S. ETFs. Canadian ShareOwner Investments Inc. has dividend reinvestment plans and low cost purchase programs on all iUnits and several U.S. ETFs. With more requests, others will certainly follow. Dividend reinvestment programs save you a commission and allow you to keep your money tracking the total return index.

Capital gains generated from the ETF's own internal buying and selling are distributed in the form of additional units of the ETF at the end of each year, but only for an instant. In December, an ETF with a capital gain distribution will issue more units of itself in an amount equal to the value of the capital gain distribution. When this distribution "in-kind" happens, more units are created but the underlying value of the assets remains unchanged. This means that the price of all the ETF units must go down so that when all the units are added up, the total value of all the units still equals the original net asset value. For an instant, you own more units at a fractionally lower price. You'll note that this is exactly what happens with conventional mutual funds when they make a distribution: the units are increased by the amount of the distribution but the value of all the units is decreased by the amount of the distribution. There is no change in the value of your total holdings.

The difference with an ETF, though, is that it immediately "consolidates" all its outstanding shares, knocks the number of units back down to the pre-distribution number, and boosts the unit price back to its pre-distribution level. After this, you are left with an unchanged number of shares at the pre-dividend price, but with a higher adjusted cost base. The value and number of your units hasn't changed, but the fund has passed on to you a capital gains tax liability in proportion to the distribution. The good news is that your adjusted cost base increases by the amount of the capital gains distribution, so when you subsequently sell your ETF your ultimate capital gain will be less than it would have been without receiving the dividends.

Remember, you are still required to pay tax on this capital gains distribution even though you received it in-kind temporarily, in the form of increased units. The unit consolidation is done so investors aren't left with fractions and odd numbers of shares from distributions. (While you can sell 103 units, it's quite impossible to sell 103.33 shares on a stock exchange.) More importantly, the ETF's divisor would be thrown off if the number of ETF units increased while the share value dropped.

The capital gains distribution and consolidation confuses many investors and advisors. The fund is no richer or better off when it has realized a gain—it has simply generated a tax liability. Think of a situation where you invested $50,000 in a stock. It goes up to $100,000 and you sell it. You had $100,000 on paper, now you have $100,000 in cash. You are no richer than before you made the sale but suddenly you owe tax on that $50,000 of capital gain. When these realized gains are distributed by an ETF, there isn't any new wealth in the fund to be passed on to unitholders. The distribution just passes on the tax liability of this realized gain. That is why the price and the number of units doesn't ultimately change.

Distributions with a traditional fund give you additional units but the price of all the units goes down by exactly the amount of the dividend, so you're not really any better off than you were before. The value of your investment is the same even though you own more units. That's not much different from what an ETF distribution achieves. In both cases, when the dust settles, the only thing that's happened is that the value of your holdings are unchanged, but the fund's liability for capital gains tax has been flowed through to unitholders.

Distributions from U.S.-based ETFs to Canadian residents are most practically treated as income and are therefore taxed at your highest marginal tax rate. (See Chapter Six for an explanation of this.) Distributions from Canadian-based ETFs are more tax-advantaged because they retain their tax character as dividends or capital gains.

The frequency of U.S.-based ETF distributions is not as easy to remember as Canadian distribution schedules. To date, all fixed income ETFs in the U.S. distribute income monthly. That's easy, but equity ETFs in the U.S. distribute dividends annually or quarterly. VIPERs, for instance, distribute annually except for broad market and large cap VIPERs which go for quarterly distributions. All ETFs distribute capital gains annually and, thankfully, these are usually modest.

Index Construction, Free Floats

Putting together an index may not seem like a tough job. Take the stocks of 100 companies with the largest market capitalization on a stock exchange and there, you've got an index. The bigger a company's capitalization, the greater that company's influence on the index. What could be more straightforward? But take a look at some of the listed securities excluded from the Russell U.S. indices:

• foreign stocks and non-U.S. incorporated stocks, ADRs
• closed-end funds
• limited partnerships
• royalty trusts
• stocks trading below $1.00
• preferred shares

Source: www.russell.com/US/Indexes/US/Methodology.asp

That's a fair number of dance partners ruled out before the music even starts, but in this big ballroom every move counts and each discrimination happens for a reason.

Indices are constructed with some primary goals. First, an index should be an accurate representation of a market or market segment, otherwise its fluctuations don't mean very much. Secondly, an index should be investable. In other words, index investors should be able to reproduce the index easily by buying its components. This is where some foreign indices fall short. A company may have a very large market capitalization, but when few of the shares are available for trading, it becomes difficult to reproduce the index. This can happen when a company holds many of its own shares or the shares of another company also on the index. Foreign ownership restrictions on stock purchases imposed by some countries further reduces the investability of an index, as does major stock holdings by controlling shareholders, company management, or governments.

Most index sponsors have addressed this issue by designing indices and their weightings based on the "free float" of a company's stock available to investors instead of being based on total market capitalization. (The TSX was one of the first index sponsors to adjust their index to free float when they introduced the TSE 300 in 1977.)

Morgan Stanley Capital International, the world's top provider of global stock indices, completed converting all its indices to free float adjusted in June 2002. This process dislodged so many stocks included in major indices that the conversion was done in stages to minimize disruption to the markets.

About the same time Morgan Stanley was transitioning to free float, MSCI aimed to increase the number of companies their indices include in each market to give their indices a more accurate representation of those markets. The changes make MSCI indices more meaningful benchmarks for investors, but global fund managers are not doing pirouettes in delight: these changes fixed some formerly notoriously easy to beat indices, such as the MCSI EAFE Index.

Even the granddaddy of liquidity itself, the S&P 500, is transitioning to free-float in stages to minimize the disruption. When this is complete in September 2005, S&P will have converted all its indices to free float.

The free float issue isn't as quite as simple as it may seem because market representation and liquidity are frequently a trade-off. This often necessitates degrees of compliance with free float ideals and the Canadian market is a good example of this. S&P disregarded ownership restrictions in its index construction for Canada's market for a long time. It was thought that Canadian restrictions on foreign ownership of media and communication companies, airlines and financial institutions would leave a Canadian index with too few companies to be representative of the market. The belief was that optimal Canadian market representation requires the inclusion of many companies on which the government has imposed foreign ownership restrictions. S&P's domestic Canadian indices opted for the best representation rather than for perfect foreign liquidity. Now S&P does a float adjustment when 20% or more of a Canadian company's outstanding shares have purchasing restrictions. Twenty percent is a high threshold for float adjustments.

The Dow Jones people, at least for the purposes of their global index, do their market cap calculations based on free float. Their free float calculations take into account block holdings of 5% or more. This is a common threshold, but still not without its issues. Consider a country such as Japan, which has many small block holdings under 5%. The Dow Jones' free float will not be sensitive enough to adjust for that.

Index construction has other issues, too. Just what kind of shares should be in an index? Exchangeable shares (shares that can be exchanged for another security either in the same company or in another company), were removed from all S&P Canadian indices. Multi-class shares were another sore spot. Some companies, like Bombardier for instance, have different classes of shares independently listed on different indices. Bombardier B was in the S&P/TSE 60 index and Bombardier A was in the S&P/TSE small cap index, but Bombardier itself is a large cap company. With Bombardier and other dual class companies like it, S&P amalgamated the classes into the largest, most liquid class and determined into which index that class should be put. The thinking is that companies rather than securities should be in an index. But again, there is pressure to be reflective of the market. With so many income trusts in Canada, S&P seems resigned to including these securities into their Canadian indices, which may happen by the end of 2005.

No doubt there will be other refinements to indices as time goes on and their uses become more diverse. "Fifteen or twenty years ago, indices were mainly used to measure markets. Today, more and more, you are seeing indices with products associated with them—derivatives and ETFs," says Glen Doody, a vice president with Standard & Poor's in Hong Kong.

For investors, knowing something about the problems involved in constructing an index puts their performance—and those of a fund manger—in perspective. All the financial sophistication in the world has yet to make it a science.

What Happens When ETFs Close Down?

When ETFs fail to gain significant assets they may be withdrawn from the market by their sponsors. One Canadian-based ETF was withdrawn in late 2002, SSgA Dow Jones Canada Titans 40. This State Street Global Advisor's ETF was withdrawn even though that product had the lowest MER of any Canadian ETF, a noteworthy 0.08%.

Perhaps the unpopularity of the underlying index was to blame for this product's poor acceptance, as the Dow Jones Canada Titans 40 Index didn't have much of a following institutionally or with retail investors.

When an ETF is withdrawn from the market, shareholders are first notified of the impending closure. The fund sponsor sets a date for trading to stop and a deadline is given for the units to be redeemed. All investors still holding units or shares in the ETF at that time must redeem their holdings, but no brokerage fees or redemption charges of any kind are imposed. That at least saves you the expense of a brokerage commission to sell the fund before it wraps up.

Don't worry about getting fair value for your ETF when it is wound down. Because the fund is liquidated for its net asset value (minus some small expenses) neither much of a premium nor a discount to NAV is likely so investors should not face a loss or a profit just because the fund is closing. Investors are given cash in proportion to their ownership interest in the fund. Institutions and others with holdings of 50,000 units or more can redeem their units for the underlying stocks.

Record Keeping

Here's a run down of some of the administrivia for ETFs—tax slips, certificates, and shareholder communication.

One of the big reasons ETFs have such low MERs is because they use the established facilities of brokerages to provide the monthly statements for investors and the tax reporting. The brokerage that holds your ETF will issue you a T-3 slip, not the ETF sponsor company. This arrangement uses to advantage an already established big, efficient distribution system.

One thing neither a sponsor nor a brokerage will do, however, is issue a certificate for an ETF. Even though ETFs have many stock-like qualities, they don't come in certificate form. No ETF will issue a certificate. Your ownership in an ETF is tracked on an electronic book-based system coordinated through the transfer agent. So don't look to tuck an ETF stock certificate into a safety deposit box or surrender a stock certificate as collateral for a loan, though they can still be used as collateral.

As for shareholder communication, you may be heartened to know that ETFs don't flood you with shareholder mailings for the underlying securities. Retail investors receive shareholder information for the ETF itself and have voting rights only with respect to the business of the ETF, not its underlying securities, similar to any conventional mutual fund. Investors with positions of 50,000 units or more of an ETF, typically institutional investors, do have voting rights on the underlying securities.

Smelling the oil yet? Understanding some of the issues in index construction and maintenance will help you choose the right index to track with an ETF. You'll find a complete list of the indices that have ETFs associated with them in Appendix B. There you'll also find mention of how the indices are constructed and run.

Before you turn back there, take a few minutes in the next chapter to review the history of ETFs, where they came from and why. It's been said that history repeats itself. Who knows, but maybe some of the failed products that came before ETFs might find the time is finally ripe to reassert themselves. In the next chapter, too, you'll find some predictions about what's next on the scene in exchange traded funds. Meanwhile, here's a preview of some important Canadian index considerations from one of Canada's leading experts on indices.

Canada's Most Momentous Index Change

Steve Rive, Vice President, Canadian Index Services, runs the Canadian index services for Standard & Poor's and is also responsible for S&P listed products globally, which include futures, options, and ETFs linked to S&P indices. He talked about important recent index developments—including the decision to add income trusts to Canada's composite index in September 2005.

Adding income trusts to the S&P/TSX Composite is the biggest Canadian index event ever. Why did S&P decide to do this and what will be the result?

Total market cap today includes only equities. You've got 8 or 9% of market cap out there in income trusts. From the perspective of running the index, we don't confer index worthiness on any particular type of security. It's the market that does that. We were concerned about representativeness, particularly in certain sectors such as energy and real estate. If you look only at stocks, there's almost no real estate sector because we're down to one name now. The energy sector was eroding away from us. We weren't covering the investment opportunities in these sectors, which are mostly in the form of income trusts now.

Including income trusts will add roughly 9% to the market cap of the composite. This is a very significant chunk of the market to be adding. In terms of numbers, it would take us back up to almost 300 securities again. The former TSX 300 composite was always fixed at 300 stocks. Three years ago we moved to a new approach whereby we took any number of stocks that met our criteria. That brought us down to about 220. Now we're getting back to around 270 with income trusts. From the number of names and dollar value, it clearly has a big impact on the index.

There was a lot of debate back and forth on income trusts. The challenge we faced here was that there are investors who don't want to invest in income trusts for various reasons. If someone says they're not going to invest in income trusts, then an index that includes income trusts wouldn't be investable. On the other hand, a lot of people like income trusts because they like the idea that management has to come back to market with a plan in order to spend money on new ventures.

We're always looking at a trade-off between representativeness and investability. If you ignored investability and only looked at representativeness, you'd probably include a lot of companies that are too small or illiquid to trade. Going too far on the investability side, then you might not be as representative as you should be.

We concluded that we would add trusts to the composite because we felt on balance there was enough investor interest to do so. In particular, since retail investors have most embraced income trusts, and the Composite is the most visible for retail investors, we thought that's really their benchmark and we ought to be including income trusts. At the same time, we made the commitment that we would continue to offer an equity-only index so there wouldn't be any disruption for somebody who wanted to track the equity-only index.

What are the latest indexing trends?

People are looking for the next frontier. The broad representative indexes are all well established. There are ETFs on them and they've attracted a lot of assets. So people are looking at alternatives to the classic market cap–weighted index. A good example of this is the S&P 500 equalweight index. As soon as you move away from a market weighted index, you're implementing a kind of active strategy, a rules-based active strategy. The equalweight index gives a higher weight to small stocks, so when smaller stocks are outperforming you've got an opportunity to get better returns. Growth and value indices are another example of this rules-based strategy.

Also there's increasing effort to bring in alternative asset classes. The two new gold ETFs in the U.S. are examples of this. People are looking to put currency and other commodities into an ETF package.

What are the big global developments with ETFs?

The biggest development was the launch of options on Spiders in January and February of this year. Those are trading very heavily now. The presence of derivatives linked to an ETF offers a good additional opportunity for hedging and greater flexibility because it gives you the possibility of classic stock option strategies, like being long an ETF and writing options against it to generate additional income. That was the big break through event of this year.

May 12, 2005

Notes

1) For the precise calculation method, visit *iunits.com* then go to "broker/dealer."

2) Data on assets and trading volume as of February 10, 2005 as reported in Morgan Stanley Equity Research, North America, "Exchange Traded Funds, Industry Overview," p. 6.

3) June 29, 2001.

Chapter Eight

The Past and Future of ETFs

Modern Portfolio Theory and the Efficient Markets Hypothesis together were the intellectual underpinnings of indexing, but indexing as an investment strategy wouldn't have been practical in real life without the technology to make trading a list of stocks all at once possible. In the late 1970s, institutions started taking advantage of new electronic order delivery systems on the NYSE and AMEX that allowed them to trade groups of shares effectively as a single basket. "Program trading" got its name from the computer programs that were designed to generate lists of stocks to be transacted through the electronic order delivery system. The new electronic system made it possible for a large number of different stocks to be bought or sold more or less simultaneously for a fixed commission, and so virtual basket trades began.

Then in 1982, the Chicago Mercantile Exchange introduced an index future on the S&P 500 that proved hugely popular because it was a more efficient way to effectively trade a whole index.[1] A future is a contract promising to buy or sell a stock, commodity, index, or other instrument, at a specified price at a set time in the future. An index future is a contract that pays you the cash equivalent of the value of the market at a set time in the future. By buying a contract that promises to pay you the cash value of an index in the future, it is as though you have bought all the stocks in the index, but all you've actually purchased is a contract.

Index futures revolutionized portfolio management. Trading index futures was a pretty good proxy for buying and selling all the stocks in an index, and an improvement over doing just that. Futures contracts were dirt cheap to trade and quickly became highly liquid.

Program trading and a heavy use of index futures were the main working parts in something known as portfolio insurance that prospered from

1982 to the market crash in October 1987, and which some have blamed for the crash itself.[2] Two finance professors at Berkeley, Hayne Leland and Mark Rubinstein, developed software in the late 1970s that was designed to control the risk of an entire portfolio. Their program calculated how much the equity component of a portfolio could go down relative to its cash position before the whole portfolio fell below a specified bottom. When stocks were going down, the software dictated how much money had to be stripped from stocks and plowed into cash. When stocks were going up, more money was taken from cash in favour of equities. Applying this program trading with S&P 500 index futures gave them a dynamic strategy to control the risk of an entire portfolio. By 1986, the professors' company, Leland, O'Brien, Rubinstein Associates, Inc. (LOR) was managing US$60 billion either directly or through software licensing agreements.

"Our computer models worked right on target. It was a really reliable product," said Rubinstein in an interview for this book. "Our simulations showed that even through the Great Depression that would have disturbed us a little bit. ...[B]ut the results might have been acceptable, and in almost all the rest of the time it works like a charm."

The charm lasted until October 19, 1987. That day the market fell so fast and furiously that portfolio insurers couldn't liquidate their positions swiftly enough to protect against losses. The market dropped 20% that dark day, and according to Rubinstein, 20% of the sales of stocks and index futures that day were from portfolio insurers who would have sold more if they could have—making it all that much harder for the market to stagger back to its feet.

Regulators had not been impressed with the resilience of futures under stress, so the SEC encouraged the development of low-cost equity basket-type products not associated with the futures market.

Index Participation Shares

After Black Monday, a number of equity basket products started being developed in parallel. The first of these was Index Participation Shares (IPS), which came in a few varieties. The most popular was AMEX's "Equity Index Participations," based on the S&P 500 Index. IPS were simply stocks that paid returns linked directly to the underlying index. They could be sold on the secondary market or redeemed for cash—but not for the underlying securities because there weren't any securities behind them. IPS were a claim on the return of a futures contract on the S&P index. The first IPS started trading in May 1989. Not long after, a Chicago court ruled that IPS were actually futures and should trade on a futures exchange and be under the jurisdiction of the Commodity Futures Trading Commission. No futures exchange picked up the innovative product, possibly because they didn't want it competing with their own index futures, and IPS died.[3]

SuperTrust

Meanwhile, Leland, O'Brien, and Rubinstein were hatching a different portfolio product. In 1988, they made an application to the SEC for something they called a SuperTrust that was to hold a basket of securities identical to the S&P 500 index. It was a complicated product containing SuperShares and SuperUnits. It took LOR five years to painfully maneuver their product through the SEC. By the time it emerged, AMEX was just a few months short of launching its own portfolio product which turned out to be kryptonite for SuperTrust.[4]

Despite having the biggest launch in the history of any fund product to that point (US$2 billion), SuperTrust failed in good part because it was too complicated. AMEX's elegantly simple product, the famous SPDRs, made it to the market three months after SuperUnits, in January 1993, and completely eclipsed LOR's regulatory groundbreaking product—the very first exchange traded fund proper.[5]

TIPS

The demise of IPS in the U.S. was something of a stroke of good fortune for Canada because the Toronto Stock Exchange had an IPS of its own in the making. In March 1990, the TSE conducted the first trade on TIPS, Toronto 35 Index Participation Units, based on the Toronto 35 Index, a collection of Canada's biggest and most liquid companies with wide industry representation. Unlike the American IPS, however, TIPS was a trust containing a basket of securities matching the Toronto 35 Index. The trust issued units as a claim on the trust. These units could be bought or sold on the TSX or in sufficiently large numbers, redeemed for the underlying securities in the trust. TIPS was immediately embraced by institutional investors and went on to popularity even among retail investors. So, by some odd reversal of our usual national fortune, the TSX launched a world first—the first successful ETF.

According to Gord Walker, Director of Derivatives, Markets and Marketing at the TSX from 1991 to 1996, TIPS was the model for SPDRs.

He believes a copy of a TIPS prospectus was attached to the SEC application for SPDRs. Walker was responsible for launching and overseeing Canada's second ETF in 1995—HIPs, based on the Toronto Stock Exchange 100 Index. TIPS and HIPs were re-branded into TIPs 35 and TIPs 100 in 1999.

Although TIPS and HIPs were an attempt to bring Bay Street to Main Street, the products were far less popular with retail investors than the TSX expected. They were, however, hugely popular with institutional investors because of their convenience and their penchant to run on nothing more than the smell of an oily rag. TIPS and HIPs did not have a management fee. The funds repaid the TSX for their operating expenses only through interest made from lending the securities of the funds to short sellers, something it could do because of being granted an exemption from the general prohibition for mutual funds against securities lending. That worked out to 0.04% annually, and as it turned out, less than the funds needed to pay their own way. The interest the fund earned on stock dividends was banked before their quarterly distribution to unitholders.

Walker is convinced that more individual Canadian investors would have bought TIPs had the retail investment community had more of a motivation to sell the product. TIPs, like all ETFs, were up against mutual funds, many of which pay a sales commission and regular trailer fees for as long as the client holds the fund. An ETF sale nets a broker a small stock trading commission and usually nothing more thereafter—nothing like the 5% or so of a typical mutual fund sale (back-end load).

Nevertheless, institutional interest in TIPs was strong, and TIPs became among the most actively traded securities on the TSE. In a way, TIPs was a victim of its own success. Its vaporous 0.04% forced the TSE to subsidize the operating expenses of the fund and tied up resources that could be directed to its equity listing services, so the exchange decided to offload responsibility for the product onto an outside provider. Barclays Global Investors Canada Limited won the shareholders' permission to manage TIPs by merging it with the already existing i60 Fund. In March 2000, TIPs 35 and TIPs 100 were both merged with Barclays Canada's i60 Fund and its comparably robust 0.17% MER. The combined entity made the i60 the largest index fund and one of the largest mutual funds in the Canadian equity category.

Spiders, of course, went on to great fame and glory. Appropriately enough, Spiders spawned WEBS (World Equity Benchmark Shares) in 1996. These ETFs were based on international equity indices and are now known as iShares MSCI Funds. There are now an impressive 23 of these representing the indices of 20 countries and 3 regions. Before there could be eentsy-weentsy ETFs, the arachnid theme was abandoned in favour of more industrial sounding names like Diamonds (January 1998) based on the Dow Jones Industrial Average, and Qubes (March 1999) for the Nasdaq 100 Index.

ETFs Today: U.S. Developments

January 2005 was a watermark for U.S. ETFs. For the first time ever, money into ETFs beat money into stock funds.[6] With fines and regulatory penalties battering mutual funds in 2004, the cheat-proof nature of exchange traded portfolios has got to be part of their recognition. More than 164 U.S.-based ETFs are taking their place in the sun and the proliferation is far from over.[7] More exciting than the sheer increase in numbers and assets, however, is the liberating expansion of investment possibilities.

VIPERs

Perhaps the biggest indication of the irreversible momentum of ETFs was Vanguard Group's launch of its own ETFs. Vanguard pioneered index mutual funds for the retail investor, and is the second largest mutual fund company in the United States with a staggering US$800 billion under administration.

Vanguard's first ETF was based on an optimized basket of Vanguard's Total Stock Market Index Fund, which is itself based on an optimized basket of stocks in the Wilshire 5000 Index. The ETFs in the Vanguard series are called VIPERs which stands for "Vanguard Index Participation Equity Receipts." The interesting thing about VIPERs is that they are ETFs and simultaneously a new share class of Vanguard's existing index funds. This is a first in the ETF world and may be imitated by other fund companies. Introduced on May 31, 2001, the VIPER series numbers 23 ETFs. As a group they are the lowest cost ETFs available, with MERs ranging from 0.07 to 0.13% for U.S. domestic broad ETFs, 0.25% for U.S. sector products, and from 0.18 to 0.30% for international ETFs. Vanguard also appears to be moving to MSCI indices throughout its offering. Clearly, Vanguard anticipates a promising future for its new version of index funds.

Some have speculated that these low cost darlings have a tax disadvantage because of their class structure. Each VIPER is a class of an underlying Vanguard index fund and must carry with it all that fund's unrealized capital gains. With a number of Vanguard's index funds being big and old, the worry of unrealized gains is not an inconsiderable one; however, Vanguard argues compellingly that the underlying index fund can sell high-cost positions and take a capital loss to offset gains the ETF might generate.[8] Time will tell whether this new ETF construction has any bearing on tax efficiency. So far, Vanguard's ETF distributions are not attracting attention to themselves.

Portfolio Services

With Vanguard nipping at its heels, Fidelity Investments still retains the distinction of being America's largest mutual fund company, and it's not going to be left out of the fun. In October 2003, Fidelity launched its own ETF, tracking the Nasdaq composite index. A little more than a year later, the fund company introduced a service that lets investors build and trade portfolios of ETFs. The Fidelity ETF Portfolio Builder helps investors select portfolios based on three approaches—sectors, market capitalization, or style and market cap. This service is part of an "ETF Center" at *www.fidelity.com* that offers ETF research and educational tools.

Amerivest is another service that helps investors design and trade ETF portfolios. This is an on-line initiative of Ameritrade Holding Corp. and offers 25 different portfolios in all for an annual fee of 0.50% of assets under US$100,000 and 0.35% of assets over $100,000 (*www.amerivest.com*).

The oldest of these portfolio services is FOLIOfn Inc., which allows American investors to buy and sell ready-made portfolios ("folios") for a flat monthly fee. FOLIOfn, at *www.foliofn.com*, offers over 100 portfolios that cover markets, sectors, risk levels, and famous investment strategies like the Dogs of the Dow. Each folio can hold up to 50 stocks, including ETFs. The web site says, "It's as easy as selecting a mutual or index fund." What's more, FOLIOfn has the even more remarkable feature of allowing investors to customize the contents of their folios with a generous number of free trades in as many as three folios—all for a modest annual or monthly fixed price from US$19.95 ($199 a year). That's the equivalent of holding C$160,000 of an i60 unit with an MER of 0.17%—without trading commission. Quite a deal, especially when you think of the added flexibility it gives you over a fixed position in an ETF. FOLIOfn has licensed its patented technology to a Japanese company, but there are no plans to deliver this economical offer to Canada.

No one yet knows just how active investors ultimately want to become, even when they're aiming for a predominantly passive investment approach. One other similar service, netFolio, shuttered its doors in 2002. Yet should a do-it-yourself, ready-made but customizable portfolio service catch on, ETF sponsors might very well be forced to join them at their own game and radically revise the nature of their offering.

This proliferation of portfolio programs is all over and above innumerable ETF managed account offerings from brokerages, insurance companies and investment counseling firms in the U.S. Beyond their increasing popularity as a bundled product, however, ETFs continue to push into new asset classes and even into advanced index construction. It's easy because the ETF structure can accommodate a vast variety of investments so long as there is a liquid market for them. Just look what's happening.

Global Sector ETFs

Global sectors are to international investing as laser surgery is to ophthalmology. Global sector ETFs contain stocks from one particular industry sector, but selected from countries around the world. They allow investors to concentrate the focus of their international investing in a way that was seldom possible before. Studies are beginning to show that good timing of sector plays can boost returns, and this applies in big letters to sectors across country boundaries.[9] Given the difficulty in individual stock picking, especially internationally, ETFs are the ideal product for sector plays. You can move in and out of them quickly, and because only a few (Canadian) ETFs hedge foreign currencies, you get full exposure to the currency effect on all the international stocks.

So far there are five global sector ETFs. These cover energy, financials, healthcare, technology, and telecommunications. (See Appendix C for more details.)

Fixed Income ETFs

Putting bonds into an ETF structure is a liberation for investors who want diversification but don't want to pay an active manager a fee to run a fixed income portfolio. (Just how many smart managers can earn enough of a premium on their fixed income strategies to compensate for their own management fees?) There are six U.S.- listed fixed income ETFs and two in Canada. More will almost certainly arrive.

ETFs have given retail investors the ability to trade a portfolio of bonds on the open market very, very close to the true value of the underlying bonds. Traditionally, bonds are traded through a brokerage's bond desk with little price transparency for the investor. In this arrangement, each bond trade is charged a commission which is discreetly subtracted from the bond's yield and seldom disclosed. Fixed income ETFs trade directly over an exchange and should save investors money on yield spreads otherwise lost to implicit commissions. They will make building a diversified bond portfolio easier and cheaper. And the MERs can't be beat. Canadian MERs range from 25 to 30 basis points, while U.S. MERs are a lithe 15 to 20 basis points.

Style and Capitalization ETFs

ETFs bringing different definitions of "growth" and "value" continue to proliferate with the latest being the iShares Morningstar series, which divides the large, mid and small cap universes into growth, value, and neutral ("core"). International growth and value ETFs would be a welcomed addition but have not yet made it to the party.

Regional ETFs

Not long ago, international coverage with ETFs was limited to developed countries. That's changing quickly. The first ETF on China stocks was launched in the third quarter of 2004 to an enthusiastic reception. Shortly thereafter, another ETF appeared comprised of U.S.-listed securities of companies that get most of their revenue from China. Regional ETF representation is growing, too with emerging markets ETFs, a Latin America iShares, along with an EAFE product that has been established for a few years. There are a few broad market Europe and global products, too, though more should be coming to beef up the regional representation.

New Asset Classes and Custom ETFs

Eventually, everything you can find in a mutual fund will likely end up as an ETF—probably even active management. But for now, asset class diversification is the main avenue of innovation.

Gold was the big story of 2004. In November, streetTRACKS Gold Trust was launched and within three months collected more than US$2 billion in assets. This was the world's first commodities-based ETF and the hunger for it bodes well for future commodity offerings such as oil and silver and perhaps even an agricultural basket. There are now two competing gold ETFs. Unlike most other ETFs, which are index linked, the U.S.-listed gold ETFs hold physical gold, so they are a pure play on the price of gold.

Dividends have also begun to sparkle as attractively as gold. There are now two dividend ETFs that contain nothing but companies with a long history of dividend payments. These ETFs are linked to indices of dividend-paying companies, which themselves have rules-based criteria for inclusions.

Because all that glitters is not gold, or dividends, social investment advocates should be happy with the introduction of an ETF on an index of companies selected from the Russell 1000 and the S&P 500 judged to be the most socially responsible of their sector. The index strictly excludes only tobacco companies.

ETFs linked to rules-based indices verge on active management, but are generally considered "enhanced" index-linked funds. These are some of the most exciting ETF developments of late. PowerShares Capital has put out 11 of these enhanced ETFs so far, with more in the offing. They use a proprietary, rules-based quantitative methodology to select stocks they think have the greatest growth potential.

The most unusual among the PowerShares lineup is the Wilderhill Clean Energy Portfolio. This ETF selects companies with greener energy sources or with technologies associated with cleaner energy, and is based on what AMEX says is the first index comprised of companies focusing on clean energy.

New indices and proprietary methodologies will likely proliferate but old indices may very well be revisited. Rydex may have given us a glimpse into the future with their S&P 500 equal-weighted ETF. This is the S&P 500 Index with every constituent given an equal weighting of 0.2%.

The financial universe is very much like a biological ecosystem. Where there's a niche, evolution ensures there will be a creature or product to fill it.

Pending Developments—A Lever, a Well, and Action!

Competition exists even among funds not yet launched. U.S. fund companies, Rydex Global Advisors, and Profunds Distributors, Inc. are snorting at the starting gate, vying to be the first to bring leveraged ETFs to investors. Some proposed ProFunds would return 200% of their index's return in either direction, others would deliver the inverse of their index's performance.

If a market could be said to be baying for a non-existent product, it is baying for commodity ETFs. The lonesome howling, and the immense popularity of the first gold ETF, has led Standard Asset Management to file a registration with the Securities and Exchange Commission to create an ETF tracking the price of oil. More commodity ETFs will certainly follow. Average investors wanting to bet on the movement of oil or silver, sugar or pork bellies, can do little other than invest in the companies that deal in these commodities, a less-than-direct route to the riches these could present. This asset class expansion will be as liberating as fixed income ETFs. Forlorn howls should turn to whoops of joy when the domain once of professional traders and highly sophisticated investors becomes open to anyone with a brokerage account. This oil ETF, in its initial design anyway, is intended to hold futures contracts for oil and options on futures, so it will be a derivative product like the original Canadian RSP-eligible EAFE fund. It will not be tracking an index, nor will it actually hold the commodity.

The last notable pending development, though hardly the least exciting, is the introduction of genuinely actively managed ETFs. That will set the mutual fund industry spinning on its ample MERs.

ETFs Today: Canadian Developments

Canada's ETF offering has grown from one pioneering TIPS in 1999 to sixteen products in 2005. The growth of ETFs is hardly likely to stop, especially in light of Canada's own mutual fund scandal. At $9.5 billion in total Canadian assets, ETFs still have a lot of room to catch up to the $513 billion Canadian mutual fund industry, but their cheat-proof nature and innovative delivery will, I believe, ultimately eclipse the mutual fund mammoth.

There is certainly no lack of innovation in Canada. The country had fixed income ETFs more than a year before the U.S. rolled theirs out. The iUnits Government of Canada 10-year Bond Fund, and iUnits Government of Canada 5-year Bond Fund were unique in a number of respects. Apart from the fact that they were the world's first fixed income ETFs, they were also the first ETFs not pegged to an index. Both bond funds held one bond each.

Now this is no longer entirely correct. The iG5 still holds one 5-year Government of Canada bond, but the iG10 has been reconceived to track the Scotia Capital Universe Bond Index, and as such is a more conventional product replicating a bond index. The iG5 remains unique in all the world.

Barclays Canada's two 100% RRSP eligible ETFs tied to foreign markets are also unique to Canada because they are designed to address the foreign content restriction on RRSP savings. They are, in fact, synthetic ETFs in that they do not hold stocks but rather buy exchange traded futures contracts on their targeted index. This is similar to the way 100% RRSP eligible foreign equity mutual funds work. (These funds, often known as clone funds, use private derivatives contracts rather than exchange traded ones.) The ETFs, however, have MERs that would make their mutual fund counterparts blush: 0.30% and 0.35% compared to 2.5% or more for most clone funds.

The two synthetic ETFs cover the S&P 500 Index and the MSCI EAFE Index. It's likely the Canadian government will eliminate foreign content restrictions in RRSP accounts, so these products may continue using derivatives, but with a different purpose. Instead of tracking a foreign index, they may very well hedge a foreign currency.

Based on the product inquiries I see daily, there's a lot of demand on the Canadian scene for an income trust ETF and a dividend ETF, and a materials ETF, too. Unfortunately, because of the technical difficulty of creating a commodities ETF, it is likely that asset class will stay the domain of closed-end funds for a while, in Canada anyway.[10]

ETFs Internationally

Global markets are introducing ETFs rapidly. As of April 2005, there were 198 ETFs listed on non–North American markets. Domestic or regional ETFs are traded on exchanges around the world—in the United Kingdom, Germany, the Netherlands, France, Finland, Sweden, Switzerland, India, South Africa, Australia, New Zealand, Hong Kong, Singapore, Japan, Israel, Mexico, and China.

The trading volume in ETFs increases substantially when options and futures are pegged to them. A small number of options are now available in Europe. This will give ETFs yet another push forward.

Interestingly, Japan has been a particularly successful market for ETFs abroad. Introduced in Japan in 2001, ETFs there achieved US$26.5 billion in assets with just 15 ETFs. Europe's numbers took longer but they have considerably surpassed Japan's now. ETFs have been available in Europe since 2000 and now number 122, with assets of US$36.9 billion.

Cross-Listings

There's long been a flurry of cross-listing going on with ETFs globally. Cross-listing allows the securities from one exchange to be traded on another exchange. Institutional investors often have foreign intermediaries through which they can trade foreign securities, but cross-listing gives retail investors the chance to buy and sell stocks that might not otherwise be available to them on a home exchange. Cross-listing also increases the liquidity of the cross-listed security. In Europe, there are more than 150 ETF cross-listings, some of them U.S.-listed ETFs.

Cross-listing isn't just good for foreign investors. It also has benefits for North American investors when the cross-listing gives reciprocal access. Suppose you own an iShare MSCI Hong Kong and you sell it at 11 a.m. Toronto time. You get a price as of 11 a.m. Toronto time, but the underlying securities are 12 hours away tucked in their beds. Your 11 a.m. price actually reflects the market sentiment about what the Hong Kong market will do when it wakes up, so it is not a perfect tracking device. If, on the other hand, you owned a Hong Kong ETF that tracked the Hong Kong market, your 11 a.m. sell order would be executed the minute the Hong Kong market opened at that exact market price.

The flexibility to trade domestic ETFs in their own time zone will enhance tracking and increase liquidity. It's the financial markets equivalent of free trade. ETFs may not just be the next generation of mutual funds: they may turn out to be the financial enterprise that boldly goes where no financial instrument has gone before.

The Evolution of ETFs (fig. 47)

1978	Program trading, trading large blocks of different stocks simultaneously based on a computer program's instructions, starts.
1982	LOR's portfolio insurance takes off with the introduction of index futures in the U.S.
1987	October stock market crash puts the lie to portfolio insurance as it was designed. Regulators call for a different kind of stock basket product.
1988	LOR files a proposal to the SEC for a SuperTrust with SuperUnits and SuperShares, the first exchange traded funds.
1989	Index Participation Shares trade on AMEX and the Philadelphia Exchange. Shortly thereafter a Chicago court rules them futures and so eligible for trading on a futures exchange only. No futures exchange picks up the product and it is discontinued.
1990	Toronto 35 Index Participation Units first traded on the TSE, becoming the first successful ETF in the world.
1992	SuperTrust units are traded on AMEX in November but are quickly eclipsed by a simpler product, Spiders (SPDRs).
1993	Standard & Poor's Depositary Receipts (Spiders) land on AMEX in January.
1995	HIPs first traded on the TSE
1996	WEBS (now iShares MSCI Funds) launched.
1998	DIAMONDS (Dow Jones Industrial Average ETF) launched.
1999	Qubes (Nasdaq 100 ETF) launched in March and becomes one of the most heavily traded securities in the US.
2000	More than 75 ETFs launch worldwide this year. Canada introduces world's first fixed income ETFs, also the first ETF not related to an index.
2001	May 31, Vanguard Group launches its long awaited initial VIPERs ETF
2001	July 31, NYSE begins trading Spiders, Diamonds, and Qubes.
2002	First U.S. fixed income ETFs (July). ETFs terminated—one in Canada, three in the U.S. NYSE adds an additional 34 ETFs; total now trading on NYSE reaches 37.
2003	First enhanced index ETFs (quasi-active) launched by PowerShares
2004	First commodity based ETFs, streetTRACKS Gold Trust and iShares COMEX Gold Trust.

ETFs in the Future

More Variety

ETFs are certain to become far more varied in kind. As long as it can be bought and sold with real time pricing, anything can be thrown into an ETF structure. A hedge fund index has been developed in the U.S. and an ETF is almost sure to follow. A Lehman Brothers' report on ETFs as far back as September 2000 predicted a hedge fund of ETFs would follow active and leveraged active fund ETFs.

Pools of ETFs

More immediately, it's not hard to imagine ETFs made up of pools of other ETFs. Spectrum Investment Management Limited in Canada did something like this within a mutual fund. "Tactonics" was a global tactical asset allocation fund that contained as many as 20 ETFs dynamically managed. Despite being recognized as the "Best New Initiative of 2001" by the Canadian Mutual Fund Awards, the product did not catch on and was withdrawn. Nevertheless, Tactonics was onto something, and an ETF holding other ETFs in a dynamic asset allocation could do something very similar without the drawbacks of a mutual fund structure.

ETFs as Product Building Blocks

Right now, ETFs are the mutual fund industry's worst nightmare, but I believe that attitude will change once their usefulness within broader investment solutions is recognized. ETFolios, the customized asset allocation service offered by Guardian Capital Advisors Inc., is a good example of this. (See Chapter Five.) These are important first steps, not only because they expand the use of ETFs, but more significantly because they allow financial planners to provide ETFs to their clients. (ETFs, being an exchange traded security, require a securities license which many financial planners do not have.)

ETFs have always been more popular among institutional investors than among individual investors, but this will change when ETFs are embedded within an attractive product solution. Even now, some prominent figures in the Canadian mutual fund industry and experts in asset allocation are working at establishing programs that integrate ETFs into mutual fund portfolios. This service is aimed squarely at planners who, because of licensing restrictions, currently have limited access to ETFs.

An all-ETF portfolio solution is about to bust out in the investment counsel, portfolio management world, too. A number of independent wealth management companies have been using ETFs extensively in their portfolios for some time, but Union Securities, an independent IDA firm, is rolling out a firm-wide program with all ETF portfolios designed for various risk/reward profiles. Union Securities hopes to differentiate itself in the marketplace with this program and to attract a greater part of their clients' more conservative money. I predict this leading edge initiative will not long be unique.

Actively Managed ETFs

Germany was the first country to claim to have actively managed ETFs, way back in November 2000.[11] Few in the international ETF community, however, consider Germany's actively managed products to be ETFs. The same is true of Australia's so-called active ETFs as well. The problem rests with the transparency of the underlying portfolios.

Institutional shareholders of Germany's actively managed "ETFs" learn about their portfolio positions with a two-day delay. Retail investors, on the other hand, get one-month-old information. This information lag makes arbitraging impossible. Since the normal arbitraging that keeps index ETF prices in line with their NAVs isn't available for the active funds, the Deutsche Borse of Frankfurt restricts the actively managed "ETFs" on its exchange from trading beyond a set bid/ask spread. To Deborah Fuhr, Global ETF analyst, those restrictions violate the defining characteristics of ETFs.

> Despite the claims of some European and Australian fund managers, to my mind, we don't yet have actively managed funds. Three things differentiate exchange traded funds from just funds that trade on exchanges. Everyday ETFs provide the underlying portfolio to the marketplace. You also have indicative net asset values, and the unique in-kind creation/redemption process. If you look at funds that trade on an exchange, they are normal mutual funds that are just trading on an exchange. You don't know the underlying portfolio, there are no indicative asset values, and there's no in-kind creation/redemption process. These are not ETFs.[12]

In Canada and the United States, ETFs are required to provide continuous portfolio disclosure, which poses a problem for active fund managers who don't want to show their hand too flagrantly. There's good reason for that reluctance. If market participants get wind of a manager's intention to buy a security, others will buy it up first and push the price up before the manager has finished establishing his position. Similarly, once it's known that a manager is selling a significant position in a stock, others will sell too and grind the price down. That manager's cold sweat is known as front running. Jurisdictions that permit actively managed ETFs will have to come to some kind of compromise between continuous disclosure and portfolio confidentiality.

So far, the North American regulatory hurdle of continuous disclosure is holding back the introduction of actively managed ETFs, but industry sources do not think that will prove insurmountable. Certainly the appetite for actively managed ETFs is enormous. Boston-based Financial Research Corporation expects actively managed ETFs to attract as much as US$200 billion in the U.S. alone within five years of their launch.[13] When you think it took nine years for index ETFs to garner US$66 billion, those are serious expectations.

Kevin Ireland, Vice President of ETF Marketing for AMEX, is of the opinion that active ETFs are definitely on their way to North America. "The first generation of active funds will be quantitative and rules-based, like the leveraged ETFs," he says. "The models being created to price these things effectively on an interday basis, with or without full disclosure, are pretty well done. Now it's just a matter of fine tuning them. Once they get the arbitrage mechanism to work within the trader's realm of risk, then you're going to be able to run an active portfolio and be able to price it effectively during the course of the day."

He believes active ETFs will not have full portfolio disclosure. "No active manager wants everybody to know what he's doing so he can just be copied," says Ireland. "These models that they're creating are going to be able to provide the necessary hedge for liquidity purposes without full disclosure." But, he says, it isn't going to happen quickly. "It will take baby steps. You aren't going to go from an index fund to a fully non-disclosed portfolio in one leap."

Whether or not actively managed ETFs ever get off the ground, there's still plenty of room for the plain index variety to proliferate. Even with current regulatory restrictions, exchange traded baskets of securities will continue to proliferate here and around the world because they're more efficient and flexible than conventional mutual funds.

Derivatives on ETFs

Mark Rubinstein who, along with his colleagues at LOR, was the U.S. ETF pioneer, feels the time is ripe for another generation of ETFs that have options associated with them, as did his SuperUnits. "Our product really [was] better than ETFs today because you could break it up and do more with it... I'm going to be quite surprised if some exchange traded funds don't effectively start doing this. In today's context, it's going to be a lot easier to get regulatory approval for things like we were doing. There's a lot more awareness of derivatives and options."

Perhaps Rubinstein's design of options within units won't materialize but there are other ways to achieve the same end. The Montreal Exchange lists three options on the i60 and one on each of four sector ETFs.

Options are widely available on a large number of U.S. ETFs. Although index futures are well established, futures on ETFs are just beginning. Futures on Qubes, Spiders and the iShares Russell 2000 are now available on the Chicago Mercantile Exchange. These are the first U.S. futures on an ETF, and a welcome addition to investor's arsenal because they are small – about one-fifth the size of E-mini futures, which are, in turn, about one-fifth the size of conventional index futures.[14]

Conventional mutual funds are not likely to lie down and play dead in the face of the ETF threat. More mutual fund companies will almost certainly launch their own ETFs, as Vanguard and Fidelity have done. Smelling the change in the wind, some fund companies might even attempt to convert some of their existing funds to exchange traded funds.[15] We've just entered the third inning of ETF development. Competition among the sponsors and exchanges will continue to spawn more choice and more innovative offerings. The game is only beginning to heat up.

From Passive to Active:
The Evolution of a Killer App

Cliff Weber, Senior Vice President of the ETF marketplace for The American Stock Exchange, is responsible for ETF product development for AMEX. He shared his thoughts about the future direction of ETFs, their evolution into actively managed vehicles, and their expanding application. AMEX lists 156 of the 181 U.S. ETFs.

Where do you see ETFs going in the future?

ETFs in the U.S. cover all kinds of slicing and dicing of the domestic equity markets, as well as the international markets, sectors, and regions, in equity and some fixed income products. (There were fixed income products in Canada before there were in the U.S.) Going forward, the product will evolve along a couple of different lines.

ETFs are expanding into alternative assets. We've seen gold-based ETFs, and now there's a filing in the U.S. for an oil ETF. To expand into other commodities and alternative asset classes, they aren't necessarily going to fit into more traditional structures that are really geared for equity or fixed income securities. The ETF structure will change somewhat to accommodate these different directions. The oil product [for instance] is structured as a partnership, as opposed to a 40 Act mutual fund structure. I think there will continue to be innovation and extension of the product into more specialized structures that will enable the product to grow into more alternative asset investments. That's definitely the way things are going.

ETFs are also expanding from a pure index-based product through to enhanced indexing and then into more active management. There's been a lot on interest in having ETFs on true, fundamental, actively managed products. I think we will get there through a series of steps where there will be enhanced indexing, then strategy-based products, which are a more active approach to an index product, but ultimately we think there will be true actively managed funds trading in the ETF format. That would allow investors—just as they buy shares of a stock—to buy shares of name-your-favourite mutual fund. And investors can buy it throughout the day just like the index-based ETFs. Active ETFs will offer some of the cost savings of ETFs that you see now. Certainly they will offer the flexibility in intraday trading, the ability to use different order types like stop and limit orders, instead of a market on close orders. They'll offer broader distribution for the fund company so that they can be marketed direct to any investor who has a brokerage account.

What form will active ETFs actually take and when can we expect them?

A fund company could set up a clone fund of an existing fund, or the fund company could issue a share class of its existing fund.

True, actively managed ETFs we don't expect to see out there trading before towards the end of next year. There's still a lot of work to be done getting the product approved through the SEC.

What are the major design hurdles for active ETFs and how have you overcome them?

For an actively managed ETF to trade efficiently in the secondary market, the specialists, market makers, the liquidity providers, and investors need to have some sense that the products are trading at a fair price, and for that to happen the market makers, specialists and liquidity providers will need to have some understanding of how the portfolio behaves and have an ability to hedge their position so they are not taking on more risk than they need to. Ideally, they want to see exactly what the fund holds so they know exactly what their risks are like and they can be as aggressive as they can in pricing it. But the fund manager is essentially selling their expertise, so they don't want to broadcast to the marketplace exactly what it is they are doing and what they hold because it allows for market participants who can, based on that information, determine what they think the manager is going to be buying next and try to front-run them by buying those securities first then turning around and selling them for a profit. That would drive up the costs to the shareholders and hurt performance. There's also the fear of free riding: instead of investing your money with a fund manager and paying them for their expertise, you can just watch what they are doing and do it yourself without having to pay them.

The trick is getting enough disclosure into the marketplace for effective and efficient trading without giving so much info that the fund manager exposes too much information.

We've spent several years developing a solution. Our solution provides info to the marketplace about the portfolio, descriptive information about the portfolio, that is available for the approximation of the value intraday. From that information the specialists and liquidity providers can get comfort in how the portfolio will react in the market. Even though they don't know exactly what that portfolio is, they can be comfortable with how it will react. It's not going to be as precise as index-based, but all our discussions with specialists, market makers, and market participants indicate it will work very well for there to be good liquidity and tight pricing for the product.

A lot of this we can't say for sure until it gets final approval from the SEC. Our guess is that you'll need a 15-second value published intra-day just like an index product.

How much demand do you see for actively managed ETFs?
I think it is a very big opportunity. If it is done as a share class of an existing [actively managed mutual] fund, I do think that it will provide a new method of distribution for the fund companies, ways to get to investment advisors and investors who are looking for more flexibility, and the cost efficiencies that ETFs provide. It has a potential to be very big.

ETFs are just starting to break into the 401K and IRA distribution platforms and the variable annuity channel. To what extent they will become more mainstream in that kind of distribution, I don't know, but that is a very significant source of where mutual fund assets come from.

They're such a versatile tool that people will always find ways to extend their uses. The question is: what direction will those alternate uses go?

Indexing itself continues to grow in popularity. That bodes well for the future continued growth in index-based ETFs. As the products become more accepted and widely used, smart people will always be developing new ways to use an effective tool like ETFs.

May 20, 2005

Notes

1) The history of index futures and other derivative products is instructively and entertainingly told in "The Whence, How and Why of OTC Equity Derivatives: An Introduction to OTC Derivatives for the Financial Investor," by Bruce Collins, Ph.D., Associate Professor of Finance, Western Connecticut State University. The paper is available at *www.wcsu.ct.stateu.edu/finance/newsletter/n/fall98.htm*.

2) For an accessible and entertaining explanation of portfolio insurance see *Capital Ideas: The Improbable Origins of Modern Wall Street*, Peter L. Bernstein, (New York: The Free Press, 1992), pp.269-294.

3) On the history of equity baskets see *The Handbook of Equity Derivatives*, Revised Edition, Jack Clark Francis, William W. Toy, J. Gregg Whittaker, editors, (New York: John Wiley & Sons, Inc., 2000); "Index Participation Units," Eric Kirzner, pp. 100-120; "Exchange-Traded Equity Funds—Genesis, Growth, and Outlook," by Gary L. Gastineau and Clifford J. Weber, pp. 121-141; also, "Why Financial Instruments Fail or Succeed," by Jack Clark Francis, pp.631-650.

4) On SuperShares and SuperUnits, a fascinating product that was fifteen years ahead of its time, see Mark Rubinstein's extraordinary web site, *www.in-the-money.com*. Click on articles about SuperShares. Also interesting is his discussion of the development of portfolio insurance.

5) Mark Rubinstein was one of three principals of Leland O'Brien Rubinstein Associates, Inc. (LOR), the California-based company that invented portfolio insurance, and subsequently SuperTrust, the first ETF in the United States. The company is no longer active and Rubinstein remains a professor of finance at The University of California at Berkeley. He very generously gave an extensive interview for this book. Here is an excerpt from that May 2001 interview, demonstrating so poignantly the heartbreak of pioneers.

Rubinstein:

We feel frustrated about the fact that now exchange traded funds are the big deal and even though we had the idea first, at least in terms of applying it, we didn't make it. We were a little company. We feel we've been cheated out of the intellectual credit for this. We were the first people to actually do it.

We spent millions of dollars on attorneys trying to convince the SEC to allow us to do this. We were doing something that was obviously right and would be in the interest of investors. If ordinary options are in the interests of investors, these certainly would be. If index funds and mutual funds are in the interest of the investors, these are. So it made no sense to me. They asked us to go through all kinds of hoops and we couldn't just sit down at a table and talk to them.

Prime and Scores* had already been approved, and our product had an even better reason to exist because we were not trading calls on individual stocks. We were going to make it possible to buy calls on a widely diversified portfolio, and, generally speaking, that's better for investors than individual stocks.

But the SEC said they were ashamed that they had approved Primes and Scores. They didn't like them and they were going to make us go through a very long procedure instead of a shortcut procedure for approval. It ended up taking five years. If the SEC had not done that, our business might be a lot different today.

By the time they ended up approving [SuperShares], index securities in general and options were becoming more popular and there was a variety of them. AMEX ended up going ahead with their own product [SPDRs], but I'm sure if we'd gotten our product out a year or two before they wouldn't have gone ahead, and they probably would have helped us more in marketing. We were way ahead of the game in our thinking.

John O'Brien ...convinced large companies to buy huge quantities of SuperUnits and then break them up and sell them off to the market. I think we had the largest initial launch of any fund to that point, $2 billion.

Our product was really better than ETFs today because you could break it up and do more with it. Unfortunately, in the practical world there are other things. The SEC won't let you do it, they'll put burdens on you.

The Achilles heel of our product was its complexity. [Because of this] the SEC said every secondary transaction must come with a prospectus. We told the brokerages you can sell SuperUnits just like an ordinary stock—but then there was the prospectus problem. Brokerage companies didn't want to change their procedures until the product got popular.

LOR exists as a shell. That's what happened to us. It shows you that when you try to innovate in financial markets you're probably going to fail, and you have to get the product just right; otherwise, someone else will come in who makes it just a little bit better and take the whole market, which is basically what SPDRs did.

SuperUnits and SuperShares stopped trading in 1995.

*Primes and Scores were a popular but unusual product first introduced in 1983 by a company called Americus. Here's how Prof. Rubinstein explains them in his unpublished paper "SuperTrust," (available on his remarkable site, www.in-the-money.com, by clicking on "Mark Rubinstein" and scrolling down the list of articles):

The first trust was based on shares of AT&T. For each share of AT&T a shareholder turned over to Americus, he was issued a trust unit. In turn, the investor could split the unit into a SCORE and a PRIME. At the end of five years, the SCORE received AT&T shares with a market value equal to the capital gains above a preset "termination value" earned over the period (if any). The PRIME received all the cash dividends, AT&T shares equal to the remaining capital value of the trust, and shareholder voting rights" (p. 8). A recombined PRIME and SCORE could be redeemed for a unit at any time and a unit could also be redeemed at any time. There were 28 different stocks being used in these Americus Trusts in 1988. An unfavourable taxing ruling in 1986 made the creation of any more of these trusts impractical. They have all since expired.

6) As reported by MarketWatch out of Boston on February 17, 2005.

7) As of April 14, 2005. Reported in "Exchange Traded Funds—End of Q1 2006 Review," published by Morgan Stanley Investment Strategies.

8) See *Business Week*, April 25, 2005, p.130, "Dividend Income without the Hassle." Also "Comparing Tax Efficiency of ETF Distributed Index Funds to Conventionally Distributed Index Funds," by Gus Sauter, *Institutional Investor*, October 2003.

9) See "The Global ETF Investor: Conference Highlights: Slicing the World—The Country versus Sector Allocation Debate," Salomon Smith Barney Equity Research publication, May 22, 2001.

10) Tellingly, in the second quarter of 2005, an affiliate of VenGrowth Asset Management launched a closed-end fund with exposure to 19 commodities via the Dow Jones—AIG Commodity Index Real Return.

11) German institutional investors seem to favour the index products while the actively managed funds are more popular with retail investors. In less than a year and a half, actively managed "ETFs" attracted over US$16 billion, no doubt owing to the costs of traditional mutual funds, which, in that country, usually carry a sales charge, annual management fees, and bank deposit fees. Coleen Moses, SEI Investments, April 24, 2001 e-mail broadcast.

12) Quoted from an interview for this book in September 2002.

13) David Haywood, Director of Alternative Investments Research, Financial Research Corp. in a telephone interview, May 12, 2005.

14) In a May 6, 2005 publication, "Three ETF Futures Set for June Launch" by John Spencer, *MarketWatch* says Morgan Stanley reports there are 94 options and 6 futures on ETFs trading around the world. The new U.S. futures will make it a total of 9. Also see *MAR ETFR*, "How Single Stock Futures Will Affect ETFs," Ellise Coroneos, issue no. 23, September 2002, p.2.

15) An article written by Gary L. Gastineau, Senior Vice President at AMEX, and Clifford J, Weber, Vice President at AMEX, has suggested that even though it is too early to say for certain, it is possible that after a certain date in the future most or all new mutual funds will be exchange traded. "...[T]he facts that exchange-traded funds have some attractive characteristics not available in conventional funds, and that these funds are frequently less costly for their sponsors to create and maintain, suggests that substantial gains in market share are likely." p.140, "Exchange-Traded Equity Funds—Genesis, Growth, and Outlook," *The Handbook of Equity Derivatives*, Revised Edition, Jack Clark Francis, et al., editor, (New York: John Wiley & Sons Inc, 2000).

Part Four

Appendix A

Fact Sheets on All Canadian ETFs

iUnits™ S&P®/TSX™ 60 Index Fund — Large Cap

Pricing and Fund Data

	March 31/05	52 Week Range
Price	$53.56	H $55.09
Net Asset Value Per Unit	$53.54	L $45.16
Fund Ticker Symbol	XIU	
Benchmark Ticker	SPTSX60	
MER	0.17%	
Fund Manager	BGI Canada	
Inception Date	Oct. 4/99	
Net Assets	$6,672.6MM	
Shares Outstanding (MM)	124.6	
Avg. Daily Trading Vol. (000)	1,214	
Underlying Securities	60	
Options Available	Yes	
Current Dividend Yield (%)	1.86	
P/E Ratio (12Mo. Trailing Earnings)	32.99	
Standard Deviation (3 Yr.)	0.12	
R^2 (3 Yr.)	0.98	
Sharpe Ratio (3 Yr.)	0.50	

Distributions	Income	Capital Gains
Frequency	Quarterly	Year End

History (per unit)	2002	2003	2004
Dividends	$0.65	$0.73	$0.78
Return of Capital	$0.04	$0.06	$0.05
Capital Gains	$-	$0.49	$0.94
Total	$0.69	$1.28	$1.77

Sector Exposure (%) March 31/05

Financials	36.4
Energy	22.9
Materials	14.3
Information Technology	6.2
Telecom Services	5.8
Consumer Discretionary	5.1
Industrials	5.0
Consumer Staples	3.2
Healthcare	0.7
Utilities	0.5

Top Ten Holdings (%)

Royal Bank	6.5%
Manulife Financial	6.4%
Bank Of Nova Scotia	5.4%
Encana	5.3%
Toronto Dominion Bank	4.9%
Bank Of Montreal	3.9%
BCE Inc.	3.9%
CIBC	3.5%
Sun Life Financial	3.2%
Suncor Energy	3.1%
Top Ten Total (%)	46.0%

Growth of $1,000: Total Return i60

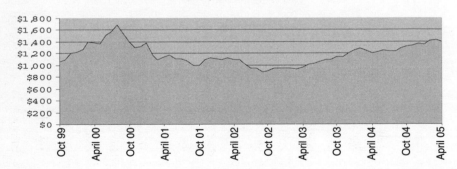

Performance % — March 31/05

	1 Mo	3 Mo	6 Mo	1 Yr	3 Yr	5 Yr	Inception
Fund NAV	0.54%	4.66%	11.63%	14.19%	8.06%	0.40%	6.67%
Quartile Ranking	1	1	2	1	1	3	

Fund Description

The iUnits S&P/TSX 60 Index Fund (i60) is an open-ended mutual fund trust, listed and traded on the Toronto Stock Exchange (TSX), designed to replicate the performance of the S&P/TSX 60 Index. The index consists of 60 large cap, liquid stocks, balanced across 10 industry sectors and represents approximately 60% of the whole market. The index is market capitalization–weighted, float adjusted, and is rebalanced quarterly.

Source: Barclays Canada, Fundata

iUnits™ S&P®/TSX™ 60 Capped Index Fund
Large Cap

Pricing and Fund Data

	March 31/05	52 Week Range
Price	$59.20	H $60.86
Net Asset Value Per Unit	$59.20	L $50.06
Fund Ticker Symbol	XIC	
Benchmark Ticker	SPTSEC	
MER	0.17%	
Fund Manager	BGI Canada	
Inception Date	Feb. 22/01	
Net Assets	$368.5MM	
Shares Outstanding (MM)	6.2	
Avg. Daily Trading Vol. (000)	15	
Underlying Securities	60	
Options Available	Yes	
Current Dividend Yield (%)	1.86	
P/E Ratio (12Mo. Trailing Earnings)	32.99	
Standard Deviation (3 Yr.)	0.12	
R^2 (3 Yr.)	0.98	
Sharpe Ratio (3 Yr.)	0.50	

Distributions

Income		Capital Gains	
Frequency	Quarterly	Year End	

History (per unit)	2002	2003	2004
Dividends	$0.76	$0.84	$0.89
Return of Capital	$0.03	$0.02	$0.42
Capital Gains	$0.26	$-	$-
Total	$1.05	$0.86	$1.31

Sector Exposure (%) March 31/05

Sector	%
Financials	36.4
Energy	22.9
Materials	14.3
Information Technology	6.2
Telecom Services	5.8
Consumer Discretionary	5.1
Industrials	5.0
Consumer Staples	3.2
Healthcare	0.7
Utilities	0.5

Top Ten Holdings (%)

Holding	%
Royal Bank	6.5%
Manulife Financial	6.4%
Bank Of Nova Scotia	5.4%
Encana	5.3%
Toronto Dominion Bank	4.9%
Bank Of Montreal	3.9%
BCE	3.9%
CIBC	3.5%
Sun Life Financial	3.2%
Suncor Energy	3.1%
Top Ten Total (%)	46.0%

Growth of $1,000: Total Return i60C

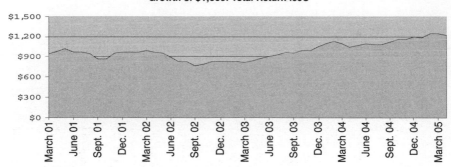

Performance %
March 31/05

	1 Mo	3 Mo	6 Mo	1 Yr	3 Yr	5 Yr	Inception
Fund NAV	0.54%	4.66%	11.63%	14.19%	8.06%	-	5.59%
Quartile Ranking	1	1	2	1	2		

Fund Description

The iUnits S&P/TSX 60 Capped Index Fund (i60C) is an open-ended mutual fund trust, listed and traded on the Toronto Stock Exchange (TSX) designed to replicate the S&P/TSX 60 Capped Index. The index consists of 60 large cap, liquid stocks, balanced across 10 industry sectors and represents approximately 60% of the whole market. The index is a constrained market capitalization–weighted, float adjusted, and is rebalanced quarterly, or when single company exposure exceeds a weighting of 10%.

Source: Barclays Canada, Fundata

iUnits™S&P®/TSX™ Canadian MidCap Index Fund ⟶ Mid Cap

Pricing and Fund Data

	Oct 31/02	52 Week Range
Price	$67.70	H $70.60
Net Asset Value Per Unit	$67.55	L $55.95
Fund Ticker Symbol	XMD	
Benchmark Ticker	SPTSXM	
MER	0.55%	
Fund Manager	BGI Canada	
Inception Date	Mar. 8/01	
Net Assets	$198.1M	
Shares Outstanding (MM)	2.9	
Avg. Daily Trading Vol. (000)	15	
Underlying Securities	60	
Options Available	Yes	
Current Dividend Yield (%)	1.61	
P/E Ratio (12Mo. Trailing Earnings)	26.23	
Standard Deviation (3 Yr.)	0.12	
R^2 (3 Yr.)	0.86	
Sharpe Ratio (3 Yr.)	0.75	

Distributions

	Income	Capital Gains
Frequency	Quarterly	Year End

History (per unit)	2002	2003	2004
Dividends	$0.30	$0.46	$0.42
Return of Capital	$0.05	$0.13	$0.11
Capital Gains	$-	$-	$2.57
Total	$0.35	$0.59	$3.10

Sector Exposure (%) — March 31/05

Financials	29.9
Materials	16.6
Energy	16.5
Industrials	9.6
Consumer Discretionary	8.8
Information Technology	5.0
Utilities	4.4
Consumer Staples	4.3
Telecom Services	3.4
Healthcare	1.6

Top Ten Holdings (%)

Power Corp	6.5%
Power Financial	5.2%
Great-West Life	4.2%
Goldcorp	3.7%
Shell Canada	3.7%
Penn West Petroleum	3.0%
IGM Financial	2.8%
PetroKazakhstan	2.6%
Brookfield Properties	2.5%
SNC-Lavalin	2.5%
Top Ten Total (%)	36.7%

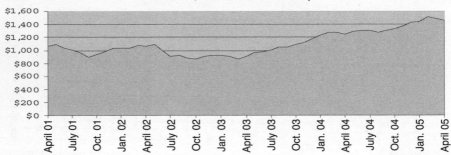

Growth of $1,000: Total Return iMidCap

Performance % — March 31/05

	1 Mo	3 Mo	6 Mo	1 Yr	3 Yr	5 Yr	Inception
Fund NAV	-1.71%	3.61%	13.41%	16.19%	11.33%	-	10.36%
Quartile Ranking	4	3	1	1	1		

Fund Description

The iUnits S&P/TSX 60 Canadian MidCap Index Fund (iMidCap) is an open-ended mutual fund trust, listed and traded on the Toronto Stock Exchange (TSX) designed to replicate the S&P/TSX Canadian MidCap Index. The index consists of 60 mid cap stocks, balanced across 10 industry sectors and represents the middle tier of Canadian companies listed on the TSX. The index is market capitalization–weighted, float adjusted, and rebalanced quarterly.

Source: Barclays Canada, Fundata

iUnits™S&P®/TSX™ Canadian Energy Index Fund   Industry Sector

Pricing and Fund Data

	March 31/05	52 Week Range
Price	$58.93	H $62.00
Net Asset Value Per Unit	$58.97	L $40.33
Fund Ticker Symbol	XEG	
Benchmark Ticker	SPTSEN	
MER	0.55%	
Fund Manager	BGI Canada	
Inception Date	Mar. 23/01	
Net Assets	$328.3MM	
Shares Outstanding (MM)	6	
Avg. Daily Trading Vol. (000)	124.1	
Underlying Securities	24	
Options Available	Yes	
Current Dividend Yield (%)	1.04	
P/E Ratio (12Mo. Trailing Earnings)	17.51	
Standard Deviation (3 Yr.)	0.16	
R^2 (3 Yr.)	0.63	
Sharpe Ratio (3 Yr.)	1.23	

Sector Exposure (%) March 31/05

Oil & Gas	100%

Top Ten Holdings (%)

Encana	18.7%
Suncor Energy	10.9%
Canadian Natural Resources	9.0%
Petro Canada	9.0%
Talisman Energy	7.5%
TransCanada	7.1%
Enbridge	5.3%
Imperial Oil	4.8%
Nexen	4.2%
Precision Drilling	2.7%
Top Ten Total (%)	79.2%

Distributions	Income	Capital Gains	
Frequency	Quarterly	Year End	

History (per unit)	2002	2003	2004
Dividends	$0.08	$0.13	$0.24
Return of Capital	$0.04	$0.05	$0.94
Capital Gains	$-	$0.17	$0.28
Total	$0.12	$0.35	$1.46

Growth of $1,000: Total Return iEnergy

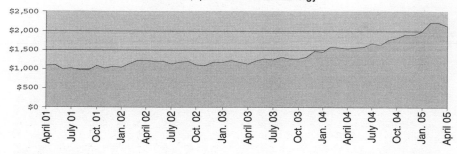

Performance %   March 31/05

	1 Mo	3 Mo	6 Mo	1 Yr	3 Yr	5 Yr	Inception
Fund NAV	0.01%	17.68%	25.99%	42.71%	22.77%	-	22.24%
Quartile Ranking	1	1	1	1	2		

Fund Description

The iUnits S&P/TSX Canadian Energy Index Fund (iEnergy) is an open-ended mutual fund trust, listed and traded on the Toronto Stock Exchange (TSX) designed to replicate the performance of the S&P/TSX Canadian Energy Index. The index consists of Canadian energy sector companies selected using Standard & Poor's industrial classifications and guidelines for evaluating company capitalization, liquidity, and fundamentals. The index is constrained market capitalization–weighted, float adjusted, and is rebalanced quarterly, or when a single company exposure exceeds a weighting of 25%.

Source: Barclays Canada, Fundata

iUnits™S&P®/TSX™ Canadian Financials Index Fund　　　Industry Sector

Pricing and Fund Data				Sector Exposure (%)	March 31/05
	March 31/05	52 Week Range		Financial	72.4
				Insurance	26.4
Price	$39.75	H $40.57		Real Estate	1.2
Net Asset Value Per Unit	$39.64	L $33.93			
Fund Ticker Symbol	XFN			**Top Ten Holdings (%)**	
Benchmark Ticker	SPTSFN			Royal Bank	15.3%
MER	0.55%			Manulife Financial	15.0%
Fund Manager	BGI Canada			Bank of Nova Scotia	12.7%
Inception Date	Mar. 23/01			Toronto Dominion Bank	11.4%
Net Assets	$226.2MM			Bank of Montreal	9.1%
Shares Outstanding (MM)	5.7			CIBC	8.1%
Avg. Daily Trading Vol. (000)	28			Sun Life Financial	7.5%
Underlying Securities	25			Brascan	3.1%
Options Available	Yes			Power Corp	3.0%
Current Dividend Yield (%)	2.32			National Bank	2.8%
P/E Ratio (12Mo. Trailing Earnings)	12.84			Top Ten Total (%)	88.0%
Standard Deviation (3 Yr.)	0.12				
R^2 (3 Yr.)	0.45				
Sharpe Ratio (3 Yr.)	0.90				

Distributions	**Income**	**Capital Gains**	
Frequency	Quarterly	Year End	
History (per unit)	**2002**	**2003**	**2004**
Dividends	$0.45	$0.56	$0.63
Return of Capital	$0.11	$0.13	$0.13
Capital Gains	$0.19	$0.13	$0.03
Total	$0.75	$0.82	$0.79

Growth of $1,000: Total Return iFin

Performance %　　　　　　　　　　　　　　　　　　　　March 31/05

	1 Mo	3 Mo	6 Mo	1 Yr	3 Yr	5 Yr	Inception
Fund NAV	0.68%	2.81%	10.58%	13.80%	13.07%	-	13.21%
Quartile Ranking	1	1	2	1	1		

Fund Description

The iUnits S&P/TSX Canadian Financials Index Fund (iFin) is an open-ended mutual fund trust, listed and traded on the Toronto Stock Exchange (TSX) designed, to replicate the performance of the S&P/TSX Canadian Financials Index. The index consists of Canadian financial sector companies selected using Standard & Poor's industrial classifications and guidelines for evaluating company capitalization, liquidity, and fundamentals. The index is constrained market capitalization–weighted, float adjusted, and is rebalanced quarterly, or when a single company exposure exceeds a weighting of 25%.

Source: Barclays Canada, Fundata

iUnits™S&P®/TSX™ Canadian Gold Index Fund

Industry Sector

Pricing and Fund Data			Sector Exposure (%)	March 31/05
	March 31/05	52 Week Range	Gold Mining	100%
Price	$48.51	H $57.89	**Holdings (%)**	
Net Asset Value Per Unit	$48.46	L $44.40	Barrick Gold	25.7%
Fund Ticker Symbol	XGD		Placer Dome	20.7%
Benchmark Ticker	SPTSEG		Goldcorp	12.9%
MER	0.55%		Kinross Gold	6.2%
Fund Manager	BGI Canada		Glamis Gold	6.0%
Inception Date	Mar. 29/01		Meridian Gold	4.9%
Net Assets	$431.8MM		Agnico Eagle Mines	3.7%
Shares Outstanding (MM)	9		Bema Gold	3.2%
Avg. Daily Trading Vol. (000)	132.9		Iamgold	2.6%
Underlying Securities	20		Eldorado Gold	2.3%
Options Available	Yes		Top Ten Total (%)	88.20%
Current Dividend Yield (%)	0.91			
P/E Ratio (12Mo. Trailing Earnings)	37.53			
Standard Deviation (3 Yr.)	0.35			
R^2 (3 Yr.)	1.00			
Sharpe Ratio (3 Yr.)	0.19			

Distributions	Income	Capital Gains	
Frequency	Quarterly	Year End	

History (per unit)	2002	2003	2004
Dividends	$-	$0.09	$-
Return of Capital	$0.06	$0.09	$0.08
Capital Gains	$1.54	$-	$-
Total	$1.60	$0.18	$0.08

Growth of $1,000: Total Return iGold

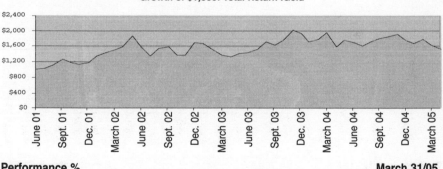

Performance %

March 31/05

	1 Mo	3 Mo	6 Mo	1 Yr	3 Yr	5 Yr	Inception
Fund NAV	-6.85%	-6.17%	-9.54%	-15.30%	3.22%	-	16.89%
Quartile Ranking	3	4	4	2	4		

Fund Description

The iUnits S&P/TSX Canadian Gold Index Fund (iGold) is an open-ended mutual fund trust, listed and traded on the Toronto Stock Exchange (TSX), designed to replicate the performance of the S&P/TSX Canadian Gold Index. The index consists of Canadian Gold sector companies selected using Standard & Poor's industrial classifications and guidelines for evaluating company capitalization, liquidity, and fundamentals. The index is constrained market capitalization–weighted, float adjusted, and is rebalanced quarterly, or when a single company exposure exceeds a weighting of 25%.

Source: Barclays Canada, Fundata

iUnits™S&P®/TSX™ Cdn. IT Index Fund

Pricing and Fund Data

	March 31/05	52 Week Range
Price	$7.11	H $9.04
Net Asset Value Per Unit	$7.15	L $6.73
Fund Ticker Symbol	XIT	
Benchmark Ticker	SPTSIT	
MER	0.55%	
Fund Manager	BGI Canada	
Inception Date	Mar. 23/01	
Net Assets	$105.6MM	
Shares Outstanding (MM)	15	
Avg. Daily Trading Vol. (000)	82.5	
Underlying Securities	20	
Options Available	Yes	
Current Dividend Yield (%)	0.38	
P/E Ratio (12Mo. Trailing Earnings)	155.96	
Standard Deviation (3 Yr.)	0.48	
R^2 (3 Yr.)	0.69	
Sharpe Ratio (3 Yr.)	0.10	

Distributions

		Income	Capital Gains
Frequency		Quarterly	Year End

History (per unit)	2002	2003	2004
Dividends	$-	$-	$-
Return of Capital	$0.01	$-	$-
Capital Gains	$-	$-	$0.54
Total	$0.01	$-	$0.54

Industry Sector

Sector Exposure (%) March 31/05

Technology	79.1
Software & Services	18.2
Commercial Services	1.7
Industrial	1.0

Top Ten Holdings (%)

Research In Motion	24.8%
Nortel Networks	24.7%
ATI Technologies	10.5%
Cognos	9.3%
Celestica	6.3%
Onex	5.5%
CGI Group	4.3%
Creo	2.2%
Open Text	2.2%
Geac Computer	1.9%
Top Ten Total (%)	91.7%

Growth of $1,000: Total Return iIT

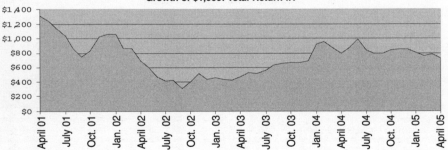

Performance %   March 31/05

	1 Mo	3 Mo	6 Mo	1 Yr	3 Yr	5 Yr	Inception
Fund NAV	2.97%	-8.53%	-1.81%	-10.57%	-3.54%	-	
Quartile Ranking	1	4	4	2	1		

Fund Description

The iUnits S&P/TSX Canadian Information Technology Index Fund (iIT) is an open-ended mutual fund trust, listed and traded on the Toronto Stock Exchange (TSX), designed to replicate the performance of the S&P/TSX Canadian Information Technology Index. The index consists of Canadian IT sector companies selected using Standard & Poor's industrial classifications and guidelines for evaluating company capitalization, liquidity, and fundamentals. The index is constrained market capitalization–weighted, float adjusted, and is rebalanced quarterly, or when a single company exposure exceeds a weighting of 25%.

Source: Barclays Canada, Fundata

iUnits™ S&P®/TSX™ Canadian REIT Index Fund   Real Estate

Pricing and Fund Data

	March 31/05	52 Week Range
Price	$11.55	H $12.50
Net Asset Value Per Unit	$11.52	L $9.90
Fund Ticker Symbol	XRE	
Benchmark Ticker	SPRTRE	
MER	0.55%	
Fund Manager	BGI Canada	
Inception Date	Oct. 22/02	
Net Assets	$103.8MM	
Shares Outstanding (MM)	9.0	
Avg. Daily Trading Vol. (000)	31.8	
Underlying Securities	13	
Options Available	Yes	
Current Dividend Yield (%)	5.65	
P/E Ratio (12Mo. Trailing Earnings)	43.34	
Standard Deviation (3 Yr.)	NA	
R^2 (3 Yr.)	NA	
Sharpe Ratio (3 Yr.)	NA	

Sector Exposure (%)   March 31/05

Real Estate (REITs)	100.0

Top Ten Index Holdings (%)

Riocan REIT	25.3%
H&R REIT	14.4%
Summit REIT	8.9%
Cdn R. E. Invest. Trust REIT	7.8%
Boardwalk REIT	7.0%
Retirement Residences REIT	6.8%
Canadian Apart. Prop. REIT	5.8%
Legacy Hotels REIT	4.8%
Calloway REIT	4.6%
InnVest REIT	4.1%
Top Ten Total (%)	89.5%

Distributions Income   **Capital Gains**
Frequency   Quarterly   Year End

History (per unit)	2002	2003	2004
Dividends	$-	$0.01	$-
Return of Capital	$-	$0.53	$0.44
Capital Gains	$-	$0.05	$0.10
Total	$-	$0.59	$0.54

Growth of $1,000: Total Return iREIT

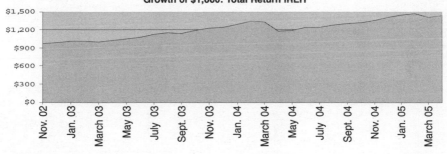

Performance %   March 31/05

	1 Mo	3 Mo	6 Mo	1 Yr	3 Yr	5 Yr	Inception
Fund NAV	-3.92%	0.39%	8.20%	5.31%	-	-	15.11%
Quartile Ranking	3	3	2	1			

Fund Description

The iUnits S&P/TSX Canadian REIT Index Fund (iREIT) is an open-ended mutual fund trust, listed and traded on the Toronto Stock Exchange (TSX), designed to replicate the performance of the S&P/TSX Canadian REIT Index. The index consists of 13 publicly traded investment trusts that invest predominantly in income producing real estate assets, such as retail, residential, office or industrial properties or special purpose properties, including hotels, or nursing homes. The index is constrained market capitalization–weighted, float adjusted, and is rebalanced quarterly, or when a single company exposure exceeds a weighting of 25%.

Source: Barclays Canada, Fundata

iUnits™ MSCI® International Equity Index RSP Fund   International Equity

Pricing and Fund Data

	March 31/05	52 Week Range
Price	$21.50	H $22.75
Net Asset Value Per Unit	$21.37	L $19.30
Fund Ticker Symbol	XIN	
Benchmark Ticker	MXEA	
MER	0.35%	
Fund Manager	BGI Canada	
Inception Date	Sept 11/01	
Net Assets	$232.5MM	
Shares Outstanding	11MM	
Avg. Daily Trading Vol. (000)	29.2	
Underlying Securities**	1,069	
Options Available	No	
Current Dividend Yield (%)**	2.72	
P/E Ratio (12Mo. Trailing Earnings)**	20.14	
Standard Deviation (3 Yr.)	0.14	
R^2 (3 Yr.)	0.99	
Sharpe Ratio (3 Yr.)	-0.01	

Distributions

	Income	Capital Gains
Frequency	Annual	Year End

History (per unit)	2002	2003	2004
Dividends	$-	$-	$-
Return of Capital	$-	$-	$-
Capital Gains	$-	$-	$1.34
Total	$-	$-	$1.34†

Sector Exposure (%) March 31/05

Financials	27.1
Consumer Discretionary	12.0
Industrials	9.7
Energy	8.8
Consumer Staples	7.9
Materials	7.6
Health Care	7.6
Telecom Services	7.0
Information Technology	6.1
Utilities	4.9

Top Ten Index Holdings (%)

BP PLC	2.6%
HSBC Holdings	2.0%
Vodafone Group	1.9%
TotalFinaElf	1.6%
GlaxoSmithKline	1.5%
Royal Dutch Petroleum	1.5%
Novartis	1.3%
Nestle	1.2%
Toyota Motor	1.2%
Royal Bank of Scotland	1.2%
Top Ten Total (%)	16.0%

Growth of $1.000: Total Return iIntR

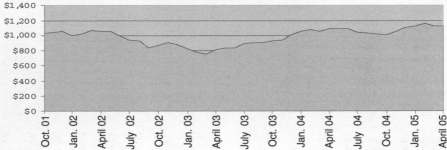

Performance % (in CAD$)   March 31/05

	1 Mo	3 Mo	6 Mo	1 Yr	3 Yr	5 Yr	Inception
Fund NAV	-3.73%	1.06%	9.70%	5.10%	1.38%	-	3.23%
Quartile Ranking	3	3	1	1	1		

Fund Description

The iUnits MSCI International Equity Index RSP Fund (iIntR) is an open-ended mutual fund trust, listed and traded on the Toronto Stock Exchange (TSX), designed to track the performance of the MSCI EAFE Index. The MSCI EAFE® Index was developed by Morgan Stanley Capital International Inc. as an equity benchmark for international stock performance. The Index includes stocks from Europe, Australasia, and the Far East.

** Underlying Securites, Current Dividend Yield, and P/E Ratio relate to the index and not the fund. The iIntR maintains 100% RSP eligibility by investing primarily in international country index futures and high quality money market instruments.

† Due to the use of futures and money market instruments, this distribution is treated as income.

Source: Barclays Canada, Fundata

iUnits™ S&P® 500 Index RSP Fund | U.S. Equity

Pricing and Fund Data

	March 31/05	52 Week Range
Price	$14.91	H $16.10
Net Asset Value Per Unit	$14.90	L $13.83
Fund Ticker Symbol	XSP	
Benchmark Ticker	SPTR	
MER	0.30%	
Fund Manager	BGI Canada	
Inception Date	May 29/01	
Net Assets	$212.3MM	
Shares Outstanding (MM)	14.2	
Avg. Daily Trading Vol. (000)	44.4	
Underlying Securities**	500	
Options Available	No	
Current Dividend Yield (%)**	1.85	
P/E Ratio (12Mo. Trailing Earnings)**	17.28	
Standard Deviation (3 Yr.)	0.14	
R^2 (3 Yr.)	0.99	
Sharpe Ratio (3 Yr.)	-0.59	

Distributions

Income		Capital Gains	
Frequency	Annual	Year End	

History (per unit)	2002	2003	2004
Dividends	$-	$-	$-
Return of Capital	$-	$-	$-
Capital Gains	$-	$-	$-
Total	$-	$-	$-

Sector Exposure (%) March 31/05

Financials	19.9
Information Technology	15.2
Health Care	13.0
Industrials	11.6
Consumer Discretionary	11.4
Consumer Staples	10.8
Energy	8.7
Utilities	3.3
Materials	3.2
Telecom Services	3.1

Top Ten Index Holdings (%)

General Electric	3.5%
Exxon Mobil	3.5%
Microsoft	2.4%
Citigroup	2.1%
Wal-Mart Stores	1.9%
Johnson & Johnson	1.8%
Pfizer	1.8%
Bank of America	1.6%
IBM	1.4%
Intel	1.3%
Top Ten Total (%)	17.8%

Growth of $1,000: Total Return i500R

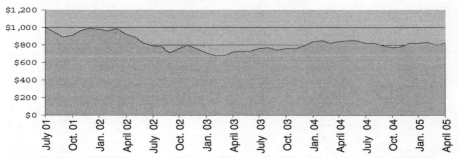

Performance % (in CAD$) March 31/05

	1 Mo	3 Mo	6 Mo	1 Yr	3 Yr	5 Yr	Inception
Fund NAV	-3.40%	-1.35%	1.93%	-2.30%	-6.80%	-	-6.67%
Quartile Ranking	2	2	2	2	2		

Fund Description

The iUnits S&P 500 Index RSP Fund (i500R) is an open-ended mutual fund trust, listed and traded on the Toronto Stock Exchange (TSX), designed to track the performance of the S&P 500 Index. The index consists of 500 large cap, liquid stocks balanced across 10 industry sectors, and is considered to be the leading barometer of U.S. market activity.

** Underlying Securites, Current Dividend Yield and P/E Ratio relate to the index and not the fund. The i500R maintains 100% RSP eligibility by investing primarily in S&P 500 index futures and high-quality money market instruments.

Source: Barclays Canada, Fundata

iUnits™ Government of Canada 5-year Bond Fund **Fixed Income**

Pricing and Fund Data

	March 31/05	52 Week Range
Price	$28.80	H $29.40
Net Asset Value Per Unit	$28.82	L $27.91
Fund Ticker Symbol	XGV	
Benchmark Ticker	-	
MER	0.25%	
Fund Manager	BGI Canada	
Inception Date	Nov. 23/00	
Net Assets	$318.7MM	
Shares Outstanding (MM)	11.1	
Avg. Daily Trading Vol. (000)	32.2	
Options Available	No	
Current Yield	3.46%	
Duration (Yrs.)	4.4	
Standard Deviation (3 Yr.)	0.03	
R^2 (3 Yr.)	0.94	
Sharpe Ratio (3 Yr.)	1.41	

Benchmark Bond	March 31/05
CAN 5.50% 06/01/10	100%
Benchmark Bond Yield:	3.71%

Distributions	Income	Capital Gains
Frequency	Semi Annual	Year End

History (per unit)	2002	2003	2004
Interest Income	$1.47	$1.41	$1.27
Return of Capital	$0.13	$0.03	$0.03
Capital Gains	$0.62	$0.01	$-
Total	$2.22	$1.45	$1.30

Growth of $1,000: Total Return iG5

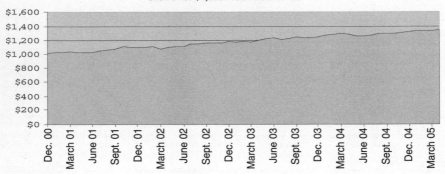

Performance % **March 31/05**

	1 Mo	3 Mo	6 Mo	1 Yr	3 Yr	5 Yr	Inception
Fund NAV	-0.08%	0.57%	2.90%	2.98%	7.22%	-	6.79%
Quartile Ranking	1	1	1	1	1		

Fund Description

The iUnits Government of Canada 5-year Bond Fund (iG5) is an open-ended mutual fund trust, listed and traded on the Toronto Stock Exchange (TSX), designed to replicate the performance of a 5-year Government of Canada (GOC) bond. Approximately once a year, the fund will sell the existing holding and select a new 5-year bond to maintain the term to maturity.

Source: Barclays Canada, Fundata

iUnits™ Government of Canada Bond Bond Market Index Fund   Fixed Income

Pricing and Fund Data

	March 31/05	52 Week Range
Price	$28.87	H $29.60
Net Asset Value Per Unit	$28.77	L $27.31
Fund Ticker Symbol	XBB	
Benchmark Ticker	-	
MER	0.25%	
Fund Manager	BGI Canada	
Inception Date	Nov. 23/00	
Net Assets	$198.1MM	
Shares Outstanding (MM)	6.9	
Avg. Daily Trading Vol. (000)	27.6	
Options Available	No	
Average Yield	3.92%	
Duration (Yrs.)	6.19	
Standard Deviation (3 Yr.)	0.05	
R^2 (3 Yr.)	0.97	
Sharpe Ratio (3 Yr.)	1.30	

Top Ten Holdings (%)   March 31/05

Cda Housing Trust 4.40% 15-Mar-08	9.77
Cda Housing Trust 4.75% 15-Mar-08	7.89
Cda Housing Trust 4.65% 15-Sep-09	4.72
Canada 8% 01-Jun-23	4.12
Cda Gov't Bond 6.00% 06-Jan-11	3.79
Ontario (Prov. of)	3.35
Cda Gov't Bond 5.25% 06-Jan-12	2.89
Canadian Government	2.82
Ontario (Prov. of) 5.20% 03-Aug-07	2.53
Canada 5.25% 01-Jun-13	2.29
Top Ten Total (%)	44.17

Distributions

Income		Capital Gains	
Frequency	Quarterly	Year End	

History (per unit)	2002	2003	2004
Interest Income	$1.34	$1.32	$1.19
Return of Capital	$-	$0.02	$0.74
Capital Gains	$0.64	$0.81	$0.59
Total	$1.98	$2.15	$2.52

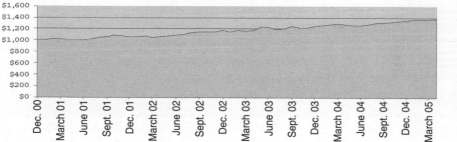

Growth of $1,000: Total Return iBond

Performance %   March 31/05

	1 Mo	3 Mo	6 Mo	1 Yr	3 Yr	5 Yr	Inception
Fund NAV	0.18%	0.97%	4.46%	5.33%	9.10%	-	7.33%
Quartile Ranking	1	1	1	1	1		

Fund Description

The iUnits Canadian Bond Broad Market Index Fund (iBond) is an open-ended mutual fund trust, listed and traded on the Toronto Stock Exchange (TSX), designed to replicate the performance of the Scotia Capital Universe Bond Index™. The fund will invest in a regularly rebalanced sample portfolio of bonds that closely matches the characteristics of the Universe Bond Index, including yield, term to maturity, credit quality, and duration.

Source: Barclays Canada, Fundata

TD S&P/TSX Composite Index Fund

Broad Market

Pricing and Fund Data

	March 31/05	52 Week Range
Price	$32.39	H $33.32
Net Asset Value Per Unit	$32.22	L $27.25
Fund Ticker Symbol	TTF	
Benchmark Ticker	SPTSX	
MER	0.25%	
Fund Manager	TD Asset Management	
Inception Date	Feb. 23/01	
Net Assets	$187.2MM	
Shares Outstanding	5.81MM	
Avg. Daily Trading Vol.	5.3M	
Underlying Securities	227	
Options Available	No	
Current Dividend Yield (%)	1.68	
P/E Ratio (12Mo. Trailing Earnings)	17.8	
Standard Deviation (3 Yr.)	0.11	
R^2 (3 Yr.)	0.99	
Sharpe Ratio (3 Yr.)	0.53	

Distributions	Income	Capital Gains
Frequency	Quarterly	Year End

History (per unit)	2002	2003	2004
Dividends	$0.34	$0.38	$0.39
Return of Capital	$-	$-	$-
Capital Gains	$-	$-	$-
Total	$0.34	$0.38	$0.39

Sector Exposure (%) March 31/05

Financials	32.0
Energy	21.0
Materials	16.2
Consumer Discretionary	6.2
Industrials	6.1
Information Technology	5.7
Telecommunication Services	5.3
Consumer Staples	4.0
Health Care	1.5
Utilities	1.4

Top Ten Holdings (%)

Royal Bank	4.9%
Manulife Financial	4.8%
Bank of Nova Scotia	4.1%
EnCana	3.9%
Bank of Montreal	2.9%
BCE	2.9%
CIBC	2.6%
Sun Life Financial	2.4%
Suncor Energy Inc.	2.3%
Top Ten Total (%)	30.8%

Growth of $1,000: Total Return TTF

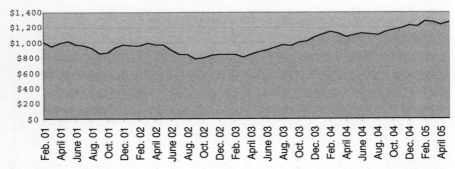

Performance %
31-Mar-05

	1 Mo	3 Mo	6 Mo	1 Yr	3 Yr	5 Yr	Inception
Fund NAV	-0.39%	4.27%	11.65%	13.54%	8.58%	-	6.00%
Quartile Ranking	2	2	2	2	2		

Fund Description

The TD S&P/TSX Composite Index Fund is an open-ended mutual fund trust, listed and traded on the Toronto Stock Exchange, designed to replicate the performance of the S&P/TSX Composite Index. The S&P/TSX Composite Index comprises approximately 71% of market capitalization for Canadian-based, Toronto Stock Exchange listed companies. The broad economic sector coverage has made the S&P/TSX Composite Index the premier indicator of market activity for Canadian equity markets since its launch on January 1, 1977.

Source: TD Asset Management

TD S&P/TSX Capped Composite Index Fund   Broad Market

Pricing and Fund Data

	March 31/05	52 Week Range
Price	$37.54	H $38.63
Net Asset Value Per Unit	$37.35	L $31.59
Fund Ticker Symbol	TCF	
Benchmark Ticker	T00CAR	
MER	0.25%	
Fund Manager	TD Asset Management	
Inception Date	Feb. 23/01	
Net Assets	$95.2MM	
Shares Outstanding	2.56MM	
Avg. Daily Trading Vol.	2.3M	
Underlying Securities	227	
Options Available	No	
Current Dividend Yield (%)	1.68	
P/E Ratio (12Mo. Trailing Earnings)	17.8	
Standard Deviation (3 Yr.)	0.11	
R^2 (3 Yr.)	0.99	
Sharpe Ratio (3 Yr.)	0.53	

Distributions	Income	Capital Gains	
Frequency	Quarterly	Year End	

History (per unit)	2002	2003	2004
Dividends	$0.38	$0.46	$0.39
Return of Capital	$-	$-	$-
Capital Gains	$-	$-	$-
Total	$0.38	$0.46	$0.39

Sector Exposure (%)   March 31/05

Financials	32.0
Energy	21.0
Materials	16.2
Consumer Discretionary	6.2
Industrials	6.1
Information Technology	5.7
Telecommunication Services	5.3
Consumer Staples	4.0
Health Care	1.5
Utilities	1.4

Top Ten Holdings (%)

Royal Bank	4.9%
Manulife Financial	4.8%
Bank of Nova Scotia	4.1%
EnCana	3.9%
Toronto Dominion Bank	3.6%
Bank of Montreal	2.9%
BCE Inc.	2.9%
CIBC	2.6%
Sun Life Financial	2.4%
Suncor	2.3%
Top Ten Total (%)	34.4%

Growth of $1,000: Total Return TCF

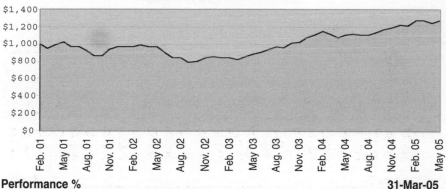

Performance %   31-Mar-05

	1 Mo	3 Mo	6 Mo	1 Yr	3 Yr	5 Yr	Inception
Fund NAV	-0.4%	4.26%	11.62%	13.50%	8.60%	-	6.10%
Quartile Ranking	2	2	2	2	2		

Fund Description

The TD S&P/TSX Capped Composite Index Fund is an open-ended mutual fund trust, listed and traded on the Toronto Stock Exchange, designed to replicate the performance of the S&P/TSX Capped Composite Index. The S&P/TSX Capped Composite Index includes all of the constituents of the S&P/TSX Composite Index. However, the relative weight of any single index constituent is capped at 10% and readjusted quarterly.

Source: TD Asset Management

TD Select Canadian Growth Index Fund

Style-Based

Pricing and Fund Data

	March 31/05	52 Week Range
Price	$9.15	H $9.41
Net Asset Value Per Unit	$9.13	L $7.39
Fund Ticker Symbol	TAG	
Benchmark Ticker	DJCNGT	
MER	0.55%	
Fund Manager	TD Asset Management	
Inception Date	Dec. 7/01	
Net Assets	$20.4MM	
Shares Outstanding	2.24MM	
Avg. Daily Trading Vol.	2.6M	
Underlying Securities	48	
Options Available	No	
Current Dividend Yield (%)	0.77	
P/E Ratio (12Mo. Trailing Earnings)	28.0	
Standard Deviation (3 Yr.)	0.17	
R^2 (3 Yr.)	0.77	
Sharpe Ratio (3 Yr.)	-0.13	

Distributions	Income	Capital Gains
Frequency	Quarterly	Year End

History (per unit)	2002	2003	2004
Dividends	$-	$-	$0.39
Return of Capital	$-	$-	$-
Capital Gains	$-	$-	$-
Total	$0.00	$0.00	$0.39

Sector Exposure (%)   March 31/05

Energy	24.8
Materials	22.5
Consumer Discretionary	12.3
Industrials	12.2
Consumer Staples	11.5
Information Technology	9.8
Financials	4.3
Health Care	1.4
Utilities	0.7

Top Ten Holdings (%)

Suncor Energy	9.3%
Canadian National Railway	9.0%
Barrick Gold	6.5%
Research in Motion Limited	6.2%
Potash Corporation of Sask.	4.9%
Imperial Oil Limited	4.1%
Cameco Corporation	3.9%
Shoppers Drug Mart Corp.	3.6%
Placer Dome Inc.	3.6%
The Thomson Corporation	3.2%
Top Ten Total (%)	54.3%

Growth of $1,000: Total Return TAG

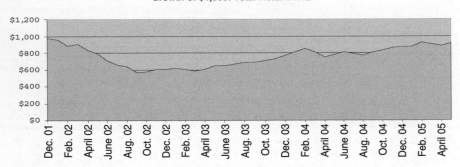

Performance %

	1 Mo	3 Mo	6 Mo	1 Yr	3 Yr	5 Yr	Inception
Fund NAV	-0.98%	4.82%	12.44%	13.00%	0.20%	-	-2.70%
Quartile Ranking	2	1	2	2	4		

31-Mar-05

Fund Description

The TD Select Canadian Growth Index Fund is an open-ended mutual fund trust, listed and traded on the Toronto Stock Exchange (TSX), designed to replicate the performance of the Dow Jones Canada TopCap Growth Index. The Index consists of stocks trading on the Toronto Stock Exchange that exhibit strong growth characteristics as determined by Dow Jones.

Source: TD Asset Management

TD Select Canadian Value Index Fund

Style-Based

Pricing and Fund Data

	March 31/05	52 Week Range
Price	$22.02	H $22.47
Net Asset Value Per Unit	$21.78	L $18.68
Fund Ticker Symbol	TAV	
Benchmark Ticker	DJCNVT	
MER	0.55%	
Fund Manager	TD Asset Management	
Inception Date	Dec. 7/01	
Net Assets	$31.1MM	
Shares Outstanding	1.43MM	
Avg. Daily Trading Vol.	2.2M	
Underlying Securities	72	
Options Available	No	
Current Dividend Yield (%)	2.34	
P/E Ratio (12Mo. Trailing Earnings)	14.3	
Standard Deviation (3 Yr.)	0.10	
R^2 (3 Yr.)	0.85	
Sharpe Ratio (3 Yr.)	0.9	

Distributions	Income	Capital Gains
Frequency	Quarterly	Year End

History (per unit)	2002	2003	2004
Dividends	$0.26	$0.35	$0.39
Return of Capital	$-	$-	$-
Capital Gains	$0.03	$0.28	$1.29
Total	$0.29	$0.63	$1.68

Sector Exposure (%) March 31/05

Financials	51.3
Energy	19.1
Materials	9.8
Telecommunication Services	7.0
Industrials	3.0
Information Technology	3.0
Utilities	2.2
Consumer Discretionary	2.0
Consumer Staples	1.2
Health Care	0.4

Top Ten Holdings (%)

Royal Bank	8.4%
Manulife Financial	8.3%
Bank of Nova Scotia	7.1%
EnCana Corporation	6.8%
The Toronto Dominion Bank	5.9%
Bank of Montreal	5.0%
BCE Inc.	5.0%
CIBC	4.5%
Sun Life Financial Inc.	4.2%
Canadian Natural Resources	3.3%
Top Ten Total (%)	58.5%

Growth of $1,000: Total Return TAV

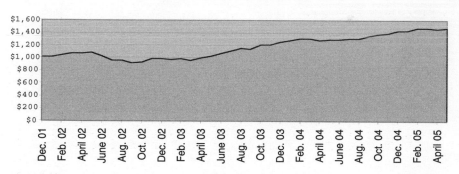

Performance %

31-Mar-05

	1 Mo	3 Mo	6 Mo	1 Yr	3 Yr	5 Yr	Inception
Fund NAV	0.24%	2.98%	10.28%	13.20%	11.40%	-	12.50%
Quartile Ranking	1	3	3	2	1		

Fund Description

The TD Select Canadian Value Index Fund is an open-ended mutual fund trust, listed and traded on the Toronto Stock Exchange, designed to replicate the performance of the Dow Jones Canada TopCap Value Index. The Index consists of stocks trading on the Toronto Stock Exchange that exhibit strong value characteristics as determined by Dow Jones.

Source: TD Asset Management

Appendix B

Making Sense of the Indices: A Reference
Guide to Canadian, U.S., International, and
Global Indices Associated with ETFs

A Reference Guide to ETF Indices

Since almost all ETFs are currently related to an index, it's important to know something about an ETFs' underlying index before you lay your money on the line. You shouldn't necessarily want to buy the top perform-ing ETF or the one you believe has the best prospects because your pri-mary consideration should be selecting an index that best suits your port-folio objectives.

Once you've decided on the kind of index you wish to capture with an ETF, you may be confronted with a selection of competing indices and their related ETFs. There are, for instance, seven large cap U.S. equity ETFs for you to choose from, each related to a different index. Because each index family has its own methodology, it's a good idea to do some homework about the underlying index before buying the ETF so you know exactly what you're buying. Sure, you can select ETFs simply based on their MERs, but understanding the pros and cons of their underlying indices is a better way to do it.

Here are some of the key points about the indices used for ETFs in Canada and the U.S. The indices are arranged in order of decreasing speci-ficity as follows:

1. U.S. Equity Major Markets Indices
2. U.S. Equity Style Indices
3. U.S. Sector Indices
4. U.S. Equity Custom Indices
5. International Equity Indices
6. Global Equity Indices
7. U.S. Fixed Income Indices
8. Canadian Equity Indices
9. Canadian Equity Style Indices
10. Canadian Equity Sector Indices
11. Canadian Fixed Income Indices

Each index is listed with its associated ETF, so once you decide on the index you want, the ETF that goes with it is easy to find.

A Note on Index Methodology and Terminology

Before jumping into the clockworks of indices, here's a brief primer on some of the basic distinguishers of index construction and maintenance.

Rebalancing and Reconstitution

Because indices reflect the market they are trying to measure, they need to be adjusted to market changes. A significant change in the market value of a stock will affect the weighting of that stock in a market capitalization–weighted index. Adjusting for stock weightings is called rebalancing the index. That is just an adjustment to the proportion of the index a company's stock takes up. Deciding what stocks to add or delete from an index is sometimes referred to as reconstitution, or constituent rebalancing. Many index sponsors post regular dates for rebalancing and reconstitution, and the criteria for these changes, so money managers who are keenly interested in an index can anticipate changes and work to adjust their holdings in a systematic way. The fewer times an index is adjusted, the more tax efficient its associated ETF will be. The more times it is adjusted, the closer it will pace its market.

Some indices experience more movement within than others. The S&P/Barra style indices, for example, bump their constituents around from value and growth generally more than the Dow Jones style indices. That is simply a function of the way the styles are defined. If you want a style related ETF, take a look at how the styles are arrived at. This will give you an idea of how much adjustment within the indices might occur so you can weigh the anticipated taxable distributions against the style definition you like best—if tax is an issue. Small cap indices graduate their holdings to mid cap indices frequently, too, so these also have relatively more reconstitution changes than a large cap index for instance. Many index methodologies try to minimize these sorts of reconstitutions by incorporating a buffer system that permits a certain leeway within the index before adjustments must be made, but again, the bigger the buffer, the looser the tracking.

Float Adjusted

The percentage of outstanding shares available for investment is known as "the free float." The size of the float affects the investability of an index; the bigger the free float, the greater the investability of the index. Since investability is one of the desiderata of index construction, most contemporary indices are float adjusted. In other words, the market capitalization–weighting is adjusted to reflect the actual market value of the shares available for investment—not just the total number of shares issued by a company. The mechanics of this adjustment are not uniform among index sponsors. For instance, Dow Jones ignores block holdings of less than 5% whereas the *Financial Times* index folks who run the FTSE indices in some cases aggregate these small block holdings and adjust the free float accordingly. The details of free float calculation are too technical for our purposes here, but you can usually obtain this information from the index sponsor's web site.

We highly recommend a stroll through Dow Jones' indexes site, *www.djindexes.com*, and S&P's web site, *www.standardandpoors.com*, and click on "Indices." These are models of fulsome information on their indices and their maintenance methodology. That's especially handy because S&P administers the major Canadian equity indices.

Eligibility for Inclusion and Maintenance

Indices are a little bit like exclusive clubs: you've got to meet the criteria to get in, but you don't necessarily have to live up to them to stay in. Indices frequently have one set of rules for eligibility to get into the index and a less stringent set of rules for staying in the index. This lessens turnover and may also help the index stay reflective of market conditions. S&P, for instance, exercises the discretion of the index committee while some other index operations are strictly rules-based.

1. U.S. Equity Major Markets Indices Broad Market and Large Cap Indices

1.1 Dow Jones Wilshire 5000 Composite Index

This is the broadest U.S. equity index with approximately 5,000 stocks. Its stated objective is to "represent all U.S. equity issues with readily available prices." It is a market capitalization–weighted index that does not adjust for free floats. For a security to be included in the index, it must be the primary equity issue of a U.S. company. Reconstitution is done when necessary. Rebalancing is done on the third Friday of every month after the close of markets.

*ETF: Vanguard Total Stock Market VIPERs**

*This ETF is actually a separate class of the Vanguard Group's Total Stock Market Index Fund, a giant low-cost U.S. index mutual fund. The mutual fund is based on an optimized basket of about 3,600 stocks in the Dow

Jones Wilshire 5000 Composite Index.
www.wilshire.com
(Sometime by the end of December 2005, this VIPERs benchmark is expected to change to MSCI US Broad Market Index.)

1.2 Dow Jones Wilshire 4500 Index

Take the Dow Jones Wilshire 5000, subtract the 500 companies in the S&P 500 and you've got the 4500 Index. It is a measure of mid and small cap U.S. stocks.

ETF: Vanguard Extended Market VIPERs*
*See note for Vanguard Total Market VIPERs. Sometime by the end of 2005, this VIPERs benchmark is expected to change to an as yet unidentified MSCI index.
www.wilshire.com

1.3 Dow Jones U.S. Total Market Index

This index captures about 95% of the total U.S. market capitalization and has no fixed number of stocks. It was designed for investability and its 1,600 or so stocks are liquid. It excludes foreign stocks, thinly traded stocks, closed-end mutual funds, unit trusts, and limited partnerships. REITs, however, are not excluded. The index includes all large and mid cap publicly traded stocks, but to preserve the index's overall liquidity, only about half of the small cap market is included.

The index is free float adjusted and market cap–weighted. It is reconstituted quarterly and when extraordinary corporate events occur. Rebalancing is also quarterly unless the number of a company's outstanding shares changes more than 10%, in which case the rebalancing is immediate. Delisted stocks are not replaced until a reconstitution date.

ETF: iShares DJ U.S. Total Market Index Fund
http://www.djindexes.com/mdsidx/downloads/gi_rulebook.pdf

1.4 Nasdaq Composite Index

This index takes in the more than 3000 common-type stocks listed on the Nasdaq exchange. The index excludes exchange traded funds, closed-end funds, and derivative products convertible debentures, but does include ADRs, REITs, and limited partnerships among others. It is a market capitalization–weighted index.

ETF: Fidelity Nasdaq Composite Index Tracking Stock
http://dynamic.Nasdaq.com/reference/Comp_Eligibility_Criteria.stm

1.5 NYSE Composite Index

At the end of 2004, this index had more than 2,000 stocks. The index is designed to measure the performance of all the common stocks listed on the New York Stock Exchange, including ADRs. REITs and tracking stocks, but excluding derivatives, ETFs, closed-end funds and limited partnerships. The NYSE says this index represents about 77% of U.S. market capitalization. It is float adjusted, capitalization-weighted, and is reconstituted "as necessary."

ETF: iShares NYSE Composite Index Fund
www.nyse.com/pdfs/nyafactsheet.pdf

1.6 Russell 3000 and 1000 Indices

This index family is constructed by the Frank Russell Company, an investment management firm based in Tacoma, Washington and owned by Northwestern Mutual Life Insurance Company. The index family is market capitalization–weighted. The broadest index, the 3000, holds the 3,000 largest common stocks in the United States. It represents around 98% of the U.S. investable equity market and is adjusted for free float. It excludes stocks under $1, stocks of companies not domiciled in the U.S., and publicly traded entities that are not the stock of an operating company such as Berkshire Hathaway, royalty trusts, limited partnerships, closed-end funds, etc. The index is reconstituted near the end of June. Capitalization rebalancing is done at the end of every month and when corporate activities such as mergers and acquisitions occur. Initial public offerings may be added to the index quarterly, but deleted stocks are not replaced between reconstitution dates, so the number of stocks in the index may fluctuate.

The largest 1,000 stocks in the Russell 3000 become the Russell 1000. The next 2,000 stocks become the Russell 2000 Index, a small cap index.

ETFs: iShares Russell 1000 Index Fund
iShares Russell 3000 Index Fund
www.russell.com/US/Indexes/US/Methodology.asp
www.russell.com/us/indexes/us/definitions.asp

1.7 S&P Composite 1500 Index

This index is the combination of the S&P 500, S&P MidCap 400, and S&P SmallCap indices. S&P says this broad market index represents approximately 90% of U.S. equities. The index methodology is the same as the component indices. (See component entries below).

ETF: iShares S&P 1500 Index Fund
http://www2.standardandpoors.com/spf/pdf/index/Factsheet_sp1500.pdf

1.8 MSCI U.S. Prime Market 750 Index

This index is composed of the 750 largest stocks from the MSCI Investable Market Index diversified with respect to growth and value styles. Float adjusted, market cap–weighted and reconstituted semi-annually. It is float adjusted quarterly though corporate actions may trigger adjustments when they occur.

ETF: Large-Cap VIPERs

www.vanguard.com   see Institutional section to find MSCI index methodology

1.9 S&P 500 Index

This is the most widely followed U.S. stock index for U.S. money managers. The index is constructed by the New York-based firm, Standard & Poor's, which is owned by McGraw-Hill, Inc. It is a market capitalization–weighted index consisting of 500 large U.S. companies. Contrary to popular belief, the S&P 500 does not contain the 500 largest stocks; rather it contains leading U.S. companies from leading industries, which may include relatively small companies with the proviso that each company's market capitalization be more than US$4 billion and that at least 50% of its shares are investable.

S&P identifies industry sectors within the U.S. equity market, approximates the relative importance of these sectors in terms of market capitalization, and then allocates a representative sample of stocks within each sector. No strict criteria are published. Closely-held companies are typically screened out. The index is rebalanced quarterly for changes to shares outstanding, though share changes in excess of 5% are implemented when they happen. The index covers about 80% of the U.S. market. With a selection of 500 companies from the U.S. equity market, the S&P 500 is not a broad market index. Starting in September 2004, S&P began transitioning their U.S. indices to float adjusted. The full transition was to be completed by September 2005. Rebalancing is done quarterly, though changes of 5% or greater are dealt with as soon as possible or at least weekly.

Deletions from the index occur due to company mergers, financial operating failure, lack of representation, or company restructuring. Inclusion, though, is somewhat more subjective and involves the judgment of seven committee members. As a result, changes in index holdings can not necessarily be forecast and they may happen at any time. There are no fixed reconstitution dates. This has led to some criticism that perhaps the S&P 500 is more actively managed than other indices. The internet craze may have helped give credence to this opinion. In 2000, the S&P index committee added 57 stocks to the respected index, 26 of them high-tech. By mid-April 2001, the 57 stocks were down on average 12.9%. The 23 stocks expelled for reasons other than mergers or acquisitions, clocked an average gain of 38.6%. (See Ken Hoover, "Did S&P Get Caught Up in Internet Mania?" *Investor's Business Daily*, April 24, 2001.)

  ETFs: *SPDRs*
      iShares S&P 500 Index Fund
      iUnits S&P 500 Index RSP Fund
www2.standardandpoors.com see "Index Methodology"

1.10 S&P Equal Weight Index

  This is the S&P 500 Index with every constituent given an equal weighting of 0.2%. It is rebalanced quarterly on the same schedule as the S&P 500.

  ETF: Rydex S&P Equal Weight ETF
www2.standardandpoors.com/spf/pdf/index/ewifactsheet.pdf

1.11 S&P 500 O-Strip Index

  "O" here stands for OTC, "over the counter." This index includes only those securities in the S&P 500 that also trade on Nasdaq. It is capitalization–weighted and the methodology is the same as the S&P 500.

  ETF: streetTRACKS SPDR O-Strip
www2.standardandpoors.com see "Index Methodology"

1.12 Fortune 500 Index

  Fortune is an American business magazine that compiles a list every year ranking the 500 U.S.-based and incorporated companies with the biggest revenue. The Fortune 500 Index takes those companies, adds some additional eligibility criteria such as minimum market capitalization, minimum share price, minimum trading volume, and being exchange traded, and ranks them according to market capitalization (not free float adjusted). As a result, the index ranking is different from the list ranking, and because some Fortune 500 companies are private, the index has fewer than 500 companies. The index was launched on December 31, 1999. Its constituents are updated the third Friday in April, naturally after the publication of the Fortune 500 list in *Fortune* magazine, though additions and deletions can happen any time due to corporate actions. Rebalancing is done quarterly, or as soon as is practicable after a share change of 5% or more.

  ETF: streetTRACKS Fortune 500 Index Fund

  There is no on-line information source for this index.

1.13 S&P 100 Index

  A subset of the S&P 500 Index, this index holds one hundred blue chip stocks selected from the S&P 500 index. Each constituent must have individual stock options.

ETF: iShares S&P 100 Index Fund
www2.standardandpoors.com/spf/pdf/index/factsheet_sp100.pdf

1.14 NYSE US 100 Index
Consisting of the 100 largest U.S. common stocks listed on the New York Stock Exchange, this index in intended to track "the best of the best," according to the NYSE.

Float adjusted, market capitalization–weighted. Quarterly reviews and ongoing adjustments for extraordinary corporate events.

ETF: iShares NYSE 100 Index Fund
http://www.nyse.com/pdfs/key_benefits_ny.pdf

1.15 Nasdaq-100 Index
Nasdaq was the world's first electronic stock market, and according to their web site, "trades more shares per day, on average, than any other U.S. market." The Nasdaq-100 Index is made up of the 100 largest non-financial companies in the Nasdaq Composite Index. The Nasdaq Composite Index tracks all the common stocks listed on the Nasdaq Stock Market of which there are more than 3,000. Major industry groups currently represented include technology, communications, retail, financial services, media, transportation, and biotechnology. The 100 Index is a modified market capitalization–weighted index which means that it caps the market weightings of its constituents to meet U.S. diversification requirements. No one company's weighting will represent more than 24% of the index, and all the companies with weightings of 4.5% or more cannot together add up to more than 48% of the index. This is a technology heavy index.

The index is reconstituted on the third Friday of December every year with quarterly reviews for weighting changes, though many corporate actions that effect weightings and changes of 5% or more are responded to promptly.

ETF: Nasdaq-100 Index Tracking Stock, otherwise known as Qubes (QQQQ)
The symbol for Qubes used to be QQQ but with the ETF's move from AMEX to Nasdaq, the symbol has gained a Q because Nasdaq tickers contain a minimum of four letters.
http://dynamic.Nasdaq.com/dynamic/Nasdaq100_activity.stm

1.16 Russell Top 50 Index
This is an index of the 50 largest companies included in the Russell 3000 index and uses the Russell index methodology.

ETF: Rydex Russell Top 50 ETF
www.russell.com/US/Indexes/US/Methodology.asp

1.17 Dow Jones Industrial Average

This is the oldest continuously published stock index in the world (est. 1896) and is unusual in that it is a price-weighted index. It has another peculiarity, too. Its 30 blue chip constituents are selected by the editors of *The Wall Street Journal*. The Dow Jones web site says, "While there are no rules for component selection, a stock typically is added only if it has an excellent reputation, demonstrates sustained growth, is of interest to a large number of investors, and accurately represents the sector(s) covered by the average." Reconstitution happens when corporate events dictate them. Because it is not a market capitalization–weighted index, it does not need to take free floats into account. Only one stock, General Electric, has remained in the average since it was established more than 100 years ago.

ETF: Diamond Trust Series 1 (DIAMONDS)
www.djindexes.com/mdsidx/index.cfm?event=showAvgOverview&averageSel ection=G

Mid Cap U.S. Equity Indices

1.18 Russell Midcap Index

The Russell Midcap index is a subset of the Russell 1000 index. The Russell Midcap Index itself is a capitalization-weighted index consisting of 800 of the smallest companies in the Russell 1000. These 800 companies make up about 25% of the market cap of the 1000 index. Russell's web site reported as of July 2004 that the latest reconstitution determined the index's average market capitalization was approximately US$4.2 billion and its median market capitalization was approximately US$3.2 billion. The largest company in the index was worth US$12.4 billion in market cap.

ETF: iShares Russell Midcap Index Fund
www.russell.com/US/Indexes/US/methodology.asp

1.19 MSCI U.S. Mid-Cap 450 Index

This index is a subset of MSCI U.S. Prime Market 750 Index and consists of the 450 smallest stocks of that index. It is a market capitalization–weighted index, adjusted for free float and market capitalization range. It changes quarterly, though corporate actions may trigger float adjustments when the actions become effective. Capitalization is determined by rank within the broader index. To minimize turnover, a buffer zone allows some capitalization flexibility.

ETF: Mid-Cap VIPERs
www.vanguard.com   see Institutional information on VIPERs for index methodology

1.20 S&P MidCap 400 Index
S&P says this index is the most widely used mid cap index. It is intended to measure the performance of the mid-sized company segment of the U.S. market. It holds the stock of 400 U.S. mid cap companies selected by market cap, liquidity, and industry representation. The median market capitalization of companies in the index as of December 31, 2004 was US$2.36 billion. It is a market capitalization–weighted index.

ETFs: MidCap SPDRs
iShares S&P MidCap 400 Index Fund
www2.standardandpoors.com/spf/pdf/index/400brochure.pdf

Small Cap U.S. Equity Indices

1.21 Russell 2000 Index
The smallest 2000 stocks of the Russell 2000 make up this index, the most widely followed index for U.S. small cap. Only common stock of U.S. companies are included. Closed-end funds, limited partnerships, royalty trusts, and other non-operating entities are excluded. The index is capitalization-weighted and float adjusted. It is fully reconstituted once a year.

ETF: iShares Russell 2000 Index Fund
www.russell.com/us/indexes/us/methodology.asp

1.22 MSCI U.S. Small-Cap 1750 Index
This index is a subset of the 2500 stock MSCI Investable Market Index. It is market cap–weighted, adjusted for free float and market capitalization. Its range changes quarterly, though corporate actions may trigger float adjustments when the actions become effective.

The capitalization range is determined by rank within the broader index and is buffered within a zone of flexibility.

ETF: Small-Cap VIPERs
www.vanguard.com   See Institutional information on VIPERs for index methodology

1.23 S&P SmallCap 600 Index
This index is intended to track the performance of the small cap segment of the U.S. market. It holds 600 U.S. small cap stocks. As of December 31, 2004, the median company size was US$.76 billion. The S&P 500, the 400,

and the 600 together make up the S&P Composite 1500 Index.

ETF: iShares S&P 600 Index Fund
www2.standardandpoors.com/spf/pdf/index/600brochure.pdf

2. U.S. Equity Style Indices

Each index provider has a different way of determining style and market capitalization. When choosing an index, keep in mind how pure the styles and how rigid the capitalization definitions. Does the definition of value, for instance, end up capturing the segment of the market you want? Is your desire for mid cap companies, and nothing but mid caps, worth the potential tax liability of investing in an index that makes frequent stock switches when capitalization values change slightly?

2.1 Dow Jones U.S. Total Market Style Indices

All the stocks in the DJ U.S. Total Market Index are first separated by capitalization. As with all Dow Jones country indices, classifying an index component as large, mid, or small cap is based on a survey of the country's cumulative capitalization. The top 70% of that total capitalization is automatically classified as large cap. The next 20% is mid cap, and the remaining 10% is screened for trading volume and market capitalization to select a final 5% that comprises the small cap segment. After that basic division, the components are ranked on the basis of six factors: projected price to earnings, projected earnings growth, trailing price to earnings, trailing earnings growth, price to book value, and dividend yield.

After some statistical work, each stock emerges identified either as growth, value or neutral, and the style indices are formed. Neutral stocks are excluded, so the resulting indices are a purer representation of growth and value styles than either the Russell or the S&P style indices (see below).

The style indices are reconstituted at the end of each March and September. Capitalization is reviewed quarterly with immediate changes for extraordinary events.

ETFs: streetTRACKS DJ U.S. Large Cap Growth Index Fund
streetTRACKS DJ U.S. Large Cap Value Index Fund
streetTRACKS DJ U.S. Small Cap Growth Index Fund
streetTRACKS DJ U.S. Small Cap Value Index Fund
www.djindexes.com/mdsidx/index.cfm?event=showStyleMethod
www.djindexes.com/mdsidx/downloads/StyleRulebook.pdf
www.djindexes.com/mdsidx/index.cfm?event=showTotalMarketMethod

2.2 Intellidex Style Indices

Intellidex indices are enhanced indices that employ proprietary methodology with the aim of selecting stocks that are representative of the market and also have appreciation potential. These indices are used by Powershares ETFs and are provided by AMEX. Powershares literature describes the Intellidex style methodology this way:

"The Style Intellidexes apply a rigorous ten-factor style isolation process to objectively segregate companies into their appropriate investment style and size universe. Next, each company is thoroughly evaluated to determine its investment merit by analyzing unique financial characteristics from four broad financial perspectives: fundamental, valuation, timeliness, and risk."

The Powershares web site (*www.powershares.com*) has back tested performance information on the Intellidex indices and comparisons with other style indices.

ETFs: *Powershares Dynamic Small Cap Growth Portfolio*
Powershares Dynamic Mid Cap Growth Portfolio
Powershares Dynamic Large Cap Growth Portfolio
Powershares Dynamic Small Cap Value Portfolio
Powershares Dynamic Mid Cap Value Portfolio
Powershares Dynamic Large Cap Value Portfolio
http://www.powershares.com/styleinvproc.asp

2.3 MSCI Style Indices

Using the MSCI US Prime Market 750 Index for the available stock universe, MSCI uses a multi-factor framework to identify stocks with growth and value characteristics to create the MSCI US Prime Market Growth Index and the MSCI US Prime Market Value Index. According to Vanguard's web site, the selection factors include book value to price value ratio, 12-month forward earnings to price ratio, and dividend yield. Growth factors include forward earnings per share growth rate, historical earning per share growth trend, and internal growth rate. MSCI uses buffer zones for capitalization ranges. The index is market cap–weighted and the free float is adjust quarterly though corporate actions may trigger adjustments when the actions become effective. Major reconstitution is done in May and November with minor ones done in August and February.

ETFs: *Vanguard Growth VIPERs*
Vanguard Value VIPERs

The MSCI US Small-Cap Growth and the MSCI US Small-Cap Value Index are both derived from the MSCI US Small-Cap 1750 Index using the same multi-factor framework as discussed above. Same index characteristics as described above.

ETFs: *Vanguard Small-Cap Growth VIPERs*
       Vanguard Small-Cap Value VIPERs
https://institutional2.vanguard for MSCI index information

2.4 Morningstar Style Indices

In their work analyzing mutual funds, Morningstar developed a nine-box capitalization and style grid with which to classify mutual funds. Now Morningstar is applying a similar grid to stocks to produce nine-style indices. Morningstar's methodology first screens stocks listed on the major U.S. exchanges for liquidity and excludes ADRs, derivatives, limited partnerships, and holding companies, among others. Then it identifies the capitalization size by establishing bands based on percentages of the overall market instead of fixed thresholds. After this, each stock is identified exclusively as either value, growth, or "core" (when neither growth nor value characteristics dominate). Style criteria for value include price to projected earnings, price to book, price to sales, price to cash flow, and dividend yield. Growth criteria include projected and historical earnings growth, sales and cash flow growth, and book value growth.

Morningstar's style matrices do not overlap and are completely objective and rules-based. Reconstitution is semi-annual and rebalancing quarterly unless a free-float changes by 10% or more, or two constituents merge, in which case rebalancing is done immediately.

ETFs: *iShares Morningstar Large Growth Index Fund*
       iShares Morningstar Large Value Index Fund
       iShares Morningstar Large Core Index Fund
       iShares Morningstar Mid Growth Index Fund
       iShares Morningstar Mid Value Index Fund
       iShares Morningstar Mid Core Index Fund
       iShares Morningstar Small Growth Index Fund
       iShares Morningstar Small Value Index Fund
       iShares Morningstar Small Core Index Fund
http://indexes.morningstar.com/Index/Methodology.asp

2.5 Russell Style Indices

The stocks in the Russell 3000, 2000, and 1000 indices are divided into growth and value styles, so there is a Russell 3000 Growth Index, a Russell 3000 Value Index, and so on, for the "thousand series" indices. The style decision is based on two variables, the price to book ratio (as with the S&P style indices), and the I/B/E/S forecasted long-term growth rate relative to its peers. (I/B/E/S International Inc. is a Thomson Corporation company well-known for its consensus earnings estimates.) The results of these two variables are combined into a score for each stock which, with more fiddling, determines style membership. Seventy percent of the stocks in each index are classified as all value or all growth, and 30% are assigned proportionately to value and growth. Growth and value determinations, then, are not mutually exclusive. Some stocks have a little of both. Although this method actively identifies growth stocks, as opposed to the S&P method that characterizes growth stocks as simply those that aren't value stocks, purists should know the Russell value and growth indices can cause a company's market cap to be divided between both growth and value. Reconstitution is in June.

ETFs: *iShares Russell 3000 Growth Index Fund*
        iShares Russell 3000 Value Index Fund
        iShares Russell 1000 Growth Index Fund
        iShares Russell 1000 Value Index Fund
        iShares Russell 2000 Growth Index Fund
        iShares Russell 2000 Value Index Fund

The Russell mid cap style indices are a subset of the Russell Midcap index. The Midcap Growth Index consists of those companies in the Russell Midcap Index with higher price-to-book ratios and higher fore-casted growth values. Similarly, the Russell Midcap Value Index contains companies in the Russell Midcap Index with lower price to book ratios and lower forecasted growth values.

ETFs: *iShares Russell Midcap Growth Index Fund*
        iShares Russell Midcap Value Index Fund
www.russell.com/US/Indexes/US/Methodology.asp

2.6 S&P Style Indices

These indices include the S&P 500/Barra Growth, the S&P MidCap 400/Barra Growth, and the S&P SmallCap 600Growth, and the corresponding S&P Value indices.

The style indices divide the respective index holdings into value or growth companies by examining their price to book (P/B) ratio, a standard yardstick for evaluating the value of a stock. Stocks with a low P/B ratio are designated value stocks, and stocks with a high P/B ratio are designated as growth stocks. These divisions are treated as mutually exclusive, and the indices are split in half by market capitalization and sorted by price-to-book. Taken together the value and growth stocks always equal the total of their respective index, be it the 500, the 400, or the 600.

This is a pretty simple system. A stock is either value or growth with nothing in-between. Critics point out that price-to-book value may be a good indication of a value play, but it doesn't say much about a growth stock except to point out the obvious; namely, that it isn't a value stock.

Reconstitution happens monthly and rebalancing on or about January 1 and July 1.

ETFs: *iShares S&P 500/Barra Growth Index Fund*
           iShares S&P 500/Barra Value Index Fund
           iShares S&P MidCap 400/Barra Growth Index Fund
           iShares S&P MidCap 400/Barra Value Index Fund
           iShares S&P SmallCap 600/Barra Growth Index Fund
           iShares S&P SmallCap 600/Barra Value Index Fund
www.barra.com/Research/Description.aspx

Index Family	Dow Jones	Morningstar	MSCI	Russell	S&P/Barra
Broad market index	Total market	US Market	US Total market	Russell 3000	Super Composite 1500
% of U.S. market	95%	97%	98%	98%	87%
Number of stocks	1,600+	2,000	2,500	3,000	1,500
Rules-based methodology	Yes	Yes	Yes	Yes	No
Weighting	Free float	Free float	Free float	Free float	Market cap (free float by Sept. 05)
Growth/value separation	Stocks not growth or value omitted from style indexes	Stocks not growth or value assigned to separate core style index	Stocks not growth or value proportionately split to each style index	Stocks not growth or value proportionately split to each style index	Each company assigned to either the value or growth index
Rebalance frequency	Semi-annual	Semi-annual	Semi-annual	Annual	Ad hoc for broad indexes. Semi-annual for style
Style rebalance dates	March, Sept.	June, Dec.	May, Nov.	June	June, Dec.
Buffer zones	No	Yes	Yes	No	No
Number of style factors	6	10	8	2	1
Value factors	P/B P/E Yield P/E forward	P/B P/E Yield P/CF P/S	P/B P/E forward Yield	P/B	P/B
Growth factors	LT earn gr 5-yr hist. earn gr	5-yr avg sales gr 5-yr avg earn gr 5-yr avg cash flow 5-yr avg book value Projected earn gr	LT earn gr ST earn gr Current gr rate LT hist earn gr LT hist sales gr	LT earn gr	None

source: Morgan Stanley

3. U.S. SECTOR INDICES

3.1 Dow Jones U.S. Total Market Sector Indices

The DJ U.S. Total Market Index is divided into the following ten industries:

> *Oil and Gas*
> *Basic Materials*
> *Industrials*
> *Consumer Goods*
> *Health Care*
> *Consumer Services*
> *Telecommunications*
> *Utilities*
> *Financials*
> *Technology*

Nestled within these industries are up to 18 supersectors, 39 sectors and 108 subsectors. For instance, the industry class "Financials" has within it three supersectors: "Banks," "Insurance," and "Financial Services." "Financial Services" includes four sectors: "Real Estate," "General Financial," "Equity Investment Instruments," and "Nonequity Investment Instruments," and so on.

This industry classification was formulated by Dow Jones working in collaboration with the London-based FTSE Group and was implemented in 2004. It is called the Industry Classification Benchmark.

There is an iShares ETF for each of the ten Dow Jones U.S. Total Market industries. A few industry sub-group indices also sport iShares ETFs. These are:

> *iShares DJ U.S. Financial Services Composite Index Fund*
> *iShares DJ U.S. Real Estate Index Fund*
> *iShares DJ U.S. Transportation Average Index Fund*

Dow Jones' new way of classifying stocks on their indices has meant that the names of a few ETFs launched under the previous industry classification may not perfectly match the current industry/sector classifications. While the few ETFs affected by this have changed their names, one in particular is out of synch: the iShares Dow Jones U.S. Energy Sector Index Fund is pegged to the Dow Jones U.S. Oil and Gas Index.
www.djindexes.com/mdsidx/downloads/gi_rulebook.pdf

3.2 MSCI Sector Indices

MSCI uses the Global Industry Classification Standard (GICS), a classification designed by Morgan Stanley Capital International, Inc. and S&P.

This classification scheme has 10 sectors, 24 industry groups, 64 industries, and 139 sub-industries. The sector indices are related to the sector positions in the broader MSCI U.S. Investable Market Index. In other words, the components within the Investable Market Index's Consumer Discretionary sector should also be within the MSCI U.S. Investable Market Consumer Discretionary Index: Float adjustments, capitalization weighting, and the same maintenance as MSCI uses in their style indices.

ETFs: VIPERs on all ten GICS industry sectors: Information Technology, Financials, Energy, Consumer Discretionary, Industrials, Telecommunication Services, Utilities, Health Care, Consumer Staples, Materials.
https://institutional2.vanguard for MSCI index information

3.3 S&P Select Sector Indices

Standard & Poor's also uses the Global Industry Classification Standard (see 3.2). This classification scheme divides the S&P 500 into ten economic sectors, so you'd expect there to be ten sector ETFs on the S&P 500, but that isn't the case.

The sector ETFs split the S&P 500 into just nine sectors (having ten sectors would not allow each one to qualify as a regulated investment company or RIC, due to security concentration issues) and are associated with Select Sector Indices published by AMEX. These are the sectors for the Select Sector SPDRs:

> Consumer Discretionary
> Consumer Staples
> Energy
> Financial
> Health Care
> Industrial
> Materials
> Technology (+Telecom)
> Utilities

Taken together, the stocks in these nine sectors make up the entirety of the S&P 500 index, so what holds for the S&P 500 index holds for the corresponding sector ETFs.

ETFs: Nine Select Sector SPDRs, one for each of the above listed sectors.
http://www.spdrindex.com/aboutspdrs/
www2.standardandpoors.com "Global Industry Classification Standard"

3.4 Goldman Sachs Technology Index

Goldman Sachs is a global investment bank and securities firm. Their technology index is made up of U.S. technology companies across every major sub-sector of technology. It is a modified capitalization-weighted index to limit dominance by a few stocks. To qualify in the index, all stocks must trade on the NYSE, AMEX, or Nasdaq, and have a minimum annual trading volume of 30% of float. If volume falls to less than 15%, the company is removed. Foreign companies, ADRs, limited partnerships, and closed-end funds are excluded. Companies with free float below 20% are not eligible and companies whose free float falls below 10% will be removed. Reconstitution takes place semi-annually to reduce portfolio turnover. There is no fixed number of constituents.

ETFs: iShares Goldman Sachs Technology Index Fund

There are now three ETFs based on corresponding Goldman Sachs Technology sub-sector indices:

iShares Goldman Sachs Networking Index Fund
iShares Goldman Sachs Semiconductor Index Fund
iShares Goldman Sachs Software Index Fund

www.ishares.com

No on-line information is available on the indices from Goldman Sachs.

3.5 Goldman Sachs Natural Resources Sector Index

An index designed to reflect U.S.-traded, natural resource–related stocks. According to the iShares prospectus, the index includes "extractive companies, energy companies, owners, and operators of timber tracts, forestry services, producers of pulp and paper, and owners of plantations." Reconstitution is semi-annual. It is a modified, capitalization-weighted index with objective rules for constituent inclusion.

ETF: iShares Goldman Sachs Natural Resources Index Fund

www.ishares.com

No on-line information is available on this index from Goldman Sachs.

3.6 Morgan Stanley REIT Index

This index is undergoing revisions to its index methodology in 2005. The index, which is said to cover two-thirds of the U.S. REIT market, contains actively traded Real Estate Investment Trusts (REITs) that meet a minimum market capitalization. IPOs may be admitted to this index before scheduled quarterly reviews if it meets other eligibility requirements.

See 2.3 for reconstitution and rebalancing frequency. As of March 2005, the index had 121 holdings.

ETF: Vanguard REIT VIPERs

3.7 Morgan Stanley Technology Index

This index comprises American electronic-based technology companies. The index is owned and maintained by Morgan Stanley, a U.S. financial services company. It is equal-dollar-weighted and rebalanced in December. The American Stock Exchange calculates this index and Morgan Stanley acts as consultant to AMEX.

ETF: streetTRACKS Morgan Stanley Technology Index Fund
http://advisors.ssga.com/etf/fund/wtb/why_this_benchmark_MTK.html

3.8 Nasdaq Biotechnology Index

This is a capitalization-weighted index that includes companies classified by the Global Classification System as either biotechnology or pharmaceutical. According to the iShares web site, the companies in the index "are primarily engaged in using biomedical research for the discovery or development of novel treatments or cures for human disease." Eligibility requirements include a market cap of at least US$200 million, and a price of US$10 or more, good daily trading volume of at least 100,000 shares a day on average, and having been publicly traded for at least six months, except for spinoffs. Semi-annual reconstitution. There were 159 companies in the index as of March 31, 2005.

ETF: iShares Nasdaq Biotechnology Index Fund
http://dynamic.Nasdaq.com/dynamic/Nasdaqbiotech_activity.stm

3.9 Wilshire REIT Index

This index tracks the performance of publicly traded U.S. real estate investment trusts. The index requires eligible REITs to have a market capitalization of at least US$200 million, and 75% or more of the company's revenue must be from real estate assets. Mortgage REITs, health care REITS, real estate finance companies, home builders, companies with more than 25% of their assets in direct mortgages, large land owners, and subdividers are not included. Reconstitution occurs at quarterly intervals and float adjustments when so done on Dow Jones Wilshire 5000 Composite Index. The index is a subset of the Wilshire Real Estate Securities Index.

ETF: streetTRACKS Wilshire REIT Index Fund
www.wilshire.com/Indexes/RealEstate/REIT/

3.10 Cohen & Steers Realty Majors Index

This index tracks the market in large, actively traded U.S. REITs or Real Estate Investment Trusts. This is geographically diversified and has REITs in many sectors of U.S. real estate. As of December 2004, the Cohen & Steers Index had REITS in apartments, office property, regional malls, industrial properties, shopping centres, and self-storage. The index is modified capitalization-weighted with a maximum constituent weight of 8%. Reconstitutions happen quarterly.

ETF: iShares Cohen & Steers Realty Majors Index Fund
www.cohenandsteers.com

4. Custom Equity Indices

4.1 KLD Select Social Index

This index is put together by the people at KLD Research & Analytics, Inc. in Boston, world-famous for their pioneering efforts in social investment advocacy and research. The KLD Domini 400 Social Index has been a standard in the social investment community since its launch in 1990. It was the first equity index whose constitution criteria involved social screens, which eliminated companies involved in tobacco, alcohol, armaments, nuclear power, adult entertainment, and gambling.

For those who think the Domini 400 Index was too exclusionary, you'll be happy to know that the KLD Select Social Index has far less judgmental screens: the only industry it excludes entirely is tobacco. This index draws on the stocks listed in the Russell 1000 Index and the S&P 500 to a maximum of 350 stocks. Companies eligible for the index are evaluated based on their social and environmental performance. KLD's web site lists community relations, corporate governance, diversity, employee relations, human rights, and product safety and quality as the performance criteria. The index is a modified capitalization-weighted index and is designed to track the Russell 1000 within 2%.

ETF: iShares KLD Select Social Index Fund
http://www.kld.com/benchmarks/factsheet/ssi_methodology.pdf

4.2 Dow Jones Select Dividend Index

Dow Jones says this is the first dividend index created by a major indexer. This index, designed for those who are looking for income, is made up of 100 liquid, dividend-yielding stocks from the Dow Jones U.S. Total Market Index. Each company's weight in the index depends on their indicated annual dividend. The index will adjust to corporate events affecting index weighting. Annual constitution review is in December, though immediate deletion from the index will result if the company is delisted or bankrupt, eliminates its dividend, or lowers its dividend to below a relative threshold established each month.

ETF: iShares Dow Jones Select Dividend Index Fund
www.djindexes.com/mdsidx/downloads/meth_info/DJUSDIV_Method.pdf

4.3 Mergent Dividend Achievers 50 Index

This index consists of the 50 highest-yielding stocks in the Mergent

Dividend Achievers universe. Mergent Inc.'s web site says this universe is drawn from U.S.-listed companies that have increased their annual dividends in every year for at least the last 10 consecutive years. It is a yield-weighted index, reconstituted annually, and rebalanced quarterly.

ETF: Powershares High Yield Equity Dividend Achievers Portfolio
http://www.mergent.com/Publish/DividendAchieverMediaDetail236.asp

4.4 Dynamic Market Intellidex Index

This index draws from the 2000 largest stocks (by market cap) of U.S.-headquartered companies trading on NYSE, AMEX or Nasdaq. The index selects stocks from each sector. A proprietary quantitative methodology identifies those stocks as having the greatest future capital appreciation. The quantitative, rules-based method involves a liquidity screen and a number of stock evaluation factors, which include financial strength, a price valuation assessment, a timeliness determination, and the risk-reward profile. AMEX produces the index. Rebalancing is quarterly.

ETF: Powershares Dynamic Market Portfolio ETF
http://www.powershares.com/dynmktinvproc.asp

4.5 Dynamic OTC Intellidex Index

The universe for this index is the 1000 largest U.S. stocks listed on Nasdaq.

The index methodology is quantitative, rules-based, and proprietary, and seeks to identify stocks with growth potential. See 2.2 and 4.4 for methodology description.

ETF: Powershares Dynamic OTC Portfolio ETF
http://www.powershares.com/dynotcinvproc.asp

4.6 Wilderhill Clean Energy Index

This is an enhanced index that is intended to deliver capital appreciation. Publicly traded companies involved with greener energy sources or renewable energy, and technologies associated with cleaner energy constitute this index. It is rebalanced and reconstituted quarterly and is a modified equal-weighted index. AMEX, the publisher of this index, says this is the first index comprised of companies focusing on clean energy. The index is named after Dr. Robert Wilder, whose company, WilderShares, LLC, is the source for the index constitution.

ETF: Powershares Wilderhill Clean Energy Portfolio
www.powershares.com/images/pdf/pbwfund.pdf
www.wilderhill.com/index.php

5. International Equity Indices

5.1 MSCI Indices/Country Indices

Morgan Stanley Capital International Inc., majority owned by the global financial services firm, Morgan Stanley, runs a large series of international indices, from broad global indices like the MSCI World Index to regional indices like the MSCI Europe Index, right down to country-specific indices like the MSCI South Korea Index. MSCI finished revamping, its international indices to full free float weightings in 2002, and with it also achieved greater market coverage from 60% to about 85%. The free float changes resulted in a lower weighting for telecommunication and utility stocks, which are commonly owned in some part by governments, or come with foreign ownership restrictions.

Stocks within each country are sorted by industry and by size in descending order with screens for free float and liquidity. Rebalancing and reconstitution are done quarterly one region at a time. All indices are reviewed every 18 months. Extraordinary corporate events affecting weightings and industry representation are addressed as they happen. Changes are announced two weeks in advance.

ETFs: The ETFs on MSCI country indices are extensive; 25 as of April 2005, all of them iShares. See Directory for a full list.
www.msci.com

5.2 MSCI EAFE Index

EAFE (pronounced E-fee) is designed to capture the market performance of developed equity markets in Europe, Australasia, and the Far East. It is a free float adjusted, market capitalization index, and as of April 2005 the index included 21 country indices. The MSCI EAFE is widely regarded as the premier index for exposure to developed countries outside of North America. The iShares fund (AMEX: EFA) that tracks this index is now the third largest ETF in terms of assets after SPY and QQQQ.

ETFs: *iShares EAFE Fund*
         iUnits MSCI International Equity Index
www.msci.com

5.3 MSCI EMU Index

Large and liquid stocks from the eleven countries in the European Economic and Monetary Union make up this index. Like all MSCI indices, it is a free float adjusted, market capitalization index.

ETF: *iShares MSCI EMU*
www.msci.com

5.4 MSCI Europe Index

An index consisting of European common stocks from 16 countries.

ETF: Vanguard European VIPERs

www.msci.com

5.5 S&P Europe 350 Index

This index is designed to track the performance of stocks on 17 European exchanges. It has three sub-indices: the S&P Euro (holding stocks from the ten EuroZone countries), the S&P Euro Plus (adds Denmark, Norway, Sweden, and Switzerland), and the S&P United Kingdom. It is intended to cover about 70% of the market capitalization of its target markets. Inclusion depends on liquidity, sector representation, fundamental analysis, and market capitalization. It has 350 stocks adjusted for free float. This index is itself a subset of the S&P Global 1200 Index.

Additions to the index generally occur when there is a vacancy arising from an index deletion. Float weights and share changes are reviewed quarterly, or as soon as a change of 5% or greater occurs.

ETF: iShares S&P Europe 350 Fund

www2.standardandpoors.com   see "Index Methodology"

5.6 Dow Jones STOXX 50 Index

One of Dow Jones' blue chip indices, the STOXX web site describes it as consisting of 50 stocks covering the market supersector leaders in the Dow Jones STOXX^{sm} 600 Index. The Dow Jones STOXX 600 Index is derived from the largest 600 stocks in the Dow Jones STOXX Total Market Index which is a European index.

STOXX 50 index is free float adjusted and market cap–weighted with a 10% weighting cap. It is reconstituted annually.

ETF: streetTRACKS Dow Jones STOXX 50 Fund

http://www.stoxx.com/indexes/guide/definitions.pdf

http://www.stoxx.com/indexes/factsheets/stoxx50_fs.pdf

5.7 Dow Jones EURO STOXX 50 Index

Like the Dow Jones STOXX 50 Index (5.6), this is another blue chip Dow Jones index based on the Dow Jones STOXX Total Market Index. The Euro STOXX 50 contains fifty market supersector leading stocks from the Dow Jones EURO STOXX Index, a eurozone index. Reconstituted annually, with a 10% weightings cap on constituents.

ETF: streetTRACKS Dow Jones EURO STOXX 50 Fund

http://www.stoxx.com/indexes/guide/definitions.pdf

http://www.stoxx.com/indexes/factsheets/eurostoxx50_fs.pdf

5.8 Bank of New York American Depositary Receipt Indexes (BLDRs)
Emerging Markets 50 ADR Index
Developed Markets 100 ADR Index
Europe 100 ADR Index
Asia 50 ADR Index

American Depositary Receipts (ADRs) are certificates that trade in U.S. markets and represent an interest in shares on a foreign market. The ADR Index tracks all Depositary Receipts, Global Receipts, and a similar product called New York Shares, traded on The New York Stock Exchange, The American Stock Exchange, and Nasdaq. The Bank of New York ADR Index is a composite of many subindices, four of which now have ETFs associated with them. The composite index, from which all the other ADR indices are derived, is capitalization-weighted and adjusted for free float utilizing Dow Jones' index methodology. It is reviewed quarterly, but may be revised when significant corporate events occur.

ETFs: *BLDRS* Emerging Markets 50 ADR Index Fund*
   BLDRS Developing Markets 100 ADR Index Fund
   BLDRS Europe 100 ADR Index Fund
   BLDRS Asia 50 ADR Index Fund

*pronounced "builders"
www.bldrsfunds.com/ and www.adrbny.com/files/RuleBook.pdf

5.9 MCSI Select Emerging Markets Index

Stocks from 18 emerging market countries in Europe, Asia, Africa, and Latin America make up this index. For MSCI methodology see 5.1

ETF: Vanguard Emerging Markets VIPERs
www.msci.com

5.10 MSCI Pacific Index

This index is comprised of stocks from companies in Hong Kong, Singapore, New Zealand, Australia, and Japan.

ETF: Vanguard Pacific VIPERs
www.msci.com

5.11 S&P/Tokyo Stock Price Index 150 Index

Described by S&P as the Japanese counterpart to the S&P 500, this index, which commonly goes by the acronym TOPIX, includes 150 stocks from each major sector of the Tokyo market. According to S&P's web site, the index "...represents approximately 70% of the market value of the Japanese equity market." Only highly liquid stocks from large Japanese companies are included. It is float adjusted, cap-weighted, and revised throughout the year.

This index is a component of S&P Global 1200 Index.

ETF: iShares S&P/TOPIX 150 Fund

www2.standardandpoors.com   see "Index Methodology"

5.12 S&P Latin America 40

This index is another subcomponent of the S&P Global 1200. S&P has designed the Latin American index to capture about 70% of the market capitalization of the key countries in Latin America. Forty companies in total are captured, the most highly liquid large cap companies from Mexico, Brazil, Argentina, and Chile.

ETF: iShares S&P Latin America 40 Fund

www2.standardandpoors.com   see "Index Methodology"

5.13 Halter USX China Index

This index is comprised of companies that are listed on the major U.S. exchanges, and which get the majority of their revenue from The People's Republic of China. To be eligible for this index, companies must have a minimum market cap of US$50 million, calculated from the average closing price of the last 40 trading days. It is a modified capitalization-weighted index where no single component can exceed 20% of the index. Large components will have a minimum weight of 4.5%, and in aggregate will not exceed 30% of the index. The amount by which the large components must be reduced will be added to the small components, none of which will be over 4.5%. Reconstitution and rebalancing is done quarterly, but corporate actions affecting a component's shares outstanding greater than 5% will be adjusted for on the market's close of the date they take effect. Halter Financial Group is the index creator and provider while AMEX is the index calculator.

ETF: Powershares Golden Dragon Halter USX China Portfolio

http://www.usxchinaindex.com/methodology.cfm

5.14 FTSE/Xinhua China 25 Index

The FTSE Group is an index and data company jointly owned by The Financial Times and the London Stock Exchange. FTSE teamed up with Xinhua Financial Network to create an index of 25 of the largest and most liquid Chinese stocks available to foreign investors.

Securities are weighted in proportion to the total market value of their shares, but individual constituents are capped at 10%. All shares trade on the Hong Kong Stock Exchange. Quarterly reviews.

ETF: iShares FTSE/Xinhua China 25 Index Fund

www.ftsexinhua.com

6. Global Indices

6.1 S&P Global 1200 Index

S&P says this is the first global index to be calculated in real time. It covers 29 local markets in 7 regions as represented by these country or regional indices: S&P 500, S&P Europe 350, S&P/TOPIX 150, S&P/TSX 60, S&P ASX 50 (Australia), S&P Asia 50 (Asia, ex-Japan), and S&P Latin America 40. The proportion of each regional component is relative to the size of its adjusted market value in the global equity market. Share changes of 5% or greater are updated immediately; those less than 5% are reflected on a quarterly basis. The index is divided into ten sectors according to the Global Industry Classification Standard. Except for the S&P 500, all the indices are float adjusted and market capitalization–weighted. (The S&P 500 is transitioning to float adjusted and should be full float adjusted by mid-September, 2005.)

ETFs: *iShares S&P Global Energy Sector Fund*
iShares S&P Global Financials Sector Fund
iShares S&P Global Healthcare Sector Fund
iShares S&P Global Technology Sector Fund
iShares S&P Global Telecommunications Sector Fund
www2.standardandpoors.com see "Index Methodology"

6.2 S&P Global 100 Index

The S&P Global 100 Index tracks the performance of 100 large multi-national companies. After determining that a company's activities are truly global in nature, each stock is screened for liquidity, sector representation, size, and fundamentals. The index is free float adjusted. Companies are removed from this S&P index for the same four reasons they would be removed from any S&P index: bankruptcy, being bought or merging, corporate restructuring, or lack of industry representation. Rebalancing is quarterly, or when a change greater than 5% occurs in the outstanding shares. Companies from the S&P Global 100 index are derived from the S&P Global 1200 Index.

ETF: *iShares S&P Global 100 Index Fund*
www2.standardandpoors.com see "Index Methodology"

6.3 Dow Jones Global Titans Index

Calling 50 of the world's largest multinational companies "Titans" is almost as poetic as it is descriptive. These companies are selected from the Dow Jones World Index and are sorted by free float, market capitalization weight, sales/revenue, and net profit. The top 50 finalists make it into the index with their weight capped at 10% of the index. Reconstitution takes place annually, rebalancing quarterly, or with a change of more than 10% in the number of a company's outstanding shares.

ETF: *streetTRACKS DJ Global Titans Index Fund*
http://www.djindexes.com/mdsidx/index.cfm?event=showGlobalTitans

7. U.S. Fixed Income Indices

7.1 Lehman Brothers 1-3 Year U.S. Treasury Index
7.2 Lehman Brothers 7-10 Year U.S. Treasury Index
7.3 Lehman Brothers 20+ Year U.S. Treasury Index

These indices share the same methodology and vary only by the duration of the bonds in the index and the amount of outstanding face value each constituent must have. All the indices are designed to reflect the public obligations of the U.S. Treasury within their respective duration periods. The indices are market capitalization–weighted, pay monthly income, and are rebalanced and reconstituted at the beginning of each month, though changes are permitted intra-month. Constituents must be U.S. dollar denominated, rated investment grade by Moody's Investors Service, be fixed rate, and have a minimum specified outstanding face value. The index does not include Targeted Investor Notes, state and local government series bonds, inflation-protected treasuries, convertible, or stripped bonds. The 1-3 year index requires $250 million outstanding face value; 7-10 requires $150 million; and the 20+ also requires $150 million.

ETFs: *iShares Lehman 1-3 Year Treasury Bond Fund*
       iShares Lehman 7-10 Year Treasury Bond Fund
       iShares Lehman 20+ Year Treasury Bond Fund
www.ishares.com "fixed income" (No index methodology is available online.)

7.4 GS $ InvesTop Index

All 100 bonds in this index are equally weighted at par (face) value. They are all U.S. dollar, highly liquid, investment grade corporate bonds. The index is rebalanced every month, though portfolio changes can occur between rebalancings. Each bond offering included in the index must have at least US$500 million in outstanding face value, be five years old or more, and have a minimum of three years to maturity. No strip bonds, callable, or convertible bonds are allowed. Distributions from income are paid monthly. This index is run by Goldman Sachs.

ETF: *iShares GS $ InvesTop Bond Fund*
www: gs.com/investop/

7.5 Lehman Brothers U.S. Treasury Inflation Notes Index

Inflation protected bonds issued by the U.S. Treasury are commonly referred to as "TIPS" for Treasury Inflation Protected Securities. TIPS have inflation adjusted principal amounts with a fixed rate of interest. The bonds in this index must have at least one year to maturity, $250 million in outstanding face value, be rated investment grade, denominated in U.S. dollars, have a fixed rate of interest, and not be convertible. As of March 31, 2005, the index had 15 constituents. It is reconstituted monthly.

ETF: iShares Lehman TIPS Bond Fund
www.ishares.com "Fixed Income"

7.6 Lehman Aggregate Bond Index

As of March 31, 2005, this index contained 5,811 constituents, and had an adjusted duration of 4.4 years. The index includes U.S. denominated bonds with at least one year remaining to maturity which are sold publicly. All constituents must be of investment grade, non-convertible, fixed rate, and taxable. U.S. government bonds, corporate bonds, asset-backed securities, and mortgage pass-through securities are eligible.

ETF: iShares Lehman Aggregate Bond Fund
www.ishares.com "Fixed Income" (No index methodology is available online.)

8. Canadian Equity Indices

8.1 S&P/TSX Composite Index

This index is the broadest measure of the Canadian equity market. Subsumed within this index are the S&P/TSX 60, and the S&P/TSX MidCap, and the S&P/TSX SmallCap indices. To be included in the index, companies must have been listed on the TSX for at least 12 months (though IPOs can be considered in certain cases), and must meet certain size and liquidity requirements. The volume, value, and number of transactions taken together must be at least 0.025% of the same sum done for all the companies trading on the TSE to be considered for the index. To stay in the index, that figure can go as low as 0.020%. A stock must not have had more than 25 non-trading days in the previous 12 months to get into the index, but can have as many as 50 non-trading days once in the index. At least 25% of the companies free float shares must turnover in one year to be included in the index, and turnover must be no lower than 20% to continue in the index.

A company must have a minimum weight of 0.05% of the index on a float adjusted basis (0.025% to stay in), and a minimum trade-weighted average price of $1 over the previous three months.

Generally, only common stocks of operating companies are allowed in the index which means limited partnerships, REITs, preferred shares, and exchangeable shares are excluded; however, S&P has indicated that income trusts will be included in the Canadian index to better reflect the realities of the Canadian market, but this eligibility change had not yet been implemented as of May 2005.

The index is float adjusted for companies with purchase restrictions on 20% or more of outstanding shares. Stocks are ranked on a float quoted market value (QMV) basis. The S&P's web site defines QMV as "the close price of that security on that day multiplied by the number of float shares." Reconstitution happens quarterly though deletions, and a subsequent replacement can occur at any time. Rebalancings occur as soon as possible with a capitalization change of 0.05% or more of relative weight.

ETF: TD S&P/TSX Composite Index Fund
www2.standardandpoors.com "Canadian Indices"

8.2 S&P/TSX Capped Composite Index

This index holds all the stocks of the TSX Composite, but their weights are limited (capped) to 10% of the index. This is to ensure diversification and was a response to the heavy weighting of Nortel Networks Corp. in early 2000. Weights are adjusted quarterly but changes of relative weights greater than 0.05% are adjusted "on the first practical date." Share capitalization changes are announced one business day before being reflected in the index.

ETF: TD S&P/TSX Capped Composite Fund
www2.standardandpoors.com "Canadian Indices"

8.3 S&P/TSX 60 Index

This index comprises 60 of Canada's largest and most liquid companies selected from the TSX Composite Index. The 60 Index is balanced across 10 sectors and float adjusted. Stocks are selected based on liquidity, size, sector representation, and their stability. Because this is an S&P index, the same four reasons for deleting a company from the index apply: acquisition by another company, bankruptcy, company restructuring, or lack of industry representation. Additions are made to replace deleted companies as required. Reconstitution is quarterly and market capitalization adjustments are made to exclude block holdings of 20% or more. Stock weight changes greater than 0.05% are implemented when they occur. Index changes are announced three days in advance. This large cap index was launched December 31, 1998 and is included in the S&P Global 1200.

ETF: iUnits S&P/TSX 60 Index Participation Fund
www2.standardandpoors.com "Canadian Indices"

8.4 S&P/TSX 60 Capped Index

This index is a capped version of the S&P/TSX 60. No one company in the index will be greater than 10%. Weights are adjusted quarterly unless components' relative weights change by more the 0.05%. In that case, the adjustment will be made when the change in weight occurs. Additions or deletions to the index due to rebalancing are announced a month in advance. See the S&P/TSX Composite index description for rules.

ETF: iUnits S&P/TSX 60 Capped Index Fund
www2.standardandpoors.com "Canadian Indices"

9. Canadian Style and Capitalization Indices

9.1 Dow Jones Canadian TopCap Growth Index
9.2 Dow Jones Canadian TopCap Value Index

For these indices, stocks are selected from among all the stocks in the Dow Jones Canada Total Market Index which, according to Dow Jones, covers 95% of Canada's market capitalization. Stocks can be judged either growth, value, or neutral. Neutral stocks are not included in either style index unless they have a market capitalization more than or equal to 2% "of its size segment's capitalization." The size segments are "large cap, mid cap, small cap, top cap, and low cap" in both growth and value. The style indices are free floated and are reviewed twice a year in March and September.

According to the Dow Jones web site, "A stock's style classification is determined by the company's performance in terms of six measures—two projected, two current, and two historical:

Projected Price-to-Earnings Ratio (P/E)
Projected Earnings Growth
Price-to-Book Ratio (P/B)
Dividend Yield
Trailing P/E
Trailing Earnings Growth.

ETFs: TD Select Canadian Growth Index Fund
TD Select Canadian Value Index Fund
http://djindexes.com/mdsidx/index.cfm?event=showStyleMethod

9.3 S&P/TSX Midcap Index

This index includes Canadian mid-size companies with their weightings adjusted across economic sectors. Capitalization, liquidity, and fundamentals determine inclusion. Acquisition by another company, bankruptcy, restructuring, or lack of sector representation can knock a component out of the index. Additions will be made to fill deletions. Float is adjusted for changes of 20% or more. Stock weightings are updated quarterly or with a change of 0.05% or more on the basis of the TSX Composite Index. Reconstitution changes are announced one month in advance. Other changes are announced three days ahead of time. This index was launched in May 1999.

ETF: iUnits S&P/TSX Canadian MidCap Index Fund
www2.standardandpoors.com "Canadian Indices"

10. Canadian Sector Indices

10.1 S&P/TSX Capped Sector Indices

Stocks included in these sector indices are drawn from the pool of stocks listed in the S&P/TSX Composite Index. The same inclusion and ranking criteria apply as for the composite, but the weighting of any one component stock is capped at 25% of the index. Sectors are defined according to the S&P/MSCI Global Industry Classification Standard (GICS). There is a capped index for each GICS sector: Information Technology, Financials, Energy, Consumer Discretionary, Industrials, Telecommunication Services, Utilities, Health Care, Consumer Staples, Materials. S&P also calculates three sub-sector Canadian capped indices: Gold, Real Estate, Diversified Metals, and Mining.

ETFs: iUnits S&P/TSX Capped Energy Index Fund
iUnits S&P/TSX Capped Financials Index Fund
iUnits S&P/TSX Capped Gold Index Fund
iUnits S&P/TSX Capped Information Technology Index Fund
www2.standardandpoors.com "Canadian Indices"

10.2 S&P/TSX Capped REIT Index

With a similar construction methodology to the S&P/TSX sector indices, this index is a sub-index of the S&P/TSX Canadian Income Trust Index. All trusts in the Trust Index must derive their income from an actual underlying business. To be considered for inclusion in the REIT index, a REIT must generally have been listed on the TSX for 12 months, be among the larger trusts of its kind, and be regularly and actively traded. No one REIT in the index can exceed a 25% weighting. Weightings are adjusted quarterly except for capped weightings falling below 20%, or uncapped weightings rising above 30%. In these cases the adjustments will be done as soon as possible.

This is a float adjusted index which excludes the value of concentrated holdings of 20% or more. Deletions from the index can occur due to bankruptcy, restructuring, or lack of representation within the REIT industry.

ETF: iUnits Capped REIT Index Fund
www2.standardandpoors.com "Canadian Indices"

11. Canadian Fixed Income Index

11.1 Scotia Capital Universe Bond Index

A well-known and widely referenced measure of the broad Canadian bond market, this index contains government and corporate investment grade bonds issued in Canada and denominated in Canadian dollars. They pay semi-annual interest with a fixed rate and must have remaining terms greater than one year. To ensure liquidity, index eligibility requires corporate bond issues to be a minimum of $100 million and government bond issues a minimum of $50 million. This is a float adjusted, weighted index; Bank of Canada holdings and bonds that have been stripped of their coupons are subtracted from the calculation of the outstanding amount of each issue. As of April 2005, the universe was valued at $584 billion dollars and is adjusted daily.

ETF: iUnits Canadian Bond Broad Market Index Fund
http://www.scotiacapital.com/ResearchCapabilities/RE_Universe.pdf

Appendix C

ETF Directory:
Vital Statistics on U.S. and International ETFs,
Both Existing and Pending

U.S. ETFs: Classified by Market Cap and Style

Exchange Traded Funds	Trading Symbol	Intraday NAV Symbol	Approx # of Positions	Inception Date	Expense Ratio (%)	◊Total Assets ($ Mil)	Avg Daily Volume (1000/shrs)	Dividend /Income Distrib.	†Listed Options (O) LEAPS® (L)
U.S. EQUITY: MAJOR MARKET FUNDS									
Broad Market									
Fidelity Nasdaq Composite	ONEQ	ONEQI	1,796	9/25/03	0.30	124	59	Q	O
iShares DJ US Total Market Index Fund	IYY	NLA	1,639	6/12/00	0.20	106	23	Q	-
iShares NYSE Composite	NYC	NJP	1,737	3/30/04	0.25	10	3	Q	O
iShares Russell 3000 Index Fund	IWV	NMV	2,990	5/22/00	0.20	907	379	Q	O
iShares S&P 1500	ISI	EIS	1,501	1/20/04	0.20	83	22	Q	-
Total Stock Market VIPERs	VTI	TSJ	3,651	5/31/01	0.07	1,025	152	Q	O
Vanguard Extended Market VIPERs	VXF	EAH	3,418	12/27/01	0.08	19	6	Q	-
Large Cap									
DIAMOND Trust Series 1	DIA	DXV	30	1/20/98	0.18	6,423	6,827	M	L
iShares NYSE 100	NY	NJT	100	4/2/04	0.20	28	4	A	O
iShares Russell 1000 Index Fund	IWB	NJBX	987	5/15/00	0.15	2,057	199	Q	O
iShares S&P 100 Index Fund	OEF	OEV	102	10/23/00	0.20	883	245	Q	L
iShares S&P 500 Index Fund	IVV	NNV	502	5/15/00	0.09	12,867	763	Q	-
NASDAQ-100 Index Tracking Stock	QQQQ	QXV	100	3/10/99	0.20	19,411	98,721	Q	L
Rydex Russell Top 50 ETF	XLG	XLR	250	5/10/05	0.20	60	29,400	A	O
Rydex S&P 500 Equalweight	RSP	RSJ	500	4/30/03	0.40	720	68	Q	-
Standard & Poors Depositary Receipts	SPY	SXV	500	1/29/93	0.10	51,214	61,002	Q	O
streetTRACKS Fortune 500 Index Fund	FFF	FFY	442	10/10/00	0.22	109	9	Q	O
streetTRACKS SPDR O-Strip	OOO	OFBX	74	9/15/04	0.36	44	22	Q	O
Vanguard Large-Cap VIPERs	VV	BVH	753	1/30/04	0.07	98	25	Q	-

Exchange Traded Funds	Trading Symbol	Intraday NAV Symbol	Approx # of Positions	Inception Date	Expense Ratio (%)	◊Total Assets ($ Mil)	Avg Daily Volume (1000/shrs)	Dividend /Income Distrib.	†Listed Options (O) LEAPS® (L)
Mid Cap									
iShares Russell Midcap Index Fund	IWR	NIZ	785	7/16/01	0.20	1,182	116	Q	O
iShares S&P MidCap 400 Index Fund	IJH	NJH	400	5/22/00	0.20	2,395	88	Q	O
Standard & Poors MidCap 400 Dep Rec	MDY	MXV	400	5/4/95	0.25	7,174	1,451	Q	L
Vanguard Mid-Cap VIPERs	VO	BVO	455	1/30/04	0.13	583	105	A	-
Small Cap									
iShares Russell 2000 Index Fund	IWM	NJM	2,003	5/22/00	0.20	5,811	10,535	Q	O
iShares S&P SmallCap 600 Index Fund	IJR	NIR	601	5/22/00	0.20	3,243	425	Q	O
Vanguard Small-Cap VIPERs	VB	BVP	1,738	1/30/04	0.10	180	65	A	-
Custom									
iShares DJ Select Dividend	DVY	DJJ	95	11/7/03	0.40	6,479	607	Q	O
iShares KLD Select Social Index Fund	KLD	JYT	260	1/31/05	0.50	47	23	Q	-
PowerShares High Yield Equity Div Ach	PEY	HEY	50	12/9/04	0.50	340	166	Q	O
PowerShares Dynamic Mkt Portfolio	PWC	FZM	99	5/1/03	0.60	291	49	Q	O
PowerShares Dynamic OTC Portfolio	PWO	FZO	100	5/1/03	0.60	68	16	Q	O
PowerShares WilderHill Clean Energy Port	PBW	BWH	38	3/3/05	0.60	37	39	Q	O
Style Funds									
Broad Market Growth									
iShares Russell 3000 Growth Index Fund	IWZ	NBE	1,991	7/24/00	0.25	129	24	Q	O
Broad Market Value									
iShares Russell 3000 Value Index Fund	IWW	NNW	2,002	7/20/00	0.25	361	32	Q	O

Exchange Traded Funds	Trading Symbol	Intraday NAV Symbol	Approx # of Positions	Inception Date	Expense Ratio (%)	◊Total Assets ($ Mil)	Avg Daily Volume (1000/shrs)	Dividend /Income Distrib.	†Listed Options (O) LEAPS® (L)
Large Cap Growth									
iShares Morningstar Large-Cap Growth JKE	EJK		82	7/4/04	0.25	53	6	Q	-
iShares Russell 1000 Growth IWF	NBF		622	5/22/00	0.20	3240	793	Q	O
iShares S&P 500/BARRA Growth IVW	NJG		178	5/22/00	0.18	2433	222	Q	O
PowerShares Dynamic Large Cap Growth Port PWB	ILH		49	3/3/05	0.60	9	33	Q	O
streetTRACKS DJ US Large Cap Growth ELG	FLG		116	9/29/00	0.21	78	2	S	-
Vanguard Growth VIPERs VUG	PVJ		433	1/30/04	0.11	119	21	Q	-
Large Cap Value									
iShares Morningstar Large Cap Core JKD	EJH		93	7/2/04	0.30	57	7	Q	-
iShares Morningstar Large Cap Value JKF	EJN		92	7/2/04	0.25	59	9	Q	-
iShares Russell 1000 Val Idx Fund IWD	NJU		678	5/22/00	0.20	4907	678	Q	O
iShares S&P 500/BARRA Value IVE	NME		324	5/22/00	0.18	2698	265	Q	O
PowerShares Dynamic Large Cap Value Port PWV	DBW		50	3/3/05	0.60	10	26	Q	O
streetTRACKS DJ US Large Cap Val Idx Fund ELV	FLV		122	9/29/00	0.21	121	8	Q	-
Vanguard Value VIPERs VTV	PVW		392	1/30/04	0.11	478	56	Q	-
Mid Cap Growth									
iShares Morningstar Mid Cap Growth JKH	FDB		250	7/2/04	0.30	32	8	Q	-
iShares Russell Midcap Growth Index Fund IWP	NIW		485	7/16/01	0.25	836	77	Q	O
iShares S&P MidCap 400/BARRA Gr Idx Fund IJK	NNK		185	7/24/00	0.25	1172	61	Q	O
PowerShares Dynamic Mid Cap Growth Port PWJ	GBW		74	3/3/05	0.60	9	12	Q	O
Mid Cap Value									
iShares Morningstar Mid Cap Core JKG	FGB		248	7/2/04	0.25	64	8	Q	-
iShares Morningstar Mid Cap Value JKI	FHB		222	7/2/04	0.30	34	6	Q	-
iShares Russell Mid Cap Value IWS	NIV		555	7/16/01	0.25	1104	130	Q	O

Exchange Traded Funds	Trading Symbol	Intraday NAV Symbol	Approx # of Positions	Inception Date	Expense Ratio (%)	◊Total Assets ($ Mil)	Avg Daily Volume (1000/shrs)	Dividend /Income Distrib.	†Listed Options (O) LEAPS® (L)
iShares S&P Mid Cap 400/BARRA Value	IJJ	NJJ	220	7/24/00	0.25	1760	85	Q	O
PowerShares Dynamic Mid Cap Value Port	PWP	HWB	75	3/3/05	0.60	10	14	Q	O

Small Cap Growth

Exchange Traded Funds	Trading Symbol	Intraday NAV Symbol	Approx # of Positions	Inception Date	Expense Ratio (%)	◊Total Assets ($ Mil)	Avg Daily Volume (1000/shrs)	Dividend /Income Distrib.	†Listed Options (O) LEAPS® (L)
iShares Morningstar Small Cap Growth	JKK	HKJ	322	7/2/04	0.30	26	6	Q	-
iShares Russell 2000 Growth	IWO	NLO	1,371	7/24/00	0.25	1741	1109	Q	O
iShares S&P SmallCap 600/BARRA Growth	IJT	NLT	245	7/24/00	0.25	946	88	Q	O
PowerShares Dynamic Small Cap Growth Port	PWT	DWB	100	3/3/05	0.60	10	7	Q	O
streetTRACKS DJ US Small Cap Growth	DSG	PSG	313	9/29/00	0.27	50	3	Q	-
Vanguard Small Cap Growth VIPERs	VBK	HVK	997	1/30/04	0.12	71	15	A	-

Small Cap Value

Exchange Traded Funds	Trading Symbol	Intraday NAV Symbol	Approx # of Positions	Inception Date	Expense Ratio (%)	◊Total Assets ($ Mil)	Avg Daily Volume (1000/shrs)	Dividend /Income Distrib.	†Listed Options (O) LEAPS® (L)
iShares Morningstar Small Cap Core	JKJ	HKG	370	7/2/04	0.25	38	6	Q	-
iShares Morningstar Small Cap Value	JKL	HKK	331	7/2/04	0.30	35	10	Q	-
iShares Russell 2000 Value	IWN	NAJ	1,313	7/24/00	0.25	2598	361	Q	O
iShares S&P SmallCap 600/BARRA Value	IJS	NJS	357	7/24/00	0.25	1432	128	Q	O
PowerShares Dynamic Small Cap Value Port	PWY	HWB	99	3/3/05	0.60	10	14	Q	O
streetTRACKS DJ US Small Cap Value	DSV	PSV	375	9/29/00	0.27	91	5	S	-
Vanguard Small Cap Value VIPERs	VBR	PVY	946	1/30/04	0.12	73	12	A	-

U.S. Equity ETFs Classified by Sector

Consumer Discretionary

Exchange Traded Funds	Trading Symbol	Intraday NAV Symbol	Approx # of Positions	Inception Date	Expense Ratio (%)	◊Total Assets ($ Mil)	Avg Daily Volume (1000/shrs)	Dividend /Income Distrib.	†Listed Options (O) LEAPS® (L)
Consumer Discretionary Select Sector SPDR	XLY	YXV	87	12/22/98	0.26	342	431	Q	O
iShares DJ US Consumer Services	IYC	NLL	257	6/12/00	0.60	229	79	Q	-
Retail HOLDRS	RTH	IRH	19	5/2/01	*	487	2,284	R	O
Vanguard Consumer Discretionary VIPERs	VCR	HVA	430	1/30/04	0.25	15	4	A	-

Exchange Traded Funds	Trading Symbol	Intraday NAV Symbol	Approx # of Positions	Inception Date	Expense Ratio (%)	◊Total Assets ($ Mil)	Avg Daily Volume (1000/shrs)	Dividend Income Distrib.	†Listed Options (O) LEAPS® (L)
Consumer Staples									
Consumer Staples Select Sector SPDR	XLP	PXV	36	12/22/98	0.27	843	736	Q	L
iShares DJ US Consumer Goods	IYK	NMJ	152	6/12/00	0.60	428	60	Q	-
Vanguard Consumer Staples VIPERs	VDC	HVP	98	1/30/04	0.25	55	10	A	-
Energy									
Energy Select Sector SPDR Fund	XLE	EXV	29	12/22/98	0.25	2,477	9,070	Q	L
iShares DJ US Energy Sector	IYE	NLE	55	6/12/00	0.60	647	153	Q	O
Oil Service HOLDRS	OIH	OXH	18	2/7/01	*	1,165	4,366	R	O
Vanguard Energy VIPERs	VDE	DVO	121	9/29/04	0.25	129	47	A	-
Financials									
Financial Select Sector SPDR	XLF	FXV	82	12/22/98	0.25	1,470	6,504	Q	L
iShares DJ US Financial Sector	IYF	NLF	296	5/22/00	0.60	303	34	Q	O
iShares DJ US Financial Services	IYG	NAG	146	6/12/00	0.60	142	10	Q	O
Regional Bank HOLDRS	RKH	XRH	19	6/23/00	*	541	687	R	O
Vanguard Financials VIPERs	VFH	HVF	531	1/30/04	0.25	26	5	A	-
Healthcare									
Biotech HOLDRS	BBH	IBH	18	11/23/99	*	1,190	846	R	L
Health Care Select Sector SPDR	XLV	NXV	55	12/22/98	0.25	1,578	684	Q	L
iShares Nasdaq Biotechnology	IBB	IBF	157	2/8/01	0.50	1,065	1,054	Q	O
iShares DJ US Healthcare Sector	IYH	NHG	175	6/12/00	0.60	1,211	169	Q	O
Pharmaceutical HOLDRS	PPH	IPH	21	2/1/00	*	2,039	1,054	R	O
Vanguard Health Care VIPERs	VHT	HVH	292	1/30/04	0.25	130	24	A	-

Exchange Traded Funds	Trading Symbol	Intraday NAV Symbol	Approx # of Positions	Inception Date	Expense Ratio (%)	◊Total Assets ($ Mil)	Avg Daily Volume (1000/shrs)	Dividend /Income Distrib.	†Listed Options (O) LEAPS® (L)
Industrials									
Industrial Select Sector SPDR	XLI	TXV	56	12/22/98	0.26	778	640	Q	L
iShares DJ Transportation Average	IYT	YET	23	10/10/03	0.60	124	117	Q	-
iShares DJ US Industrial Sector	IYJ	NIJ	251	6/12/00	0.60	239	55	Q	-
Vanguard Industrials VIPERs	VIS	DVL	316	9/29/04	0.25	11	5	A	-
Materials									
iShares DJ US Basic Materials Sector	IYM	NLBX	73	6/12/00	0.60	426	95	Q	-
Materials Select Sector SPDR	XLB	BXV	32	12/22/98	0.26	873	1,520	Q	L
Vanguard Materials VIPERs	VAW	HVW	122	1/30/04	0.25	40	13	A	-
Natural Resources									
iShares Goldman Sachs Natural Resources	IGE	NGJ	124	10/22/01	0.50	607	51	Q	-
Real Estate									
iShares Cohen & Steers Realty Majors	ICF	ICG	31	1/29/01	0.35	1,338	168	Q	O
iShares DJ US Real Estate	IYR	NLR	79	6/12/00	0.60	667	893	Q	O
streetTRACKS Wilshire REIT	RWR	EWR	92	4/27/01	0.26	606	28	S	-
Vanguard REIT VIPERs	VNQ	NVZ	120	9/29/04	0.12	253	37	Q	-
Technology-Broad Based									
iShares DJ US Technology Sector	IYW	NJW	263	5/15/00	0.60	386	69	Q	O
iShares Goldman Sachs Technology	IGM	IPM	239	3/13/01	0.50	167	60	Q	O
Technology Select Sector SPDR	XLK	KXV	32	12/22/98	0.26	1,085	808	Q	L
Vanguard Information Technology VIPERs	VGT	HVI	445	1/30/04	0.25	25	5	A	-
Technology-Internet									
B2B Internet HOLDRS**	BHH	BUX	6	2/24/00	*	25	102	R	O

Exchange Traded Funds	Trading Symbol	Intraday NAV Symbol	Approx # of Positions	Inception Date	Expense Ratio (%)	◊Total Assets ($ Mil)	Avg Daily Volume (1000/shrs)	Dividend /Income Distrib.	†Listed Options (O) LEAPS® (L)
Internet HOLDRS**	HHH	HHI	13	9/23/99	*	283	473	R	L
Internet Architecture HOLDRS	IAH	XAH	20	2/25/00	*	64	32	R	O
Internet Infrastructure HOLDRS**	IIH	YIH	14	2/25/00	*	30	67	R	-

Technology-Other

Broadband HOLDRS**	BDH	XDH	23	4/6/00	*	89	84	R	O
iShares Goldman Sachs Networking	IGN	NVK	35	7/10/01	0.50	138	102	Q	O
iShares Goldman Sachs Semiconductor	IGW	NVW	58	7/10/01	0.50	270	165	Q	O
iShares Goldman Sachs Software	IGV	NVV	47	7/10/01	0.50	115	171	Q	O
Semiconductor HOLDRS**	SMH	XSH	20	5/5/00	*	1,654	27,349	R	O
Software HOLDRS**	SWH	XWH	17	9/27/00	*	233	306	R	O

Telecommunications

iShares DJ US Telecommunications Sector	IYZ	NJZ	26	05/22/00	0.60	310	165	Q	O
Telecom HOLDRS**	TTH	ITH	13	2/1/00	*	259	489	R	O
Vanguard Telecom Services VIPERs	VOX	DVT	41	9/29/04	0.25	15	3	A	-
Wireless HOLDRS**	WMH	IWH	20	11/1/00	*	59	25	R	O

Utilities

iShares DJ US Utilities Sector	IDU	NLU	74	6/12/00	0.60	644	65	Q	O
Utilities HOLDRS	UTH	XUH	19	6/23/00	*	313	459	R	O
Utilities Select Sector SPDR	XLU	UXV	33	12/22/98	0.26	1,645	1,502	Q	L
Vanguard Utilities VIPERs	VPU	HVJ	91	1/30/04	0.25	68	8	A	-

Transportation

iShares Dow Jones Transportation Average	IYT	YET	24	10/6/03	0.60	124	117	Q	-

Exchange Traded Funds	Trading Symbol	Intraday NAV Symbol	Approx # of Positions	Inception Date	Expense Ratio (%)	◊Total Assets ($ Mil)	Avg Daily Volume (1000/shrs)	Dividend /Income Distrib.	†Listed Options (O) LEAPS® (L)
International									
Broad Based Global									
iShares S&P Global 100	IOO	OON	100	12/5/00	0.40	341	46	Q	-
Market 2000+ HOLDRS	MKH	XKH	57	8/30/00	*	48	4	R	O
streetTRACKS DJ Global Titans	DGT	UGT	45	9/20/00	0.54	108	9	Q	O
Global Sectors									
iShares S&P Global Energy	IXC	XGC	55	11/12/01	0.65	316	44	Q	-
iShares S&P Global Financial	IXG	XGG	217	11/12/01	0.65	71	8	Q	-
iShares S&P Global Healthcare	IXJ	XGJ	82	11/12/01	0.65	345	68	Q	-
iShares S&P Global Technology	IXN	XGN	125	11/12/01	0.65	42	9	Q	-
iShares S&P Global Telecom.	IXP	XHP	43	11/12/01	0.65	42	8	Q	-
Broad Based									
iShares MSCI EAFE	EFA	EFV	801	8/14/01	0.35	16,043	923	S	O
Regional									
BLDRS Asia 50 ADR Index	ADRA	ADRAI	50	11/13/02	0.30	27	6	Q	-
BLDRS Developed Markets 100 ADR	ADRD	ADRDI	100	11/13/02	0.30	20	4	Q	-
BLDRS Emerging Markets 50 ADR	ADRE	ADREI	50	11/13/02	0.30	56	10	Q	-
BLDRS Europe 100 ADR	ADRU	ADRUI	100	11/13/02	0.30	10	2	Q	-
Europe 2001 HOLDRS**	EKH	EKI	44	01/18/00	*	18	2	R	O
StreetTRACKS DJ EUROSTOXX 50	FEZ	FEZIV	50	10/21/01	0.30	140	47	Q	-
Fresco Dow Jones STOXX 50	FEU	FEUIV	50	10/21/01	0.35	30	8	Q	-
iShares MSCI Emerging Markets	EEM	EEV	259	4/7/03	0.75	3,915	245	A	-
iShares MSCI EMU	EZU	WWE	289	7/25/00	0.59	557	58	S	-
iShares MSCI Pacific ex-Japan	EPP	EPK	161	10/25/01	0.50	1,287	117	Q	-

Exchange Traded Funds	Trading Symbol	Intraday NAV Symbol	Approx # of Positions	Inception Date	Expense Ratio (%)	◊Total Assets ($ Mil)	Avg Daily Volume (1000/shrs)	Dividend /Income Distrib.	†Listed Options (O) LEAPS® (L)
iShares S&P Europe 350	IEV	NJG	355	7/25/00	0.60	1,160	106	Q	-
iShares S&P Latin America 40	ILF	NIH	38	10/25/01	0.50	340	85	Q	-
Vanguard Emerging Markets VIPERs	VWO	HVO	684	3/10/05	0.30	87	63	A	-
Vanguard European VIPERs	VGK	SVK	511	3/10/05	0.18	74	43	A	-
Vanguard Pacific VIPERs	VPL	SVY	391	3/10/05	0.18	50	39	A	-

Country Specific International

Americas

Exchange Traded Funds	Trading Symbol	Intraday NAV Symbol	Approx # of Positions	Inception Date	Expense Ratio (%)	◊Total Assets ($ Mil)	Avg Daily Volume (1000/shrs)	Dividend /Income Distrib.	†Listed Options (O) LEAPS® (L)
iShares MSCI Canada	EWC	WPB	91	3/18/96	0.59	325	179	S	-
iShares MSCI Brazil	EWZ	WWC	43	7/14/00	0.74	398	918	S	-
iShares MSCI Mexico	EWW	INW	29	3/18/96	0.59	220	373	S	-

Asia/Pacific

Exchange Traded Funds	Trading Symbol	Intraday NAV Symbol	Approx # of Positions	Inception Date	Expense Ratio (%)	◊Total Assets ($ Mil)	Avg Daily Volume (1000/shrs)	Dividend /Income Distrib.	†Listed Options (O) LEAPS® (L)
iShares FTSE/Xinhua China 25	FXI	JYV	26	10/5/04	0.74	893	164	A	O
iShares MSCI Australia	EWA	WBJ	72	3/18/96	0.59	340	370	A	-
iShares MSCI Hong Kong	EWH	INH	39	3/18/96	0.59	601	596	A	-
iShares MSCI Japan	EWJI	NJ	280	3/18/96	0.59	6,571	8,691	A	-
iShares MSCI Malaysia	EWM	INM	75	3/18/96	0.59	316	446	A	-
iShares MSCI Singapore	EWS	INR	37	3/18/96	0.59	282	312	A	-
iShares MSCI South Africa	EZA	FZA	46	2/3/03	0.74	139	34	A	-
iShares MSCI South Korea	EWY	WWK	72	5/12/00	0.74	525	88	A	-
iShares MSCI Taiwan	EWT	WWM	105	6/23/00	0.74	789	889	A	-
iShares S&P/TOPIX 150	ITF	NIT	150	10/23/01	0.50	95	7	A	-
Powershares Golden Dragon USX China	PGJ	TGJ	47	12/8/04	0.60	50	40	Q	O

Europe

Exchange Traded Funds	Trading Symbol	Intraday NAV Symbol	Approx # of Positions	Inception Date	Expense Ratio (%)	◊Total Assets ($ Mil)	Avg Daily Volume (1000/shrs)	Dividend /Income Distrib.	†Listed Options (O) LEAPS® (L)
iShares MSCI Austria	EWO	INY	22	3/18/96	0.59	175	176	S	-

Exchange Traded Funds	Trading Symbol	Intraday NAV Symbol	Approx # of Positions	Inception Date	Expense Ratio (%)	◊Total Assets ($ Mil)	Avg Daily Volume (1000/shrs)	Dividend /Income Distrib.	†Listed Options (O) LEAPS® (L)
iShares MSCI Belgium	EWK	INK	23	3/18/96	0.59	78	58	S	-
iShares MSCI France	EWQ	WBF	58	3/18/96	0.59	57	35	S	-
iShares MSCI Germany	EWG	WDG	48	3/18/96	0.59	154	115	S	-
iShares MSCI Italy	EWI	INE	42	3/18/96	0.59	41	31	S	-
iShares MSCI Netherlands	EWN	INN	27	3/18/96	0.59	55	30	S	-
iShares MSCI Spain	EWP	INP	40	3/18/96	0.59	64	40	S	-
iShares MSCI Sweden	EWD	WBQ	47	3/18/96	0.59	61	35	S	-
iShares MSCI Switzerland	EWL	INL	38	3/18/96	0.59	61	39	S	-
iShares MSCI United Kingdom	EWU	INU	150	3/18/96	0.59	490	324	S	-
Commodity									
iShares COMEX Gold Trust	IAU	IAV	-	1/28/05	0.40	140	37	-	-
streetTRACKS Gold Trust	GLD	GLDIV	-	11/18/04	0.40	2,445	1,684	-	-
Fixed Income									
iShares GS $ InvesTop Corporate Bond	LQD	DLL	101	3/26/02	0.15	2,518	130	M	O
iShares Lehman 1-3 Year Treasury	SHY	SHZ	12	3/26/02	0.15	3,713	353	M	O
iShares Lehman 7-10 Year Treasury	IEF	IEN	7	3/26/02	0.15	843	237	M	O
iShares Lehman 20+ Year Treasury	TLT	TLZ	14	3/26/02	0.15	647	1,258	M	O
iShares Lehman Aggregate Bond	AGG	AKG	122	9/22/03	0.20	993	106	M	O
iShares Lehman TIPS Bond	TIP	TBK	17	12/4/03	0.20	1,513	93	M	O

Source: Morgan Stanley, Barclays Global Investors, State Street Global Advisors, Bank of New York, Goldman Sachs, AMEX

*   Expenses for HOLDRS consist of a custody fee of $2 per round lot (100 shares) per quarter.
      However, according to the HOLDRS prospectus, the trustee will waive that portion of the fee which exceeds the total cash dividends and other cash distributions.

**   HOLDRS that are no longer exempt from the rules of short selling under Securities and Exchange Commission (SEC) Rule 10a-1

◇   Total Assets as of May 6, 2005

† Listed Options
O=Options, L=LEAPS®
LEAPS® - Long-term Equity AnticiPation Securities®
LEAPS® are put and call options on underlying stocks that have January expirations up to three years from their time of listing. Conventional options with expirations up to nine months are also traded on all stocks for which LEAPS® are available. LEAPS®, which have their own ticker symbols, meld into conventional options each January when their expirations fall to one year out.

Dividend/Income Distribution
Q - Quarterly
R - As Received
S - Semi Annually
M - Monthly
A - Annually

INTERNATIONAL EXCHANGE TRADED FUNDS

Trading Symbol	Exchange Traded Fund	Sector/ Country	Inception Date	Expense Ratio (%)
Europe (Euro denominated unless otherwise specified)				
Australia (AUD denominated)				
AXSBAE	Access BNP Paribas AU Equity	Active Australia	Jul-01	1.90%
AXSMGE	Access BNP Paribas Global	Active Global	Jul-01	2.10%
AXSBMD	Access BNP Paribas Managed	Active Balanced	Jul-01	1.90%
AXSBSC	Access BNP Paribas Small Co.	Active Small Cap	Jul-01	2.15%
CDF	Commonwealth Div. Share Fund	Active Australia	Jun-98	0.95%
GOLD	Gold Bullion Ltd.	Commodity	Mar-03	0.24%
IDX AU	Indexshares Fund	Broad Market	Mar-01	0.95%
STW	streetTRACKS ASX S&P 200 Index	Large Cap	Aug-01	0.29%
SFY	streetTRACKS ASX S&P 50 Index	Large Cap	Aug-01	0.29%
SLF	streetTRACKS ASX S&P 200 Prop.	Aus. real estate	Aug-01	0.40%
WHTMAE	Wilson HTM Australian Equities	Active Australia	Sep-99	0.99%
WHTMFI	Wilson HTM Fixed Interest	Aus. Fixed Interest	Dec-00	0.55%
WHTMOS	Wilson HTM Overseas Share	International Equity	Oct-98	0.99%
Borsa Italiana				
B1EU	Beta1 MSCI Euro	Regional EuroZone	Dec-02	0.60%
B1PE	Beta1 MSCI Pan Euro	Regional Europe	Sep-04	0.50%
DJMC	iShares DJ Euro STOXX MidCap Fund	Europe Mid Cap	Feb-05	0.40%
DJSC	iShares DJ Euro STOXX SmallCap Fund	Europe Small Cap	Feb-05	0.40%
EM1015	Lyxor ETF Euro MTS 10-15 Y	Euro. Fixed Income	Jul-04	0.17%
EM35	Lyxor ETF Euro MTS 3-5 Y	Euro. Fixed Income	Apr-04	0.17%
EMG	Lyxor ETF EuroMTS Global	Euro. Fixed Income	Apr-04	0.17%
EQQQ	NASDAQ 100	U.S. Large Cap	Jun-03	0.20%
ETFMIB	Lyxor ETF S&P/MIB	Country Europe	Nov-03	0.35%
EUE	DJ STOXX 50 LDRS	Europe Large Cap	Apr-00	0.50%
EUN	iShares DJ STOXX 50	Europe Large Cap	Sep-02	0.35%
IBCS	iBoxx EUR Liquid Corporates	Euro. Fixed Income	Apr-04	0.20%
IEUR	iShares FTSE Eurofirst 80	Europe non-U.K.	Apr-04	0.40%
IEUT	iShares FTSE Eurofirst 100	EMU Large Cap	May-02	0.40%
FXC	iShares FTSE/Xinhua China 25	Asia Country	Feb-05	0.74%
IJPN	iShares MSCI Japan	Japan Large Cap	Feb-05	0.59%
MSE	Lyxor ETF DJ Euro STOXX 50	EMU Large Cap	Sep-02	0.35%
SPDRE	SPDR Europe 350	Europe Large Cap	Oct-02	0.35%
SPDRO	SPDR Euro	EMU Large Cap	Feb-02	0.35%
UST	Lyxor ETF MSCI US Tech	U.S. Technology	Nov-02	0.50%
DeutscheBorse				
DAXEX	IndEXchange DAX EX	German Large Cap	Jan-01	0.52%
DDAXKEX	IndEXchange DivDAX EX	Country Europe	Apr-05	0.30%
DJGTE	IndEXchange DJ Global Titans EX	Global Large Cap	Aug-02	0.50%
EUN1	iShares DJ STOXX 50	Europe Large Cap	Apr-00	0.35%
EUN2	iShares DJ EuroSTOXX 50	EMU Large Cap	Apr-00	0.25%
FDGETI	UBS-ETF DJ Germany Titans 30	Country Germany	Sep-02	0.50%
FDUK50	USB-ETF DJ UK Titans 50	Country U.K.	Mar-02	0.50%
FDUSTC	UBS-ETF DJ US Technology	U.S. Technology	Nov-01	0.60%

INTERNATIONAL EXCHANGE TRADED FUNDS

Trading Symbol	Exchange Traded Fund	Sector/ Country	Inception Date	Expense Ratio (%)
FRC1	Fresco Euro STOXX 50	EMU Large Cap	Mar-02	0.50%
FRC2	Fresco DJ Industrial Average	U.S. Industrials	Mar-02	0.50%
FRC4	Fresco DJ US Tech	U.S. Technology	Mar-02	0.60%
FRC6	Fresco DJ UK Titans 50	U.K. Large Cap	Mar-02	0.50%
FRE	UBS-ETF DJ Euro STOXX 50	EMU Large Cap	Jul-04	0.24%
FSEU50	UBS-ETF DJ Euro STOXX 50	EMU Large Cap	Mar-02	0.50%
FXC	iShares FTSE/Xinhua China 25	Asia Country	Feb-05	0.74%
IBCS	iBoxx EUR Liquid Corporates	Fixed Income	Mar-03	0.20%
IJPN	iShares MSCI Japan	Japan Large Cap	Feb-05	0.59%
INDUEX	IndEXchange DJ Industrial Av. EX	U.S. Industrials	Sep-01	0.52%
MGT	Lyxor ETF DJ Global Titans 50	Global Large Cap	Oct-03	0.40%
RXRGEX	eb.rexx Gov. Germany Ex	Fixed Income	Feb-03	0.16%
RXP1EX	eb.rexx Gov. Germany 1.5-2.5 Ex	Fixed Income	Jun-03	0.13%
RXP2EX	eb.rexx Gov. Germany 2.5-5.5 Ex	Fixed Income	Jun-03	0.12%
RXP5EX	eb.rexx Gov. Germany 5.5-10.5 Ex	Fixed Income	Jun-03	0.13%
R1JKEX	eb.rexx Jumbo Pfandbriefs Ex	Fixed Income	Dec-04	0.10%
IQQ8	iShares FTSE Eurofirst 80	Europe non-U.K.	Feb-05	0.40%
IQQ1	iShares FTSE Eurofirst 100	EMU Large Cap	Jun-04	0.40%
IQQM	iShares DJ Euro STOXX MidCap Fund	Europe Mid Cap	Feb-05	0.40%
IQQS	iShares DJ Euro STOXX SmallCap Fund	Europe Small Cap	Feb-05	0.40%
LCXPEX	IndEXchange DJ STOXX Large 200	German Large Cap	Apr-05	0.19%
LYSX	Lyxor ETF DJ Euro STOXX 50	EMU Large Cap	Nov-02	0.35%
MCXPEX	IndEXchange DJ STOXX Mid 200	German Mid Cap	Apr-05	0.19%
MDAXEX	IndEXchange MDAX EX	German Mid Cap	Apr-01	0.52%
NDQ GR	NASDAQ 100 QQQ	U.S. Large Cap	Mar-99	0.18%
NMKXEX	NEMAX 50 EX	German Large Cap	Apr-01	0.50%
SCXPEX	IndEXchange DJ STOXX Small 200	German Small Cap	Apr-05	0.19%
SMIEX GR	IndEXchange SMI Ex	Swiss Large Cap	Apr-01	0.52%
SRD	SPDRs SPY	U.S. Large Cap	Jan-93	0.12%
SX2P	DJ STOXX 600 Cyclical Goods	Euro. Cyclical Goods	Jul-02	0.50%
SX3P	DJ STOXX 600 Food	Europe Food	Jul-02	0.52%
SX4P	DJ STOXX 600 Chemicals	Europe Chemicals	Jul-02	0.53%
SX5E	Deutsche Bank DJ Euro STOXX 50	EMU Large Cap	Jan-05	0.15%
SX5EEX	IndEXchange DJ Euro STOXX 50 Ex	Euro Large Cap	Jan-01	0.42%
SX5P	IndEXchange DJ STOXX 50 Ex	Europe Large Cap	Dec-00	0.52%
SX6P	DJ STOXX 600 Utilities	Europe Utilities	Jul-02	0.53%
SX7E	DJ Euro STOXX Banks	EMU Financials	May-01	0.50%
SX7P	DJ STOXX 600 Banks	Europe Financials	May-01	0.52%
SX8E	DJ Euro STOXX Technology	EMU Technology	May-01	0.52%
SX8P	DJ STOXX 600 Technology	Europe Technology	May-01	0.52%
SXAP	DJ STOXX 600 Autos	Europe Automotive	Jul-02	0.52%
SXDE	DJ Euro STOXX Healthcare	EMU Healthcare	May-01	0.52%
SXDP	DJ STOXX 600 Healthcare	Europe Healthcare	May-01	0.52%
SXEP	DJ STOXX 600 Energy	Europe Energy	Jul-02	0.52%
SXFP	DJ STOXX 600 Financial Services	Europe Fin. Serv.	Jul-02	0.55%
SXHP	DJ STOXX 600 Non-Cyclical	Euro. Non-Cyclical	Jul-02	0.50%
SXIP	DJ STOXX 600 Insurance	Europe Insurance	Jul-02	0.52%

INTERNATIONAL EXCHANGE TRADED FUNDS

Trading Symbol	Exchange Traded Fund	Sector/ Country	Inception Date	Expense Ratio (%)
SXKE	DJ Euro STOXX Telecomm.	EMU Telecoms	May-01	0.52%
SXKP	DJ STOXX 600 Telecomm.	Europe Telecoms	May-01	0.52%
SXMP	DJ STOXX 600 Media	Europe Media	Jul-02	0.52%
SXNP	DJ STOXX 600 Industrial Goods	Euro. Indust. Goods	Jul-02	0.52%
SXOP	DJ STOXX 600 Construction	Europe Construct.	Jul-02	0.53%
SXPP	DJ STOXX 600 Basic Resources	Europe Resources	Jul-02	0.52%
SXQP	DJ STOXX 600 Personal	Euro. Person. & House.	Jul-02	0.53%
SXRP	DJ STOXX 600 Retail	Europe Retail	Jul-02	0.50%
SXTP	DJ STOXX 600 Travel & Leisure	Euro. Travel & Leis.	Jul-02	0.53%
SXXPIEX	IndEXchange DJ STOXX 600	Europe Sector	Apr-05	0.19%
TDXPEX	IndEXchange TecDAX EX	German technology	Apr-01	0.52%
UKXEX	IndEXchange FTSE 100 EX	U.K. Large Cap	Jan-01	0.50%
UNMSEUR	UNICO I-tracker MSCI Europe	Europe Large Cap	Mar-02	0.50%
UNMSWLD	UNICO I-tracker MSCI World	Global Large Cap	Mar-02	0.50%
UNO2	Unico MSCI Europe Financials	Europe Financials	Mar-02	0.50%
UNO3	Unico MSCI Europe Health Care	Europe Healthcare	Mar-02	0.50%
UNO4	Unico MSCI Cons Discretionary	Euro. Cons Discret.	Mar-02	0.50%
UNO5	Unico MSCI Europe Energy	Europe Energy	Mar-02	0.50%
UNO6	Unico MSCI Europe Telecom	Europe Telecoms	Mar-02	0.50%
UNO7	Unico MSCI Europe Cons Staples	Euro. Cons Staples	Mar-02	0.50%
XMMSE	XMTCH (Lux) on MSCI Euro	Euro Large Cap	Sep-03	0.59%

Euronext - Amsterdam

Trading Symbol	Exchange Traded Fund	Sector/ Country	Inception Date	Expense Ratio (%)
AEXT	streetTRACKS AEX Index Fd	Netherlands Large Cap	May-01	0.30%
DIA	Diamonds	U.S. Large Cap	Sep-03	0.18%
DJMC	iShares DJ Euro STOXX MidCap Fund	Europe Mid Cap	Feb-05	0.40%
DJSC	iShares DJ Euro STOXX SmallCap Fund	Europe Small Cap	Feb-05	0.40%
EUE	iShares DJ Euro STOXX 50 LDRS	EMU Large Cap	Apr-00	0.50%
EUNA	iShares DJ STOXX 50	Europe Large Cap	Sep-01	0.35%
EUEA	iShares DJ Euro STOXX 50	EMU Large Cap	Jan-01	0.25%
FXC	iShares FTSE/Xinhua China 25	China Large Cap	Feb-05	0.74%
IBCX	iBoxx EUR Liquid Corporates	European Corp.	Jul-04	0.20%
IERA	iShares FTSE Eurofirst 80	Europe non-U.K.	Dec-00	0.40%
IETA	iShares FTSE EuroTOP 100	Europe Large Cap	Oct-02	0.50%
IJPN	iShares MSCI Japan	Japan Large Cap	Feb-05	0.59%
ISFA	iShares FTSE 100	U.K. Equities	Apr-00	0.40%
IUSA	iShares S&P 500	Euro. Large Cap	Jul-04	0.40%
STUK	streetTRACKS MSCI UK Index	U.K. Broad Market	Jul-01	0.30%

Euronext - Brussels

Trading Symbol	Exchange Traded Fund	Sector/ Country	Inception Date	Expense Ratio (%)
BEL	Lyxor ETF BEL 20	Belgian Large Cap	Oct-02	0.50%

Euronext - Paris

Trading Symbol	Exchange Traded Fund	Sector/ Country	Inception Date	Expense Ratio (%)
C40	CAC 40 Indexis	French Large Cap	Mar-05	0.25%
CAC	Lyxor ETF CAC 40	French Large Cap	Jan-01	0.25%
DEX	TrackinDex DJ STOXX Sustainability	Europe Large Cap	Jun-03	0.40%
DJE	Lyxor ETF DJ Industrial Average	U.S. Industrials	Apr-01	0.50%

INTERNATIONAL EXCHANGE TRADED FUNDS

Trading Symbol	Exchange Traded Fund	Sector/ Country	Inception Date	Expense Ratio (%)
E40	EasyETF CAC40	Europe Large Cap	Mar-05	0.25%
EEE	EasyETF EPRA Eurozone	EMU Large Cap	Dec-04	0.45%
ERO	streetTRACKS MSCI Pan-Euro	Broad Market	Jun-01	0.50%
ETE	EasyETF Euro STOXX 50	EMU Large Cap	Apr-01	1.00%
ETN	EasyETF STOXX 50 Europe	Europe Large Cap	Apr-01	0.45%
ETT	EasyETF Global Titans 50	Global Large Cap	Apr-01	1.00%
EUE	iShares DJ Euro STOXX 50	EMU Large Cap	Jan-01	0.25%
EUE	iShares DJ Euro STOXX 50 LDRS	EMU Large Cap	Jan-01	0.40%
EUN	DJ STOXX 50 LDRS	Europe Large Cap	Apr-00	0.50%
EUNE	iShares DJ Euro STOXX 50	EMU Large Cap	Jan-01	0.25%
FRE	UBS-ETF DJ Euro STOXX 50	Europe Large Cap	Jan-03	0.24%
GWT	Lyxor ETF MSCI EMU Growth	EMU Large Cap	Apr-05	0.40%
GXE	DJ Euro STOXX 50 SM EX	EMU Large Cap	Jan-01	0.40%
GXN	DJ STOXX 50 SM EX	Europe Large Cap	Jan-01	0.40%
MFE	Lyxor ETF FTSEEurofirst 80	Euro Large Cap	Sep-03	0.35%
MGT	Lyxor ETF DJ Global Titans 50	Global Large Cap	Jul-03	0.40%
MMS	Lyxor ETF MSCI EMU Small Cap	Euro. Small Cap	Apr-05	0.40%
MSE	Lyxor ETF DJ Euro STOXX 50	EMU Large Cap	Mar-01	0.35%
MTB	Lyxor ETF Euro MTS 3-5 Y	Fixed Income	Mar-04	0.17%
MTE	Lyxor ETF Euro MTS 10-15 Y	Fixed Income	Mar-04	0.17%
MTX	Lyxor ETF EuroMTS Global	Fixed Income	Jan-04	0.17%
SPE	SPDR Europe 350	EMU Large Cap	Nov-02	0.35%
SPO	SPDR Euro	EMU Large Cap	Feb-02	0.35%
STK	streetTRACKS MSCI Euro IT	EMU Info. Tech.	Aug-01	0.50%
STN	streetTRACKS MSCI Euro Energy	EMU Energy	Aug-01	0.50%
STP	streetTRACKS MSCI Euro Materials	EMU Materials	Sep-01	0.50%
STQ	streetTRACKS MSCI Euro Industrials	EMU Industrials	Sep-01	0.50%
STS	streetTRACKS MSCI Euro Cons Stap	EMU Con. Staples	Sep-01	0.50%
STT	streetTRACKS MSCI Euro Telecom	EMU Telecom	Sep-01	0.50%
STU	streetTRACKS MSCI Euro Utilities	EMU Utilities	Sep-01	0.50%
STV	streetTRACKS MSCI Euro Cons Disc	EMU Cons. Disc.	Sep-01	0.50%
STW	streetTRACKS MSCI Euro Health.	EMU Healthcare	Sep-01	0.50%
STZ	streetTRACKS MSCI Euro Fin.	EMU Financials	Aug-01	0.50%
SX5	IndEXchange DJ STOXX 50 Ex	Large Cap	Sep-01	0.52%
SX5EEX	IndEXchange DJ Euro STOXX 50 Ex	EMU Large Cap	Sep-01	0.42%
SYA	EasyETF Euro STOXX Autos	EMU Autos	Dec-03	0.45%
SYB	EasyETF Euro STOXX Banks	EMU Banks	Mar-02	0.45%
SYC	EasyETF Euro STOXX Construct.	EMU Construction	Dec-03	0.45%
SYE	EasyETF Euro STOXX Energy	EMU Energy	Mar-02	0.45%
SYH	EasyETF Euro STOXX Healthcare	EMU Healthcare	Mar-02	0.45%
SYI	EasyETF Euro STOXX Insurance	EMU Insurance	Mar-02	0.45%
SYM	EasyETF Euro STOXX Media	EMU Media	Mar-02	0.45%
SYQ	EasyETF Euro STOXX Technology	EMU Technology	Mar-02	0.45%
SYT	EasyETF Euro STOXX Telecom	EMU Telecom	Mar-02	0.45%
VAL	Lyxor ETF MSCI EMU Value	EMU Large Cap	Apr-05	0.40%
SYU	EasyETF Euro STOXX Utilities	EMU Utilities	Mar-02	0.45%
SYV	EasyETF ASPI Euro	Europe Large Cap	Feb-02	0.60%

INTERNATIONAL EXCHANGE TRADED FUNDS

Trading Symbol	Exchange Traded Fund	Sector/ Country	Inception Date	Expense Ratio (%)
UST	Lyxor ETF MSCI US Tech	U.S. Technology	Dec-01	0.50%
Finland				
IHEX25	HEX 25 Index Share	Large Cap	Feb-02	0.25%
Helsinki Stock Exchange				
H25ETF	HEX25 Index Share	Finnish Large Cap	Feb-02	0.25%
Hong Kong (Asset & price values in USD)				
2801	iShares MSCI-China Tracker	China	Nov-01	0.99%
4362	iShares MSCI-S. Korea Index Fd	South Korea	May-00	0.99%
4363	iShares MSCI-Taiwan Index Fd	Taiwan	Jun-00	0.99%
2800	SSgA TraHK	Hong Kong L. Cap	Nov-99	0.10%
2823	iShares FTSE/Xinhua A50 China Tracker	China Large Cap	Nov-04	0.99%
2828	Hang Seng H-Share Index	China Large Cap	Dec-03	0.40%
2833	Hang Seng Index ETF	China Large Cap	Sep-04	0.10%
Iceland (ISK denominated)				
ICEQ	ICEX-15	Iceland Large Cap	Dec-04	0.50%
India (INR denominated)				
NBEES	Nifty BeES	India Large Cap	Jan-02	0.80%
JBEES	Junior BeES	India Mid Cap	Feb-03	1.00%
ICSPICE	PRUDENTIAL ICIC-SENSEX SPIcE	India Financial	Jan-03	0.80%
SUNDER	SUNDER	India Large Cap	Jul-03	0.50%
LBEES	Liquid BeES	India Large Cap	Jul-03	0.70%
BBEES	CNX Bank Index	India Banks	May-04	0.55%
Israel (ILS denominated)				
TALI IT	TALI 25	Israeli Large Cap	May-00	0.80%
KSM100	KSM TA 100	Israeli Broad Mrkt	Nov-03	1.00%
KSMTEC15	KSM Tel Aviv Technology 15	Israeli Technology	Dec-03	1.00%
KSMSX5E	KSM EuroSTOXX50	Euro Large Cap	Jan-04	0.50%
KSM75	KSM 75	Israeli Mid cap	Jan-05	1.00%
KSM30	KSM30	Israeli Small Cap	Jan-05	1.00%
KSMFN	KSM FN	Israeli Financial	Jan-05	0.50%
KSMRE15	KSM REIT	Israeli REIT	Jan-05	0.50%
KSMTABK	KSM Banks	Israeli Banks	Feb-04	0.50%
KSMDJIA	KSM DJIA	Israeli Large Cap	Mar-04	0.50%
KSMBOND	KSM TA Bonds	Fixed Income	May-04	0.40%
KSMMA	KSM TA MAALA 20	Israeli Soc. Resp.	Mar-05	0.50%
Istanbul (TRY denominated)				
DJIST	Dow Jones Istanbul 20	Istanbul Large Cap	Jan-05	0.95%
Japan (Tokyo & Osaka) (U.S. denominated)				
1320	Nikkei 225 Daiwa	Broad Cap	Jul-01	0.23%

INTERNATIONAL EXCHANGE TRADED FUNDS

Trading Symbol	Exchange Traded Fund	Sector/ Country	Inception Date	Expense Ratio (%)
1329	Nikkei 225 iShares	Broad Cap	Sep-01	0.22%
1330	Nikkei 225 Nikko	Broad Cap	Jul-01	0.23%
1321	Nikkei 225 Nomura	Broad Cap	Jul-01	0.24%
1305	S&P/TOPIX 150 Daiwa	Large Cap	Jul-01	0.20%
1307	S&P/Topix 150 iShares	Large Cap	Aug-01	0.22%
1315	S&P/Topix 150 iShares	Large Cap	1-Aug	0.29%
1308	S&P/Topix 150 Nikko	Large Cap	Dec-01	0.11%
1306	S&P/Topix 150 Nomura	Large Cap	Jul-01	0.24%
1612	Topix Banking Daiwa	Japan Banking	Mar-02	0.22%
1615	Topix Banking Nomura	Japan Banking	Apr-02	0.22%
1310	Topix Core 30	Large Cap	Apr-02	0.22%
1311	Topix Core 30 Nomura	Large Cap	Apr-02	0.22%
1610	Topix Electrical Appliances Daiwa	Japan Appliances	Mar-02	0.22%
1613	Topix Electrical Appliances Nomura	Japan Appliances	Apr-02	0.22%
1611	Topix Transportation Equipment Daiwa	Japan Trans Equip.	Mar-02	0.22%
1614	Topix Transportation Equipment Nomura	Japan Trans Equip.	Apr-02	0.22%

New Zealand (NZD denominated)

Trading Symbol	Exchange Traded Fund	Sector/ Country	Inception Date	Expense Ratio (%)
WIN	AMP Investments World Index	Global	Aug-97	0.80%
OZY	Australian 20 Leaders Index Fund	Large Cap	Feb-97	0.60%
FNZ	NZSX 50 Portfolio IDX (FONZ)	N. Z. L. Cap	Dec-04	0.90%
MDZ	NZ MidCap Index Fund	Mid Cap	Jun-97	0.75%
MZY	NZX Aust. MidCap Index Fund	Mid Cap	Sep-04	0.90%
TNZ	NZSE 10 Index Fund	Large Cap	Jun-96	0.75%

OM Sweden (SEK denominated)

Trading Symbol	Exchange Traded Fund	Sector/ Country	Inception Date	Expense Ratio (%)
XACTOMX	XACTOMX	Swed. Large Cap	Oct-00	0.30%
XACTSBX	XACTSBX	Swed. Large Cap	Jun-03	0.30%
XACBEAR	XACT OMX Bear	Swed. Large Cap	Feb-05	0.60%
XACBULL	XACT OMX Bull	Swed. Large Cap	Feb-05	0.60%

Oslo (NOK denominated)

Trading Symbol	Exchange Traded Fund	Sector/ Country	Inception Date	Expense Ratio (%)
OBXEDNBN	DnB NOR OBX	Norw. Large cap	Mar-05	0.30%
OBXEXACT	XACT OBX	Norw. Large cap	Apr-05	0.30%

Peru Stock Exchange (PEN denominated)

Trading Symbol	Exchange Traded Fund	Sector/ Country	Inception Date	Expense Ratio (%)
QQQ	Nasdaq 100 QQQ	U.S. Large Cap	Mar-99	0.20%

Shanghai Stock Exchange (CNY denominated)

Trading Symbol	Exchange Traded Fund	Sector/ Country	Inception Date	Expense Ratio (%)
510050	China 50 ETF	Chinese Large Cap	Feb-05	0.50%

Singapore (SGD denominated)

Trading Symbol	Exchange Traded Fund	Sector/ Country	Inception Date	Expense Ratio (%)
DIA	DIAMONDS Trust Series 1	U.S. Large Cap	Jan-98	0.18%
IYW	iShares DJ US Tech. Index Fd	U.S. Technology	May-00	0.60%
EWS	iShares MSCI-Singapore Index Fd	Singapore L. Cap	Mar-96	0.84%
IVV	iShares S&P 500 Index Fd	U.S. Large Cap	May-00	0.09%
SPY	SPDRs	U.S. Large Cap	Jan-93	0.12%

INTERNATIONAL EXCHANGE TRADED FUNDS

Trading Symbol	Exchange Traded Fund	Sector/ Country	Inception Date	Expense Ratio (%)
STTF	streetTRACKS STRAITS TIMES	Broad Market	2-Apr	0.30%
South Africa (SAR denominated)				
STX40	SATRIX 40	S. A. Large Cap	Nov-00	0.80%
STXIND	SATRIX Industrial Index	S. A. Industrials	Feb-02	0.80%
STXFIN	SATRIX Financial Index	S. A. Financials	Feb-02	0.80%
NRD	NewRand	S. A. Large Cap	Jun-03	0.80%
GLD	Gold Bullion Debentures	S. A. Gold	Nov-04	0.40%
South Korea (KRW denominated)				
069500	Kodex 200	Korean Large Cap	Oct-02	0.52%
069660	KOSPI 200 ETF - KOSEF	Korean Large Cap	Oct-02	0.67%
072350	KodexQ	Korean Large Cap	Apr-03	0.67%
074170	KodexKODI	Korean Large Cap	Oct-03	0.52%
Switzerland (CHF denominated)				
DJE	Lyxor ETF DJ Industrial Average	U.S. Industrials	Apr-01	0.50%
DJMC	iShares DJ Euro STOXX MidCap Fund	Europe Mid Cap	Feb-05	0.40%
DJSC	iShares DJ Euro STOXX SmallCap Fund	Europe Small Cap	Feb-05	0.40%
DJSXE	DJ Euro STOXX 50 Ex	EMU Large Cap	Sep-03	0.42%
DJSXP	DJ STOXX 50 Ex	Europe Large Cap	Sep-03	0.52%
EQQQ	NASDAQ 100	U.S. Large Cap	Jun-03	0.20%
EUN	DJ STOXX 50 LDRS	Europe Large Cap	Apr-00	0.50%
EUNE	DJ Euro STOXX 50 LDRS	EMU Large Cap	Apr-00	0.50%
FDJPHU	UBS-ETF DJ Japan Titans 100	Japan Large Cap	Nov-01	0.70%
FDUKFI	Fresco DJ UK Titans 50	U.K. Large Cap	Nov-01	0.50%
FDUSIA	UBS-ETF DJ Industrial Average	U.S. Large Cap	Nov-01	0.50%
FDUSLC	UBS-ETF DJ US Large Cap	U.S. Large Cap	Nov-01	0.50%
FDUSTC	UBS-ETF DJ US Technology	U.S. Technology	Nov-01	0.60%
FRE	UBS-ETF DJ Euro STOXX 50	Euro Large Cap	May-04	0.24%
FRESMI	USB-ETF SMI	Swiss Large Cap	Dec-03	0.35%
FSEUFI	UBS-ETF DJ Euro STOXX 50	EMU Large Cap	Nov-01	0.50%
FXC	iShares FTSE/Xinhua China 25	China Large Cap	Feb-05	0.74%
IBCX	iBoxx EUR Liquid Corporates	Fixed Income	Jun-04	0.20%
IEUR	iShares FTSE Eurofirst 80	Europe non-U.K.	Jun-04	0.40%
IEUT	iShares FTSE Eurofirst 100	EMU Large Cap	Jun-04	0.40%
IJPN	iShares MSCI Japan	Japan Large Cap	Feb-05	0.59%
MGT	Lyxor ETF DJ Global Titans 50	Global Large Cap	Sep-04	0.40%
MSE	Lyxor ETF DJ Euro STOXX 50	EMU Large Cap	Nov-02	0.35%
SMIEX	IndEXchange SMI	Swiss Large Cap	Aug-01	0.52%
XMMSE	XMTCH (Lux) on MSCI Euro	Europe Large Cap	Oct-02	0.59%
XMSMI	SMI-XMTCH	Swiss Large Cap	Mar-01	0.35%
XMSMM	SMM-XMTCH	Swiss Large Cap	Dec-04	0.45%
XTBG	XMTCH Swiss Bond Idx. Dom. Gov't 7+	Fixed Income	Nov-03	0.20%
XTBID	XMTCH Swiss Bond Idx. Dom. Gov't 3-7	Fixed Income	Nov-03	0.20%

INTERNATIONAL EXCHANGE TRADED FUNDS

Trading Symbol	Exchange Traded Fund	Sector/ Country	Inception Date	Expense Ratio (%)
Taiwan (NTD denominated)				
0050	Polaris Taiwan 50	Taiwan Large Cap	Jun-03	0.37%
United Kingdom (GBP denominated)				
DJMC	iShares DJ Euro STOXX MidCap Fund	Europe Mid Cap	Nov-04	0.40%
DJSC	iShares DJ Euro STOXX SmallCap Fund	Europe Small Cap	Nov-04	0.40%
EUE	iShares DJ Euro STOXX 50	EMU Large Cap	Apr-00	0.50%
EUN	iShares DJ STOXX 50	Europe Large Cap	Sep-01	0.35%
FXC	iShares FTSE/Xinhua China 25	China Large Cap	Oct-04	0.74%
IBCX	iBoxx EUR Liquid Corporates	Euro Corp. Bond	May-03	0.20%
IEUR	iShares FTSE Eurofirst 80	Europe non-U.K.	Dec-00	0.40%
IEUT	iShares FTSE EuroFirst 100	EMU Large Cap	Oct-01	0.40%
IJPN	iShares MSCI Japan	Japan Large Cap	Oct-04	0.59%
ISF	iShares iFTSE 100 Index	U.K. Large Cap	Apr-00	0.40%
IUSA	iShares S&P 500 ETF	U.S. Large Cap	Mar-02	0.40%
LQDE	iShares GS$ Investop Corp. Bond Fund	Fixed Income	May-03	0.20%
MIDD	iShares FTSE 250	Europe Large Cap	Mar-04	0.40%
SLXX	iBoxx Corporate Bond Fund	Euro Corp. Bond	Mar-04	0.20%
Virt-X				
DJMC	iShares DJ Euro STOXX MidCap Fund	Europe Mid Cap	Nov-04	0.40%
DJSC	iShares DJ Euro STOXX SmallCap Fund	Europe Small Cap	Nov-04	0.40%
EUN	iShares DJ STOXX 50	Europe Large Cap	Jun-02	0.35%
EUNE	iShares DJ Euro STOXX 50	Europe Large Cap	May-02	0.50%
FDUSIA	UBS ETF DJ Industrial Average	U.S. Large Cap	May-02	0.50%
FDUSLC	UBS ETF DJ US Large Cap	U.S. Large Cap	May-02	0.50%
FDUSTC	UBS ETF DJ US Technology	U.S. Technology	Nov-01	0.60%
FSEUFI	UBS-ETF DJ Euro STOXX 50	EMU Large Cap	Mar-02	0.50%
FXC	iShares FTSE/Xinhua China 25	China Large Cap	Dec-04	0.74%
IEUT	iShares FTSE Eurofirst 100	EMU Large Cap	May-02	0.50%
IEUR	iShares FTSE Eurofirst 80	Europe non-U.K.	May-02	0.40%
IJPN	iShares MSCI Japan	Japan Large Cap	Dec-04	0.59%
ISF	iShares FTSE 100	U.K. Equities	May-02	0.40%
iUSA	iShares S&P 500	U.S. Large Cap	Jan-02	0.35%
SPE	SPDR Europe 350	EMU Large Cap	Nov-02	0.35%
SPO	SPDR Euro	EMU Large Cap	Feb-02	0.35%

Source: Barclays Global Investors, Morgan Stanley, Bloomberg.com,

Pending ETFs*

ASSET CLASS

Europe

CAC Tracker (Crédit Agricole Asset Management)
CAC Tracker (Harewood Asset Management)
DAX DVG
DJ EUR 50 DVG
Dow Jones Istanbul
EasyETF EPRA Europe
EasyETF EPRA Europe ex-UK
EasyETF EPRA UK
IndEXchange Dow Jones Italy Titans 30
ISEQ 20
streetTRACKS MSCI Europe Smallcap

US

DB (Deutsche Bank) Commodity Index Tracking Fund
Firsthand Capital Management Technology Fund
iShares CSFB Liquid U.S. Agency Bond Index
iShares Lehman Treasury Bond Fund
iShares Lehman Government/Credit Bond Fund
iShares Lehman Credit Bond Fund
iShares MSCI EAFE Growth
iShares MSCI EAFE Value
iShares Russell Microcap Index Fund
iShares Silver Fund
PowerShares Dynamic Large Cap Growth
PowerShares Dynamic Large Cap Value
PowerShares Dynamic Mid Cap Growth
PowerShares Dynamic Mid Cap Value
PowerShares Dynamic Small Cap Growth
PowerShares Dynamic Small Cap Value
PowerShares Dynamic Aerospace & Defense Portfolio
PowerShares Dynamic Biotechnology & Genome Portfolio
PowerShares Dynamic Brand Name Products Portfolio
PowerShares Dynamic Consumer Electronics Portfolio
PowerShares Dynamic Food & Beverage Portfolio
PowerShares Dynamic Hardware Portfolio
PowerShares Dynamic Internet Software & Services Portfolio
PowerShares Dynamic Leisure and Entertainment Portfolio
PowerShares Dynamic Media Portfolio
PowerShares Dynamic Networking Portfolio
PowerShares Dynamic Pharmaceuticals Portfolio
PowerShares Dynamic Semiconductors Portfolio
PowerShares Dynamic Software Portfolio
PowerShares Dynamic Telecommunications Services Portfolio
PowerShares Dynamic Wireless Portfolio
PowerShares Value Line #1 Timelines and Safety Portfolio

PowerShares Wilder Alternative Power Technologies Portfolio
PowerShares Zacks Rank Large Cap Portfolio
ProFund Ultra500
ProFund Ultra100
ProFund Ultra30
ProFund Ultra400
ProFund UltraShort500
ProFund UltraShort100
ProFund UltraShort30
ProFund UltraShort400
Rydex Euro Currency Trust
Standard Asset Management Oil Fund
Vanguard® European Stock Index Fund
Vanguard® Pacific Stock Index Fund
Vanguard® Emerging Markets Stock Index Fund
Voskian Citigroup Semiconductor 50 Index

China
Shanghai Stock Exchange (SSE) 50 Index ETF
Shanghai 180 A Index

Source: Morgan Stanley
* List of planned ETF products as of June 2005
Some or all of these ETFs may or may not be subsequently launched.

Appendix D
Web Directory

For Canadian ETF Products

www.iunits.com

Covers information on the Barclays Canada iUnits family of ETFs including daily fund data, ETF related investment strategies, news articles, and more.

www.m-x.ca

Montréal Exchange site. Options on five iUnits including the popular i60s are traded on the Montréal Exchange. Offers outstanding explanation of options and futures in their Derivatives Institute section (www.derivatives-institute.com/accueil_en.htm).

www.tdassetmanagement.com

Deals with ETFs, closed-end funds, and pooled indexed and quantitative funds. Includes daily NAV and related information.

www.tsx.com

The Toronto Stock Exchange site, which is home to all Canadian-based ETFs.

For U.S.-Based ETF Products

www.amex.com

Information on all AMEX-listed ETFs and HOLDRS including quotes, holdings, and premium/discount data.

www.amextrader.com

Outstanding ETF section with distribution history on all AMEX-listed ETFs from inception. Gives volumes, premiums/discounts, last trade to NAV, and arranges for delivery of paper or electronic prospectus.

www.bldrsfunds.com

Information on BLDRS, the NASDAQ-sponsored family of ETFs, based upon The Bank of New York ADR Indices.

www.cboe.com

Chicago Board Options Exchange: Major U.S. marketplace trading equity, index, interest rate, and ETF options.

www.ubs.com (search word: etf)

Overview of Fresco Index Shares funds.

www.holdrs.com

Devoted to news and market information on HOLDRS, a Merrill Lynch exchange traded basket security.

www.ishares.com

Information on Barclays U.S.-based ETF offerings, iShares. A robust site that offers rich fund data and numerous tools helpful with portfolio construction. The site requires registration as an individual, advisor or institutional investor.

www.morningstar.com

Information and research from the mutual fund ranking giant. U.S.-listed ETFs are covered.

www.nasdaq.com

Coverage includes the NASDAQ ETF family and the ETF Dynamic Heatmap, a colour-coded guide ranking 100 ETFs by their daily percentage price change (updated every minute).

www.nyse.com

(Go to: Products & Services / Securities / Funds)
The "Big Board" site provides data on their listed and traded ETFs.

www.powershares.com

PowerShares Capital Management, a relative newcomer to the space, already has the second most ETFs including many using rules-based "active" strategies.

www.spdrindex.com

Information and data on Select Sector SPDRs.

www.streettracks.com

Information on State Street Global Advisors' ETF offerings, including resources for advisors.

www.vanguardvipers.com

Information on the share class of Vanguard index funds that are exchange traded. Sections are available for investors, advisors, and institutions.

General ETF and Indexing Sites

www.bylo.org

Site run by a Canadian private investor about do-it-yourself mutual fund investing and indexing.

www.exchangetradedfunds.com

Provides global listings of ETFs as well as industry information and news.

www.indexfunds.com

Excellent site for news, articles, and information on index funds, indexing, and ETFs. Comprehensive listing of available ETFs.

www.indexinvestor.com

Information to help investors improve investment performance through enhanced asset allocation and indexing.

www.journalofindexes.com

An open discussion of index issues based upon a cooperative effort between Index Funds International and Financial Advisor magazine.

Index Providers

www.barra.com

Detailed information on the S&P/BARRA family of indices.

www.bnyadr.com

The Bank of New York depositary receipts site.

www.djindexes.com

Revamped site full of information on methodology and maintenance of Dow Jones indices.

www.lehman.com

(Go to: Global Family of Indices)

Listing of Lehman Brothers global family of fixed income benchmarks.

www.msci.com

Morgan Stanley Capital International Inc. ("MSCI") is a leading provider of equity, fixed income, and hedge fund global benchmarks.

www.russell.com

Site for information on Russell indices, family of U.S. equity indexes.

www2.standardandpoors.com

Site for extensive information on S&P indices, their methodology and maintenance.

www.stoxx.com

Provider of Dow Jones STOXX indexes.

www.wilshire.com

Wilshire index information including the Wilshire 5000, the broadest U.S. Equity index.

Mutual Fund Sites

www.globefund.com

Exceptionally good site for information about all Canadian mutual funds with benchmark comparisons.

www.ici.org

Offers a monthly assets report on ETFs not including HOLDRS. This is the site of the Investment Company Institute, the American trade organization for mutual fund companies.

www.ific.ca

The Investment Funds Institute of Canada. Provides information and services for its members, investors, and the media.

www.morningstar.ca
>
> Canadian mutual fund site with the famous five-star rating system. Extensive articles commissioned for the site.

Miscellaneous

www.closed-endfunds.com
>
> Closed-End Fund Association site that includes tools and an education centre.

www.financialengines.com
>
> Nobel Prize–winning economist William Sharpe's site.

www.in-the-money.com
>
> Site run by Mark Rubinstein, inventor of portfolio insurance.

www.vanguard.com/bogle_site/bogle_speeches.html
>
> Archived speeches and information from the founder of the Vanguard Group, John Bogle.

ETF Portfolio Services

www.agileinvesting.com
>
> AgileInvesting is an investment advisory service based on the use of Exchange Traded Funds to construct cost-efficient, diversified investment portfolios.

www.ETFolios.com
>
> Guardian Capital Advisors' asset allocation service offering customized ETF portfolios directly to investors or through accredited investment advisors.

www.foliofn.com
>
> Low-cost FOLIOtrades brokerage service allows you to trade individual stocks or to build a diversified portfolio with a single click.

www.hahninvest.com
>
> Hahn Investment Stewards offers separately managed ETF wrap portfolios through accredited advisors.

www.shareowner.com
>
> Aimed at self-reliant investors, Canadian ShareOwner offers education, a "Stocks to Study" program, and a discount brokerage service.

Technical Analysis

www.barchart.com
>
> On-line financial quotes, charts, and technical analysis for stock and commodity traders.

www.bigcharts.com
>
> Provides free, comprehensive, and easy-to-use investment research like

interactive charts, quotes, industry analysis, intraday stock screeners, as well as market news and commentary.

www.csta.org

Not-for-profit professional organization that seeks to encourage the development of technical analysis, to educate the financial community about the uses of technical analysis, and to assist the exchange of TA information among its members.

www.decisionpoint.com

Technical analysis site offering education and prepackaged chart books covering over 1,800 stocks, mutual funds, and market/sector indexes including ETFs.

www.dorseywright.com

A leading source of information and education on the point and figure charting methodology.

www.dvtechtalk.com

Don Vialoux CMT, past president of the Canadian Society of Technical Analysts (CSTA) and a former technical analyst at RBC Investments, offers his free daily newsletter covering fundamentals, technical, and seasonality in the global markets.

www.gettingtechnical.com

Provides a blend of technical and quantitative data to create your own index-timing and stock-filtering models.

www.globeinvestorgold.com

Canadian site offering investment information including news, portfolio tracking, technical analysis, and instant alerts.

www.stockcharts.com

Provides dynamic financial information such as investors' interactive charting tools, stock quotes, analysis, and education for on-line investors.

www.stockmarkettiming.com

Stock Market Timing is a financial service for investors that offers a system for trading the popular ETFs: DIA, SPY, and QQQ.

www.stocktradersalmanac.com

The web site provides information on seasonality in the market-based upon 39 years of research.

www.traders.com

Home of the *Technical Analysis of Stocks & Commodities* magazine, one of the longest running monthly publication for traders.

Appendix E

Recommended Reading

Why Smart People Make Big Money Mistakes—and How to Correct Them, Gary Belsky and Thomas Gilovich, Simon & Schuster, New York, 1999.

Against the Gods: The Remarkable Story of Risk, Peter L. Bernstein, John Wiley & Sons, New York, 1996.

Capital Ideas, Peter L. Bernstein, The Free Press, New York, 1993.

The Four Pillars of Investing: Lessons for Building a Winning Portfolio, William J. Bernstein, McGraw-Hill, New York, 2002.

The Intelligent Asset Allocator: How to Build Your Portfolio to Maximize Returns and Minimize Risk, William J. Bernstein, McGraw-Hill, New York, 2000.

Bogle on Mutual Funds: New Perspectives for the Intelligent Investor, John Bogle, McGraw-Hill, New York, 1994.

Common Sense on Mutual Funds, John Bogle, John Wiley & Sons, New York, 1999.

John Bogle on Investing, John Bogle, McGraw-Hill, New York, 2001.

The Power of Index Funds, revised edition, Ted Cadsby, Stoddart Publishing Co., Toronto, 2001.

So You Want More Money... second edition, George Caners, B.Sc., CA., M.B.A., C.F.P, Estate Services Inc., Brockville, 2001.

The Professional Financial Advisor: Ethics, Unbundling and Other Things to Ask Your Advisor, John J. De Goey, Insomniac Press, Toronto, 2003.

The Wealthy Boomer: Life After Mutual Funds, Low Cost Alternatives in Managed Money, Jonathan Chevreau, Michael Ellis and S. Kelly Rodgers, Key Porter Books, Toronto, 1998.

Point and Figure Charting: The Essential Application for Forecasting and Tracking Market Prices, second edition, Thomas J. Dorsey, John Wiley & Sons, New York, 2001.

Investment Policy: How to Win the Loser's Game, second edition, Charles D. Ellis, Irwin Professional Publishing, Chicago, 1993.

Classics: An Investor's Anthology, Edited by Charles D. Ellis and James R.Vertin, Business One Irwin, Homewood, Illinois, 1989.

Classics II: Another Investor's Anthology, Edited by Charles D. Ellis and James R.Vertin, Business One Irwin, Homewood, Illinois, 1991.

The Index Fund Solution, Richard E. Evans, Simon & Schuster, New York, 2000.

The Handbook of Equity Derivatives, revised edition, Edited by Jack Clark

Francis, William Toy and J. Whittaker, John Wiley & Sons, New York, 2000.

How to be an Index Investor, Max Isaacman, McGraw-Hill, New York, 2000.

A Random Walk Down Wall Street, revised edition, Burton G. Malkiel, W.W. Norton & Company, New York, 1996.

The Empowered Investor: A Guide to Building Better Portfolios, Keith Matthews, Book Coach Press, 2005.

Money Logic, Moshe A. Milevsky, Michael Posner, Stoddart Publishing Co., Toronto, 2000.

Technical Analysis of the Financial Markets: A Comprehensive Guide to Trading Methods and Applications, John J. Murphy, Prentice Hall Press, New York, 1999.

The Visual Investor: How to Spot Market Trends, John J. Murphy, John Wiley & Sons, New York, 1996.

Technical Analysis Explained: The Successful Investors Guide to Spotting Investment Trends and Turning Points, third edition, Martin J. Pring, McGraw-Hill Trade, New York, 1997.

The Naked Investor: Why Almost Everybody But You Gets Rich on Your RRSP, John Lawrence Reynolds, Penguin Canada, Toronto, Canada, 2005.

Active Index Investing: Maximizing Portfolio Performance and Minimizing Risk through Global Index Strategies, Steven A. Schoenfeld, John Wiley & Sons, Inc, 2004.

Stocks for the Long Run, Jeremy J. Siegel, McGraw-Hill, New York, 1998.

The Future for Investors: Why the Tried and the True Triumph Over the Bold and the New, Jeremy J. Siegel, Crown Publishing, New York, 2005.

What Wall Street Doesn't Want You To Know: You Can Build Real Wealth Investing in Index Funds, Larry E. Swedroe, Truman Talley Books, New York, 2001.

The Only Guide to a Winning Investment Strategy You'll Ever Need, Larry E. Swedroe, Truman Talley Books/Dutton, New York, 1998.

Fooled By Randomness: The Hidden Role of Chance in the Markets and in Life, Nassim Nicholas Taleb, Texere LLC, New York, 2001.

Time In, Time Out, Brooke Thackray & Bruce Lindsay, Upwave Media Inc., Toronto, 2000.

Core and Explore: The Investing Rush Without the Ruin, Duff Young, Prentice Hall Canada, Toronto, 2000.

Glossary

Actively managed Portfolios can be actively managed or passively managed. Actively managed portfolios employ an investment manager to make investment decisions according to investment objectives, usually with the goal of beating a benchmark index.

Asset allocation The practice of dividing a portfolio into investment categories known as asset classes such as cash, fixed income, equities, real estate, tangibles, etc. Strategic asset allocation places investment in asset classes for the long term. Tactical asset allocation positions some or all of the asset classes temporarily to capture expected short- or intermediate-term market movements.

Authorized participant A U.S. term for large investors, institutions, exchange specialist, and arbitrageurs who place creation/redemption unit orders with an exchange traded fund.

Basis point One one-hundredth of a percentage point or 0.01%; 100 basis points equals 1 percentage point.

Benchmark Something against which to measure performance. The S&P/TSE 60 Index, for instance, is a benchmark for the performance of large cap Canadian equity managers.

Cap or Capitalization Refers to market capitalization, the value of a public corporation's outstanding shares. It is calculated by multiplying the current market price of a company's share by all its outstanding shares.

Capped An index or a fund is capped when there is a limit to the concentration of its holdings. For instance, the TSE 300 Capped Index limits all constituents to no more than 10% of the index. This ensures diversification in a market situation in which a few large companies can dominate an index.

Cash drag Under-performance due to cash in a portfolio.

Closed-end funds A fund that has a fixed number of issued shares and is traded on a stock exchange. Often trades at a discount or premium. Is opposed to an open-end fund that continually issues shares (units) and doesn't trade on a stock exchange.

Correlation How the movement of two variables is related. When asset classes respond similarly to market conditions, they are said to be positively correlated. When they respond differently, they are said to be negatively correlated.

Creation unit The smallest number of securities that can be cashed in for exchange traded fund (ETF) shares. Correspondingly, a redemption unit is the smallest number of ETF units that can be cashed in for the underlying securities. Most ETFs require a minimum of 50,000 of their own shares in order to be exchanged for the underlying securities.

Derivatives Contracts whose value is based on the performance of another asset or index. Derivatives include forwards, futures, and options.

Designated broker (Cdn.) Registered brokers and dealers who enter into agreements with an exchange traded fund to perform certain brokerage related funtions.

Dividends Earnings paid out to shareholders.

Diversification In portfolio management, spreading investments among different asset classes to mitigate risk .

Distributions Payment by a mutual fund to unitholders of earnings within the fund.

Duration A measure of the present value of the lifetime cash flows on a bond. A higher duration suggests greater volatility of the price of a bond as interest rates change.

Enhanced indexing An index fund or ETF constructed with the goal and potential of achieving returns superior to a specified index. Usually this involves managers over or underweighting index constituents. Some enhanced ETFs employ an objective, quantitative, rules-based methodology.

Efficient frontier In portfolio theory, the curve that depicts the points that maximize expected return for a pre-determined level of risk.

Exchange traded funds (ETFs) A basket of securities that trades on a stock exchange.

Ex-dividend A stock is said to be ex-dividend during the time a dividend is declared and the time it is issued. Anyone buying a stock during this ex-dividend period will not be entitled to the forthcoming dividend.

Forward contracts A promise to buy or sell a specific investment at a set time in the future for the current price when the contract is made. This is different from a futures contract, which is a promise to buy or sell at the future price at a set time in the future.

Futures A promise to buy or sell a specific investment at a set time in the future for the then-current price.

HOLDRS A fixed and mostly unchanging basket of investments traded on a stock exchange. Issued by Merrill Lynch. Stands for "holding company depositary receipts." Some consider HOLDRS a kind of exchange traded fund (ETF), but they are more properly known as exchange traded baskets.

Index A collection of stocks designed to be reflective of a market.

Indexing An investment management strategy which tries to track an index.

Liquidity The ease and speed with which an investment can be sold without affecting the price of the investment.

Margining Borrowing money from a brokerage to buy securities. Done through a margin account which charges interest on borrowings, collateral must be kept in the account to cover some percentage of the margined stock.

Market timing The practice of darting in and out of investments with the aim of catching them during their upward movement, and only then.

Marginal tax rate The tax rate at which your next dollar of income is taxed.

Management Expense Ratio (MER) Fees charged by a manager of a fund, and other expenses (excluding security commissions), divided by the assets of the fund to arrive at a percentage of costs to assets.

Modern Portfolio Theory A study of the relationship between investments and asset classes, and their expected risk and return.

Mutual fund A pool of securities managed on behalf of unitholders that is bought or redeemed by the fund company. Units are continually offered (open-ended).

Net Asset Value (NAV) The value of an individual unit in a fund. It is calculated by taking the total value of the fund, including cash, and dividing it by the number of outstanding shares.

Optimization In index management, the practice of buying selected components of an index to match the movement of the index as closely as possible without actually buying all the index constituents. This is opposed to replication of the index.

Options Contracts granting the right to buy or sell an investment at a set price by a specified date.

Over-the-counter (OTC) A market for securities that is apart from a stock exchange. Bonds are sold OTC. Transactions are arranged over the phone or through computer networks connecting dealers.

Passively managed An investment style in which a portfolio is structured to track a specific index. See "Actively managed."

Price limit order An order to buy a stock at a specific price or better.

R^2 A statistical measure that represents the percentage of a fund's or security's movements that are explained by movements in a benchmark index. For fixed income securities, the benchmark is the T-bill, and for U.S. equities the benchmark is the S&P 500.

Rebalancing In portfolio management, adjusting back to ideal asset allocation.

REITs Real Estate Investment Trusts

Replication An indexing strategy that involves buying everything in the index; i.e., replicating the index. This is one of a few indexing strategies. Also see "optimization."

Reversion to the mean The habit of investment manager performance to revert to the mean performance of the asset class over time.

Risk-free return The risk-free return represents the interest on an investor's money they would expect from an absolutely risk-free investment, usually a government treasury bill, or T-bill, over a specified period of time.

Secondary market The market in which shares are bought and sold after their initial public offering. All stock exchanges and over-the-counter markets are secondary markets.

Secular Long term, not seasonal or cyclical.

Sharpe ratio Average return, less the risk-free return, divided by the standard deviation of return. The ratio measures the relationship of reward to risk in an investment strategy. The higher the ratio, the safer the strategy.

Standard Deviation A measure of the dispersion of a set of data from its mean. The more spread apart the data, the higher the deviation. In finance, standard deviation is applied to the annual rate of return of an investment to measure the investment's volatility (risk). A volatile stock would have a high standard deviation. In mutual funds, the standard deviation tells us how much the return on the fund is deviating from the expected normal returns.

Tracking error The deviation from the index's price or return of any investment whose purpose is to keep pace with an index.

Short selling Selling a stock without owning it. This is done by those who expect the price of the stock to fall before the borrowed shares must be returned.

Segregated 1) In mutual funds, a fund in which all or most of the principal is guaranteed. 2) With respect to investment accounts, this refers to keeping an investor's holdings separate from those of other investors, as opposed to comingling them.

Stop loss An order to sell a stock when the price goes below a designated threshold.

Style drift In mutual funds, style drift occurs when a fund manager makes investments not completely in keeping with the fund's declared investment style or bias. A value fund loaded with a popular growth stock to boast returns would be an example of a fund experiencing style drift.

Underwriters Registered brokers and dealers who subscribe for and buy units of an exchange traded fund as they are issued.

Table of Figures

Index